The Master Musicians Series

GRIEG

Series edited by Stanley Sadie

VOLUMES IN THE MASTER MUSICIANS SERIES

Bach *E. & S. Grew*
Bartók *Lajos Lesznai*
Beethoven *Marion M. Scott*
Bellini *Leslie Orrey*
Berlioz *J. H. Elliot*
Bizet *Winton Dean*
Brahms *Peter Latham*
Bruckner *Derek Watson*
Chopin *Arthur Hedley*
Debussy *Edward Lockspeiser*
Dvořák *Alec Robertson*
Elgar *Ian Parrott*
Franck *Laurence Davies*
Grieg *John Horton*
Handel *Percy M. Young*
Haydn *Rosemary Hughes*
Mahler *Michael Kennedy*
Mendelssohn *Philip Radcliffe*
Monteverdi *Denis Arnold*
Mozart *Eric Blom*
Mussorgsky *M. D. Calvocoressi*
Purcell *Sir Jack Westrup*
Rakhmaninov *Geoffrey Norris*
Ravel *Roger Nichols*
Schoenberg *Malcolm MacDonald*
Schubert *Arthur Hutchings*
Schumann *Joan Chissell*
Sibelius *Robert Layton*
Smetana *John Clapham*
Richard Strauss *Michael Kennedy*
Stravinsky *Francis Routh*
Tchaikovsky *Edward Garden*
Vaughan Williams *James Day*
Verdi *Dyneley Hussey*
Wagner *Robert L. Jacobs*

IN PREPARATION

Britten *Michael Kennedy*
Liszt *Derek Watson*
Prokofiev *Rita McAllister*
Puccini *Mosco Carner*
Rameau *Neal Zaslaw*
Shostakovich *Geoffrey Norris*
Vivaldi *Michael Talbot*

THE MASTER MUSICIANS SERIES

GRIEG

by John Horton

With eight pages of plates and music examples in text

J. M. DENT & SONS LTD
London, Melbourne and Toronto

Printed in Great Britain
by
Billing & Sons Ltd · Guildford · Surrey
for
J. M. DENT & SONS LTD
Aldine House · Albemarle Street · London
First published 1974
Paperback edition 1976
Last reprinted 1979

This book is set in 11 on 12 pt Fournier 185

Hardback ISBN: 0 460 03135 X
Paperback ISBN: 0 460 02169 9

Preface

During the years immediately following Grieg's death in 1907, the English-speaking world's main source of biographical information and critical opinion about this most popular of composers was the American writer Henry T. Finck, who wrote a small book on Grieg in 1906 and expanded it into a larger study in 1929. Finck had the advantage of receiving some valuable written communications from the composer a few years before his death, and of being able to visit him in Norway. Finck's writings are characterized by a light journalistic style and by a naïve enthusiasm for his subject which prevents him from entertaining the slightest adverse criticism of Grieg's work, much less from attempting a balanced assessment of it, which in any case would have been difficult at the time. Even Finck himself admits that Grieg had expressed some embarrassment, when reading the proofs of the earlier book, at its 'excess of superlatives', though he offers the excuse that he has intentionally concentrated on what he believes to be Grieg's best compositions.

The first Norwegian biography, by Gerhard Schjelderup, appeared in 1903, and was amplified and made more widely accessible by being incorporated in *Edvard Grieg: Biographie und Würdigung seiner Werke*, written in German by Gerhard Schjelderup and Walter Niemann, and published by Peters of Leipzig in 1908. Though more systematic and sober in presentation, this was hardly less adulatory than Finck's books. Not until 1932 was it given a complementary volume of the composer's letters, with notes and commentary by Elsa von Zschinsky-Troxler, whose *Edvard Grieg: Briefe an die Verleger der Edition Peters 1866–1907* presents a picture of the composer as a European rather than a Scandinavian figure. In the meantime, several other selections from Grieg's vast correspondence had been published. Some, written (like the Leipzig letters) in German, were included in Julius Röntgen's biography of the composer, which appeared at The Hague in 1930. Röntgen deals in some detail with the later years of Grieg's life, and gives lively accounts of tours with him in the Jotunheim Mountains. Even more valuable are the selections from Grieg's Danish and Norwegian correspondence in *Breve fra Grieg* edited by Gunnar Hauch (Copenhagen, 1922) and Marie Beyer's *Breve fra Edvard Grieg til Frants Beyer 1872–1907* (Christiania, 1923), though these two books were available to comparatively few readers.

In 1934 David Monrad Johansen published in Norway a new full-length biography. Not only was this on a much more ambitious scale than any previous study in any language, but it also quoted extensively from letters and other documents to which Finck and other authors had no direct access. As a Norwegian, and himself a composer of standing, Monrad Johansen was in a position to survey Grieg's life and artistic achievements with considerable authority and insight, combining enthusiasm no less warm than Finck's with much greater objectivity. Monrad Johansen's book was translated, with some omissions, into English in 1938, reissued in Norwegian in 1943 and 1956, and republished in a revised English version in 1945.

The second edition of Monrad Johansen coincided with the centenary of Grieg's birth. This year (1943) also stimulated the production (as far as war-time conditions allowed) of a number of more specialized articles and essays on aspects of the composer's work. Øystein Gaukstad's Grieg bibliography and list of works, published in Oslo, is a compact but thorough collection of data. In England, Kathleen Dale wrote on 'Edvard Grieg's Piano Music' in *Music and Letters* (Vol. XXIV, 1943), Astra

Desmond having already dealt with the songs in the same journal (Vol. XXII, 1941). These two essays were reprinted in revised forms in the *Symposium* on Grieg edited by Gerald Abraham and published in London in 1948—a volume also containing studies of 'Grieg the Man' by Gerik Schjelderup, 'The Orchestral Music' by Hubert Foss, 'The Piano Concerto' by the Editor, 'The Chamber Music' by Alan Frank, 'Choral Music' by Edmund Rubbra, and 'Works for the Stage' by the present writer.[1]

In 1957 Øystein Gaukstad, of the Music Department of Oslo University Library, published *Edvard Grieg: Artikler og Taler*, a comprehensive and finely edited miscellany of Grieg's writings in private and open letters, journals, speeches on various occasions, and other documents. This splendid contribution to Grieg materials, which unfortunately is already out of print, illuminates many aspects of the composer's career and artistic development, and is frequently referred to in the most recent biographical and critical study of Grieg, that of the Norwegian scholar Dag Schjelderup-Ebbe, who, after producing in 1953 a monograph on *Grieg's Harmony*, followed it in 1964 with his *Edvard Grieg 1858–1867* which throws much fresh light on the composer's youth and early manhood, including his student years in Leipzig and the beginnings of his career up to the time when he settled in Christiania.

I acknowledge with gratitude my indebtedness to the literature mentioned above, and I further wish to thank the following persons, institutions, and publishers who have helped me in various ways, not least by granting permission for the use of copyright material: Dr O. M. Sandvik; Mr F. J. Backer-Grøndahl; Bergen Public Library; Rasmus Meyers Samling, Bergen; Munch Museum, Oslo; H. Aschehoug & Co. (W. Nygaard), Oslo; J. W. Eides Forlag A/S, Bergen; Kruseman's

[1] References to these essays will be found in subsequent footnotes under the key-word *Symposium*.

Uitgevers Mij n.v., The Hague; Peters Edition, London; Constable & Co., Ltd.; Dr John Wray and the Council of the Royal Manchester College of Music; The Trustees of the British Museum; London University Library (Music Department); Essex County Library; Dr philo. Dag Schjelderup-Ebbe and Universitetsforlaget, Oslo; Universitetsbibliotekar Øystein Gaukstad and Gyldendal Norsk Forlag, Oslo; The Royal Norwegian Embassy, London.

My thanks are also due to Mr Graham Green for compiling the Index.

Brentwood, Essex, 1974 J. H.

Note to the 1979 reprint

I have taken the opportunity to make a number of corrections and additions and to bring the Bibliography up to date. Among those to whom I am grateful for pointing out errors of fact or offering other suggestions I should like to mention in particular Brian Schlotel, Alan Jefferson, F. B. Sutton, and above all Øystein Gaukstad, whose Norwegian translation of the book was published by Dreyers Forlag, Oslo, in 1978.

J. H.

Contents

	PREFACE	v
	LIST OF ILLUSTRATIONS	xi
	NOTES ON SPELLING	xiii
1	Childhood and student years (1843–62)	1
2	The making of a nationalist composer (1862–8)	13
3	'The great tone-poet' (1868–77)	32
4	In Hardanger country (1877–87)	53
5	The climax of international fame (1887–97)	71
6	The final decade (1897–1907)	97
7	Grieg and Norwegian folk-music	119
8	Works for keyboard (other than those based on folk-music) and for strings with piano	136
9	Various instrumental works, and music for the stage	149
10	The solo songs	165
11	Grieg's personality and influence	196
APPENDICES		
A	Calendar	203
B	Catalogue of works	212
C	Personalia	234
D	Bibliography	240
E	The Greig Collection, *Bergen, Norway*	245
	INDEX	247

Illustrations

BETWEEN PAGES 112 AND 113

Verses written by Henrik Ibsen in Grieg's album, March 1866

Grieg's pen-and-ink sketch of Troldhaugen

Title page of the second part of L. M. Lindeman's *Ældre og nyere Fjeldmelodier*, 1867 (*by kind permission of the British Museum*)

Autograph of Grieg's setting of Ibsen's *En Svane* (*by kind permission of Bergen Public Library*)

Portrait of Grieg by Eilif Petersson (*by kind permission of the National Museum, Oslo*)

The Griegs in Leipzig during the winter of 1887–8

Poster by Edvard Munch for the Paris production of *Peer Gynt* in 1896 (*by kind permission of the Munch Museum, Oslo*)

Notes on spelling

Throughout Grieg's lifetime, and for a long while afterwards, the orthography of Danish, Dano-Norwegian, the many Norwegian dialects, *riksmål*, and *landsmål* was unsettled, particularly as regards spelling and the use of capital letters. Even today these matters are not entirely agreed upon in practice by native writers, whatever official rules may have been laid down, and it would have been pedantic and cumbersome to aim at complete consistency or to list all possible alternatives in a small book such as this intended chiefly for English readers.

When in doubt I have kept to the spellings Grieg himself used in his programmes, correspondence and printed editions, making as the main exceptions such names as *Solveig* and *Bergliot* which are in common usage today, and substituting these forms for the more archaic *Solvejg*, *Bergljot* etc. In quoting folk-music titles the versions taken by Grieg from the original collections (especially Lindeman's) have usually been adhered to.

Almost everywhere the symbol ø has been preferred to ö (as in such names as Bjørnson, Asbjørnsen), but aa and å occur more frequently as alternatives; for example, the former is retained in the name of the composer *Nordraak* but the latter is adopted for *Åse*, another name not uncommon in modern Norway. Among other inconsistencies I have kept some old-fashioned spellings of place-names like *Trondhjem* (now *Trondheim*) and *Christiania* (rather than *Kristiania*; as is well known, the Norwegian capital reverted to its ancient name of *Oslo* in 1924). Capital letters for common nouns were used in both Norwegian and Danish (as in modern German) in Grieg's time, and were not abolished officially in Danish until 1948; I have therefore felt justified in retaining them in song-titles in Danish, but have used them rather more sparingly in Norwegian.

When the Leipzig firm of Peters became Grieg's sole publishers, German-language titles of individual and collected works tended to predominate over, and even supersede altogether, those in the Scandinavian languages. In some of the Peters publications, such as the Op. 17 folk-music arrangements which were originally published in Denmark, the Norwegian titles did not appear at all but were replaced by German ones, usually more generalized and condensed than the originals. Now that Grieg's works are in the public domain there seems to be no reason for giving precedence to German, except where there may be difficulty in recognizing a more or less familiar composition under a Norwegian, Danish, or English heading. For this reason a few German alternatives have been included in the List of Works (Appendix B).

I am indebted to Mr Ø. Johnsen, Cultural Counsellor to the Royal Norwegian Embassy, for helpful advice on some of the above problems.

TO OLWEN

1 Childhood and student years 1843–62

The surname Grieg is by no means uncommon in modern Norway. Other distinguished men besides the composer have added to its lustre, among them Harald Grieg, director of the great Norwegian publishing firm of Gyldendal, and his younger brother Nordahl, the poet, who was killed in 1943 in a bombing raid over Berlin. But the whole family, with its many branches, traces its descent from a Scotsman, Alexander Greig, born in 1739 in the parish of Rathen, Aberdeenshire. The gravestone of Alexander's father John, tenant of the farm of Mosstown, can still be seen in Rathen kirkyard, with its inscription carrying, by a prophetic slip of the stonemason's, the later Norwegian spelling of the family name.[1]

Alexander emigrated to Bergen in Norway at some time between 1760 and 1770. That he did so on account of the economic depression that followed the Jacobite rebellion and the disaster of Culloden (1746), as often conjectured, is doubtful; in any case, Scotsmen had been seeking wider career opportunities in the flourishing Norwegian seaport for more than a century.[2] Alexander did well in Bergen, catching and exporting lobsters and stockfish and in time acquiring his own fishing-fleet. He married in succession two Norwegian sisters, took

[1] A connection with the Scottish Admiral Greig, though claimed by the composer, has not been substantiated.

[2] Prominent figures like the seventeenth-century poet Petter Dass (Dundas) and W. F. K. Christie, the first Norwegian parliamentary President in 1814, were of Scots immigrant descent.

Dano-Norwegian citizenship in 1779, changed the spelling of his name to the now familiar form, and was appointed British consul in Bergen in 1803. He is said to have revisited his native country twice a year, partly in order to take communion in Rathen kirk. His tenure of the consulship, however, must have been very brief, as he died in 1803.

His son John (1772–1844) and grandson, also named Alexander (1806–75), father of the composer, carried on the family mercantile tradition and in their turn assumed consular responsibilities. With these generations musical interests begin to appear; John married Maren Regina Haslund, a daughter of one of the first directors of the Bergen music society *Harmonien* founded in 1765, and from this time the family became regular supporters of the musical life of Bergen. The younger Alexander Grieg, a Dickensian-looking figure who greatly admired the works of that author, is said to have enjoyed playing piano duets with his wife, an accomplished pianist. Her name before marriage was Gesine Judith Hagerup. She was the daughter of a *stiftamtmann* or provincial governor and member of Parliament, whose imposing funeral in 1853 made a deep impression on the ten-year-old Edvard Grieg. Gesine's ancestry also included a branch of the Christie family and, further back, a vigorous, semi-legendary character named Kjeld Stub, who was in turn army engineer, church pastor and resistance leader against the Swedes in the war of 1643–5. Gesine seems to have inherited a considerable share of the family energy and versatility, becoming well known in Bergen both as a pianist and also as a writer of poems and plays. It is clear that Edvard Grieg, who was born on 15th June 1843—the fourth of five children—owed his literary flair, as well as his musical talents, to his mother.[1]

Ever since its development by the Hanseatic merchants in the

[1] Despite the statement of many reference books, the composer never adopted 'Hagerup' as his middle name.

later Middle Ages, Bergen had stimulated cultural life along with commercial development, counting among its citizens the eighteenth-century dramatist Ludvig Holberg, the painter J. C. Dahl, who caught the animation and colour of his native town on his canvases about the time of Edvard Grieg's birth, the poet J. S. Welhaven, and the violinist Ole Bull. Protected on the seaward side by skerries and on the eastern side by steeply-rising mountain ranges, its atmosphere washed with abundant rain, noisy with the constant traffic of its harbour and pungent from the adjacent fish-quay, Bergen had a vitality and proud sense of independence which the composer was to acknowledge to the end of his days. Speaking on the occasion of his sixtieth birthday on 15th June 1903, at the Grand Hotel in Bergen, he said:

> My material has been drawn from the whole of the surroundings of Bergen. Its natural beauty, the life of its people, the city's achievements and activities of every kind have been an inspiration to me. I find the odour of the German Quay exciting; in fact, I am sure my music has a taste of codfish in it.

The Griegs' town-house at 152 Strandgaten, one of the city's oldest thoroughfares, running along the promontory called Nordnes which encloses one side of the inner harbour, disappeared in the last war. Also vanished are the neighbouring alleys, where, according to Harald Grieg,[1] the composer was reluctant to set foot, for fear of meeting some of his illegitimate relatives; apparently some of the older merchant Griegs had the benevolent habit of dropping in at their fishermen's homes to see that all was well with the women-folk while their men were at sea.

To all outward appearances, however, the male Griegs were models of commercial and official respectability, while on the

[1] Harald Grieg, *En forleggers erindringer*, 2nd ed. (Oslo, 1971), p. 20.

Hagerup side the vocations of government servant and Lutheran pastor were guarantees of intellectual and moral rectitude. As a child, Edvard himself showed an early fondness for the spoken word, both religious and secular, improvising sermons and declaiming verse to his long-suffering parents; and all his life he had considerable natural facility in speech and writing and was sensitive in his appreciation of poetry.

At six years of age he began piano lessons with his mother, though like many other exceptionally gifted children he preferred extemporizing to practising scales and studies. Two years before his death[1] he recalled an early experiment in keyboard harmony: 'First a third, then a chord of three notes, then a full chord of four; ending at last, with both hands,—O joy! a combination of five, the chord of the ninth.' It was not to be the last time he savoured this kind of effect: he repeated it over forty years later, in the second movement of the unfinished F major String Quartet:

Harmonic discovery was from first to last one of his strongest

[1] In 'My First Success', the English version of an autobiographical sketch published in *The Contemporary Review*, July 1905.

instinctive drives, as he told his American biographer, Finck: 'The realm of harmonies always was my dream-world, and the relationship between my harmonic sensibility and Norwegian folk music was a mystery even to myself.' There is no doubt that this aspect of his musical personality owed much to hearing in childhood his mother's playing of keyboard works by her favourite composers, Mozart, Beethoven, Weber and Chopin.

Gesine inherited a country house at Landås, a few miles outside Bergen, at the foot of the dominating feature of the landscape, Ulrikken,[1] and here the family spent the summer months from Edvard's tenth year. He and his elder brother John had to walk daily to school in Bergen, rain or shine, and Edvard soon took any opportunity of avoiding an institution which he came to hate as strongly as he reacted, a few years later, to the Leipzig Conservatory. Not least among the mortifications he suffered was the sarcastic comment of one of the school staff who caught him bringing into the classroom his first ambitious manuscript, entitled 'Variations on a German Melody for the Piano, Opus 1.' His memories of this incident, and others, were still bitter half a century later:

> School life was in the last degree unsympathetic to me; its materialism, its coarseness, its coldness were so abhorrent to my nature that I thought of the most incredible ways of escaping from it, if only for a short time.

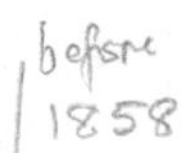

He was to escape for ever before reaching the age of fifteen, and the agent of his deliverance was no less a person than Ole Bull, who rode over from his estate at Valestrand on an Arab thoroughbred to visit the Griegs at Landås. Already Bull had become almost a folk-hero, a symbol of the new Norway with an ancient past which had broken free in 1814 from three centuries'

[1] The new buildings of the Bergen Teachers' Training College now stand close to Landås.

domination by Denmark. He had a touch of Paganini's wizardry and showmanship on the concert platform, rivalled Liszt in generosity, and possessed a bold, restless temperament that suggested some Viking ancestry. The Bergen music society *Harmonien* had bent its rules to admit him as a playing member at the age of nine. He had quickly developed into a mainly self-taught virtuoso, touring the musical centres of Europe and, in the year of Edvard's birth, paying his first visit to America, where he was rapturously welcomed by the Norwegian immigrant communities. Returning to Norway in 1848, he tried to realize his dream of founding a Norwegian national theatre (as distinct from those performing only Danish plays) in Bergen, and engaged an almost unknown young author named Henrik Ibsen as house playwright and producer. On a subsequent visit to America, Bull lost much money, and nearly his life, in the attempt to establish a Norwegian colony in Pennsylvania, under the name of Oleana.

Bull's impact on the career of the young Grieg was decisive. First, there was the thrill of meeting the most famous man in Norway, shaking hands with him—'I felt something like an electric current pass through me when his hand touched mine'—and hearing accounts of adventures which nowadays might provide material for a television Western. Then followed a request that the boy should play some of his own music, and Bull's immediate recommendation that he should be sent to study at the Leipzig Conservatory. The Griegs acted on this advice without question, and Edvard was packed off to Germany a few months later, in October 1858, feeling 'like a parcel stuffed with dreams'. It was not by any means the last time that he was to be impelled onwards by a more dynamic personality than his own: Nordraak, Svendsen and Bjørnson were among those who succeeded Bull in this role of helping him over his natural diffidence and, even more, presenting to him various aspects of nationalism. Within the field of Norwegian folk-music Bull may, as we shall see later, have taught Grieg more than was formerly realized.

Most descriptions of Grieg's years at the Leipzig Conservatory have taken at their face value his own reminiscences included in 'My First Success' which, as already noted, belongs to the last years of his life. Only recently have the researches of Norwegian scholars been able to build up a more balanced picture.[1] Undoubtedly the initial homesickness and the later physical breakdown were real enough; added to which there was a rooted distaste for institutional rules and regulations, which other promising young musicians besides Grieg have found intolerable. Such absurdities of organization as dividing a student's work in the same branch of musicianship between two teachers holding different views might be found even today in music schools of high reputation. But the records surviving from Grieg's Leipzig studentship, including his exercise books, reports and student recital programmes, show that although he may have had to endure dull lessons from reactionaries like Plaidy, who kept him—born Romantic as he was—to the works of Czerny, Kuhlau and Clementi, which he 'loathed like the plague', the majority of his teachers, among them Papperitz, E. F. Richter, Reinecke, Hauptmann and Moscheles, seem to have taught him on the whole not only conscientiously but also liberally.

For Moscheles at least he came to have the warmest admiration, nourished on the study of Beethoven's Sonatas and Moscheles's own 24 Studies. From Richter he learnt the principle that even an exercise should always sound well, while Hauptmann demonstrated that the rules of harmony and counterpoint were derived from natural laws; Grieg remembered how Hauptmann gave him special praise for an academic fugue on the name GADE, murmuring after Grieg had played it:

[1] Especially important is Dag Schjelderup-Ebbe's study, *Edvard Grieg 1858–1867* (Oslo and London, 1964).

'Sehr hübsch, sehr musikalisch.' There is in fact plenty of evidence that Grieg got on well with both professors and fellow-students, and that he finally departed from the Conservatory with the foundations of his pianoforte and composition techniques securely laid and with his gifts understood and appreciated. Certainly his later contention, repeated at times of frustration and low spirits, that he learnt nothing at Leipzig will hardly stand up to examination.

Reading between the lines of Grieg's own account it is possible to discern in the student many of the lifelong characteristics of the mature man and artist. Shy and nervous though he was by temperament, when aroused to make a stand against injustice or bigotry (as was to happen in connection with the Dreyfus case, the first Bergen Festival, and the Swedish crisis) he could call upon unsuspected reserves of courage. While he was still at the Conservatory a general reprimand for unpunctuality brought him the next day to the Principal's office to make a formal protest on behalf of the whole student body:

> Without beating about the bush, I spoke straight out from my heart. I told him how inconsiderate and wounding his conduct had been in treating us all alike, and that for my part I was not prepared to stand such treatment. He went into a furious rage, jumped up and showed me the door. But I was in a fighting mood: 'Certainly, sir, I will go: but not before I have said what I have to say.' Then came the astonishing thing . . . Schleinitz[1] suddenly knuckled under. . . . We became the best of friends, and he did not know how to do enough for me.

To quote Schjelderup-Ebbe: 'It appears likely that during his early period in Leipzig Grieg was no different from the sort of person he was later known to be: a lively Bergen fellow, outspoken, quick-tempered, and enthusiastic.'[2]

[1] H. C. Schleinitz (d. 1881) had become Director on Mendelssohn's death in 1847.

[2] Schjelderup-Ebbe, op. cit., p. 34.

Nor does it seem true that the Conservatory restricted his musical development, or tried to suppress his tendency towards harmonic experiments or his interest in contemporary trends in composition. The books of exercises now preserved in the Bergen Public Library show that even in academic counterpoint Richter and Hauptmann allowed him a fairly loose rein in his spurts of chromatic part-writing: a fugue[1] for string quartet written for Richter in December 1861 testifies to the freedom of style they were prepared to tolerate and even encourage. Equally unjust appears to have been Grieg's retrospective criticism of Reinecke for setting him to write a complete string quartet without first instructing him in the medium. If the result of this omission was, as Grieg said, to make him study the quartets of Mozart and Beethoven, it is hard to imagine a more effective way of teaching an intelligent and talented student. It appears that Schleinitz wanted Grieg's Quartet to be given public performance, but according to Grieg the suggestion was opposed by Ferdinand David: 'He thought the people would say it was futuristic [*Zukunftsmusik*], but he was wrong; there was no trace of the future in it—the style was derived from Schumann, Gade and Mendelssohn.' As for the accusation that interest in the works of Schumann was discouraged at Leipzig, Grieg acknowledged as one of his best teachers E. F. Wenzel, a personal friend of Schumann's, and dedicated to him the *Four Piano Pieces* (Op. 1), in which his devotion to Schumann (and Chopin) at this time is unmistakable. Grieg must also have learnt to play a good deal of Schumann's piano music under Wenzel, for soon after leaving Leipzig he was able to put *Kreisleriana* and the Piano Quartet into his earliest Scandinavian concert programmes. Even if the range of contemporary or recent music studied within the Conservatory classrooms left something to be desired (again, a

[1] Three movements of this Quartet (in D minor) were performed in Bergen in 1862, but Grieg parted with score and parts to a fellow-student, and they have disappeared.

not uncommon shortcoming of major teaching institutions), there was plenty to be heard outside, and of this Grieg availed himself to the full, attending performance after performance of *Tannhäuser* and hearing recitals of Schumann's piano music by Clara Schumann and of his songs by Wilhelmine Schröder-Devrient.

It may be asked why Grieg became so persistent in his denigration of the Leipzig Conservatory. The traumatic effects of his illness in the earlier months of 1860 must be held partly responsible; not only did a severe attack of pleurisy leave him with permanent damage to one lung, but there was the unsettling effect of a return to Bergen under his mother's care, a month's absence for convalescence, and the resumption of his course at Leipzig the following autumn. But it has also been suggested that he projected on to his own experience the dissatisfaction communicated by other students, emotionally less stable than himself: his brother John, who had joined him at the Leipzig Conservatory to study cello; the excitable Dane, Emil Horneman; and Rikard Nordraak, who at this time was submitting himself intermittently to academic discipline in Berlin. More generally, the effort of breaking away from the German classical-Romantic tradition hallowed by Mendelssohn and turning in new directions, first towards Scandinavian Romanticism and soon afterwards to Norwegian nationalism, may have contributed to Grieg's embittered attitude towards his student days. His natural sense of justice did, however, cause him to make some amends for his strictures:

If, in the course of these sketches of the Leipzig Conservatory, I may have blamed certain people or many tendencies of that institution, I hasten to add that it was chiefly due to my own nature that I left the institution almost as stupid as I entered it. I was a dreamer, without any talent for the battle of life. I was awkward, sluggish, unattractive, and quite unteachable. We Norwegians take a long time to develop; few of us show what we have in us before our eighteenth year. I myself had no idea of what I wanted. The atmosphere of Leipzig was like a veil before my eyes.

But at least he stayed the course at Leipzig, where he returned for the autumn term of 1861, having apparently recovered his health to the extent of being able to give a concert on the way back to Germany in the town of Karlshamn on the south coast of Sweden. His programme was made up of piano works by Mendelssohn, Moscheles and Schumann (*Kreisleriana*). A local newspaper referred to him as 'a modest young artist'. Why he should have chosen this particular town for his recital is not known, but there may have been a personal attraction: a girl named Theresa Berg, daughter of a Karlshamn business man, seems to have acquired manuscript copies of Grieg's three piano pieces written in Leipzig the previous year.[1]

Grieg ended his studentship at Leipzig at Easter, 1862, after taking part by election in the *Hauptprüfung* or final public concert. He played three of his *Four Piano Pieces* (Op. 1) and accompanied his *Four Songs for Alto* to texts by Heine and Chamisso (Op. 2). Although these were his first works to be published, they are by no means the only ones to survive from the Leipzig period. A collection of twenty-three short piano pieces (*Smaastykker for Pianoforte*) exists in a manuscript marked: 'To be destroyed after my death. Not to be printed.' It contains mainly work of about 1859, along with a few juvenilia. The *Three Piano Pieces* played at Karlshamn were written about a year later, perhaps during his convalescence in Bergen. The outstanding feature of most of these early compositions is their harmonic adventurousness, though the Op. 1 pieces have, despite the composer's poor opinion of them, many points of rhythmic and melodic interest and show a well-developed sense of texture and form.

[1] Olav Gurvin: 'Three Compositions from Edvard Grieg's Youth', in *Norsk Musikkgranskning Årbok, 1951–3,* pp. 90 fol.

The report and testimonials Grieg carried away from Leipzig were entirely favourable. Even Carl Reinecke, whose teaching was later to be the particular object of Grieg's complaints, wrote enthusiastically of his 'significant musical talent, especially for composition', while Hauptmann described him as 'an outstanding pianist . . . and in both the theoretical and practical aspects of composition among the best of our students'.

2 The making of a nationalist composer 1862–8

On leaving Leipzig, Grieg had to face the problem of many a successful student before and since: into what direction to turn his talents and energies. He could not look to his father for further support, his first application to the Norwegian government for a travelling scholarship was rejected, and there remained no alternative to the slow and painful process of building up a professional connection in his native town. He began by giving a concert in Bergen in May 1862, playing three of his Op. 1 piano pieces, some studies by Moscheles, Beethoven's *Sonate pathétique*, and the piano part in the Schumann Quartet for piano and strings. Movements from the D minor String Quartet (now lost) were also included in the programme, and he accompanied a local singer named Wibecke Meyer in three of his German songs (Op. 2). In March of the following year (1863) he played Beethoven's C minor Violin and Piano Sonata (Op. 30, No. 2) with the conductor of *Harmonien*, and in April a choral group performed a composition for mixed voices and piano, *Rückblick*, which also has since disappeared.

Between the concert seasons, in the summer months of 1862, Grieg seems to have made holiday trips to Paris and London with members of his family. It may also be assumed that he tried to establish himself as a private teacher in Bergen, though there can only have been limited scope in a town[1] where such few

[1] The population of Bergen was then about 25,000, a number only recently surpassed by the capital, Christiania, which by the middle of the century had expanded to about 30,000 inhabitants.

musical institutions as existed, even the famous *Harmonien*, were run chiefly by amateurs. Ole Bull's Norse Theatre, which had held out some promise for musicians as well as actors and playwrights, was obliged to suspend its activities in 1863.

Norway had now been politically independent of Denmark for nearly half a century, after four hundred years of subservience; but in spite of the vigorous upsurge of national aspirations in literature and pictorial art she still had far to go before attaining cultural autonomy. It was not only her musicians who had to seek their higher education in Germany, but her artists also, though for them the acknowledged centre was not Leipzig but Dresden or Düsseldorf. The real focus of Norwegian intellectual and artistic life was still Copenhagen, where a Norwegian Society had had its original headquarters as far back as 1772; only in 1859 had the Society been re-founded in the Norwegian capital itself, to become the meeting-place of the writers Ibsen and Bjørnson and the musicians L. M. Lindeman and Ole Bull. Most Norwegians of the urban, professional, official and business classes (to which, of course, the Grieg family belonged) had close connections with Denmark, going back to the period when Norway was ruled and administered from Copenhagen, and some of the most influential of Norway's new leaders, like the poet Welhaven, believed that the cultural ties between the two countries should never be broken. Even that ardent spokesman for an independent Norway, Bjørnstjerne Bjørnson, could write to Ibsen in 1867: 'Hold fast to Denmark . . . Denmark for us means culture.'

It was understandable then that Edvard Grieg should feel himself attracted towards Denmark, and should find it a vital stage in his artistic education and development to spend most of the next three years in or near Copenhagen. The two great father-figures of Scandinavian music were still active there: Niels Gade, who had deputized for Mendelssohn on the rostrum of the Leipzig Gewandhaus, and had been praised by Schumann for the 'imprint of a definite Northern character' to be found in his early concert overture, *Echoes of Ossian*; and J. P. E. Hartmann, then in his late fifties, but with close on another half-century of life before him. Hartmann's influence on Norwegian music in general, and Grieg's in particular, was probably stronger than Gade's. His interest in Romantic legend was not restricted to Danish traditions, but embraced the whole of the Nordic world of the past. His opera *Liden Kirsten* was performed six times during the years 1863–4, and his ballet *Valkyrien*, to choreography by Bournonville, had sixteen performances between 1862 and 1864; Grieg knew this work, and conducted parts of it in Christiania in 1871. Hartmann's cantata *Völvens Spaadom* ('The Witch's Prophecy'), written in 1872, must have given Grieg a useful stylistic model for his *Olav Trygvason* (1873). Grieg also associated with a group of younger Danish composers, some of whom had been at the Leipzig Conservatory and were to remain among his closest friends; these included Emil Hartmann (son of J. P. E.), C. F. E. Horneman, August Winding, and Gottfred Matthison-Hansen. Rikard Nordraak, of whom much more must be said later, was half-Danish and belonged to the same circle.

Grieg arrived in Copenhagen in the spring of 1863, and soon waited upon Gade with his Op. 1 piano pieces and Op. 2 songs. Gade did not conceal his impatience with what he thought were trifles; his own reputation had been built on his large-scale orchestral, chamber and choral works, and he advised Grieg to embark at once on a symphony. In trying to follow this counsel, Grieg began the painful process of discovering that his lyrical talent and preoccupation with harmonic colour were ill at ease in the larger classical forms. A Symphony in C minor was completed within a year (the autograph score is dated 2nd May 1864), and three movements were played under H. C. L. Lumbye in the Tivoli concert hall on 4th June 1864. There were also performances of the entire work in Bergen on 1st January and

28th November 1867, after which the composer suppressed it, marking the score 'never to be performed', though he arranged the two middle movements for piano duet and published them in that form as his Op. 14.

The two and a half years Grieg spent mainly in Denmark were to be among his happiest and most productive. The gently rolling countryside, the neat farms, the secluded manor-houses, and the never far distant seas made up the most agreeable of backgrounds to the leisurely life of a young artist, into which an element of personal romance had now entered. He had met his cousin Nina Hagerup, a girl two years younger than himself and likewise a native of Bergen, though she had grown up in Denmark. She and Edvard became engaged in July 1864, and from that time onward her delightfully sympathetic voice and poetic sensitivity were the inspiration of his song-writing. Nearly eighty years later a relative of Edvard and Nina, and the architect of their villa Troldhaugen, recalled her instinctive artistry:

> She sang as a bird sings, as though the idea of which she was singing were being born at that instant—at that very moment on her lips. She laid bare the innermost feelings or her soul. She would stand at the side of the piano with her eyes turned upwards, her hands clasped behind her back, her breast raised and an expression on her face as though she were experiencing the situation personally. . . . Her voice was like an inexhaustible well—it was like a pool of sound poured forth over the audience.[1]

Her singing was even compared to that of Jenny Lind by the few who could remember hearing the Swedish nightingale in her youth. As late as 1897, when Nina only exceptionally sang in public, the Dutch critic D. de Lange wrote: 'We shall never

[1] Schak Bull, 'Edvard and Nina Grieg as I remember them', in a symposium *Edvard Grieg* (J. W. Eide's Boktrykkeri, Bergen, 1953), p. 40.

hear Grieg's songs performed as Mevrouw Grieg interpreted them to us. The greatest simplicity, the warmest fervour, the finest possible attention to detail, supreme wit, in brief, the utmost vivacity and truth of expression, under the control of artistry.'[1]

The songs Grieg wrote during his engagement include a further German set (Op. 4, with texts by Heine, Chamisso, and Uhland), dedicated to 'Fräulein Nina Hagerup', and the earliest of his Danish settings. He had made the acquaintance of Hans Christian Andersen, then at the height of his renown not only as a writer of fairy stories but also as a lyric poet, and Grieg's *Melodies of the Heart* (Op. 5) consists entirely of Andersen settings, including two that were to attain immediate popularity: 'Two brown eyes' and the impassioned 'I love thee'. The four *Romances* (Grieg now began to use this Danish term for lyric songs) to verses by the lesser poet Christian Winther (Op. 10) are thought to date from this period. The *Romances* published in two books as Op. 18 were composed a few years later (chiefly during 1868–9) but should be mentioned here as they are again inspired mainly by Andersen's poetry in such delightfully spontaneous but finely wrought miniatures as 'Wandering in the Woods', 'The Cottage' and 'The Rosebud', though the collection also includes some of the earliest settings of Norwegian texts, such as Jørgen Moe's 'The Young Birch Tree'.

Grieg was in Norway during the summer of 1864, staying with his parents and giving a recital in Bergen with his brother John, who was now an accomplished cellist but earning his living in the family business. Edvard spent some time with Ole Bull on his Osterøy estate. They played Mozart sonatas together, and the visit may also have introduced Grieg to living Norwegian folk-music, since Bull was on excellent terms with local har-

[1] In *Het Nieuws van den Dag*, 20 February 1897. Quoted by Jules Cuypers, *Edvard Grieg* (Haarlem, 3rd impression, 1966), pp. 133–4.

danger-fiddle players and enjoyed imitating their traditional style on his own violin. Bull's piano transcriptions of fiddle dance-tunes included as an appendix to Tönsberg's splendid folio *Norwegian National Costumes*[1] foreshadow in a modest way the Halvorsen-Grieg *Slåtter* of fifty years later.

Back in Copenhagen in the autumn, Grieg encountered the second of the leading figures in Norwegian national music whose influence was to determine the lines of his future development. This was the twenty-two year old Rikard Nordraak,[2] who had just returned from a desultory course of study in Berlin. He was only half Norwegian, his mother being of Danish birth, but his ardent nature had been fired with enthusiasm for anything and everything that could be viewed as distinctively Norwegian—saga-literature, old ballads, mountain scenery, traditional costumes and festivals, and above all folksong and dance—in fact, the whole world of national Romanticism. His patriotism reached its fullest and most enduring expression in the choral setting of the national hymn, whose text, by his cousin Bjørnstjerne Bjørnson, begins: 'Yes, we love this land ...' The pianist Erika Lie Nissen, who was for a time engaged to Nordraak, said that he resembled Bjørnson in the way he seemed at once to fill any room he entered: 'It was not that he was particularly witty or amusing. He was not one of those with whom one does nothing but laugh. But he was interesting; he himself was interested in everything, and he knew how to interest others.'[3]

Bjørnson himself thought Nordraak the most gifted man he had ever met. 'To be with him', he said, 'was a feast from beginning to end.' Older men, however, like Nordraak's own father and Alexander Grieg, sometimes thought him over-conceited, a trait that seems to be aptly illustrated by his often-quoted words

[1] Chr. Tönsberg, *Norske Nationaldragter* (Christiania, 1852).

[2] Originally Richard Nordraach: he changed first the surname and then the Christian name from Danish to Norse forms.

[3] Liv Greni: *Rikard Nordraak*, Oslo, 1942, pp. 18, 36–7.

to Grieg when they were introduced to each other in the Tivoli gardens: 'Well, so we two great men meet at last.'[1] Ole Bull, whom Nordraak revered to the extent of hoarding his half-smoked cigars, said that the young man had talent but was lazy. Nordraak was impatient of technical discipline; he complained that his Berlin teacher, Kullak, could not give him what he needed and asked for, and he broke off his lessons with the internationally famous Norwegian concert pianist Neupert, in the belief that he was capable of forming his own technique, 'like Ole Bull'. Erika Lie Nissen confirmed that Nordraak never played the piano with much facility, but that his touch had 'the deepest musical understanding and feeling', while 'his accompanying was the most beautiful one can imagine'.

As a composer, Nordraak likewise sought to work by intuition, under the inspiration of nationalist ideals:

> When grief and anxiety threatened, art whispered something in my ear, and then the water-sprite played, and the fairy-folk danced to me so that I forgot everything but the sounds from over there in Norway, and I heard them clearer every day. And what I heard, I wrote down.[2]

Nordraak left behind only about forty works, more than half of them songs, among the best of these being his settings of lyrics by Bjørnson. His most substantial piano piece, *Fjeldbækken* (*The Mountain Brook*), may have been among the music Nordraak insisted on playing to Grieg soon after their meeting in Tivoli, together with some of his incidental music to Bjørnson's historical dramas *Sigurd Slembe* and *Maria Stuart*. Like other relatively unschooled composers with strong creative personalities (Mussorgsky is an obvious comparison), Nordraak wrote with simplicity, directness, and disregard for conventional

[1] This formal introduction was made by Magdalene Thoresen, Ibsen's mother-in-law, but it is possible that Grieg and Nordraak already knew each other slightly.

[2] Liv Greni: *Rikard Nordraak*, Oslo, 1942, pp. 18, 36–7.

harmonic procedures; his boldness in the use of dissonance owes much to folk-music, and especially to the character of the hardanger-fiddle tunes, with their drone basses, direct and inverted pedal notes, the scale with a sharpened fourth degree, much use of the intervals of the second, seventh, and perfect and augmented fourths and fifths, final cadences falling on to the dominant, suggestions of pre-classical modes, elaborate ornamentation, and frequent dotted rhythms and irregularities of accent. Some of these features were already latent in Grieg's own style, and certainly became more prominent from this time onwards, as in the piano *Humoresques* (Op. 6) he dedicated to Nordraak. Of the second of these dance-like pieces, the opening of which almost quotes a folk-tune,[1] Nordraak made the characteristic remark: 'I might have written it myself.'

The friendship that developed between the two young men was cemented by an understanding that they should make it their main purpose in life to express in music the spirit of Norway, and thus bring to fulfilment what Ole Bull had begun. The tragic death of Nordraak in 1866 seems to have intensified Grieg's sense of responsibility for carrying out his side of the compact, and at the same time to have caused his earlier biographers to exaggerate his indebtedness, both ideological and stylistic, to Nordraak. More recent scholarship in Norway, and particularly the researches of Gurvin and Schjelderup-Ebbe, has shown that other factors were at work, both in Denmark and in Norway, in moulding Grieg's musical personality during this period.

In the spring of 1865 Grieg and Nordraak, with the Danish musicians C. F. E. Horneman, Louis Hornbeck, and Gottfred Matthison-Hansen, formed the organization they called *Euterpe* for the promotion of contemporary Scandinavian music. This

[1] 'Alle Mand hadde Fota': folksong from the Trondhjem region, No. 26 in Lindeman's collection.

they intended to counteract the influence of the conservative Musical Association (*Musikforeningen*) over which Gade held almost unchallenged sway. *Euterpe* gave two concerts in the early part of that year; at the first (18th March) Nordraak conducted his music to Bjørnson's *Sigurd Slembe*, and at the second (1st April) the two middle movements of Grieg's Symphony were performed.

The *Humoresques*, already mentioned, were only one of a series of works Grieg produced during the spring and summer of 1865, when he and a companion named Benjamin Feddersen[1] rented three furnished rooms in an inn at Rungsted, on the coast north of Copenhagen and about half way to Helsingør. They made tea at intervals with an ancient samovar which Grieg also used for warming his fingers at the piano on the chilly spring mornings. He composed with such concentration that even the noises from the adjacent billiard room failed to disturb him—a remarkable exception to his usual edginess when at work. Besides the *Humoresques* he wrote at this time the Piano Sonata (Op. 7), which, while doing homage to the twin pillars of the Danish musical establishment, Gade and the elder Hartmann, develops further the new, terse manner of the *Humoresques*; the Sonata in F major for Violin and Piano (Op. 8), dedicated to Feddersen; several songs to texts by H. C. Andersen; and one to a poem by Christian Richardt, 'Autumn Storm', which in the following year was to become the basis of the Concert Overture, *In Autumn*.

After this burst of creative activity, Grieg took a holiday in North Zealand with Feddersen and Horneman, and kept a diary of the tour in which some amusing incidents are intermingled

[1] A manuscript has recently (1971) come to light containing some of the music Grieg wrote for a comedy, *Frieriet paa Helgoland*, by Ludvig Schneider, which was adapted by Feddersen for a series of performances in Copenhagen between 1865 and 1867 (see *Norsk Musikkgranskning Årbok 1962–71*, p. 8).

with notes on the scenery; he was surprised at the wildness of the heather-covered moors, bounded by the seething Cattegat, which at times even reminded him of the Norwegian Westland.[1] During the vacation, or soon afterwards, he sent to the Copenhagen paper *Flyveposten* a laudatory but careful review of Nordraak's recently published songs to words by Bjørnson and Jonas Lie.[2]

Forty years later, near the end of his life, Grieg was to recall the serenity of this Danish interlude in a letter to Matthison-Hansen:

The glorious days of youth, when the air and the sea and the beechwoods in lovely Zealand were filled with music and beauty. True, it was not more beautiful then than now; but we made it beautiful, because we ourselves gave expression to all our feelings of beauty in the landscape and the life of the people, in saga and history.[3]

Grieg and Nordraak had planned to spend the autumn and winter of 1865 in Italy, then the goal of so many sun-starved Scandinavians; living was cheap and there was plenty of company for northerners who wanted to relax in their own languages with authors, artists and musicians. Ibsen had only recently settled in Rome, a voluntary exile mainly on account of disillusionment with his own country after its failure to support Denmark in the war with Germany of 1864.

But while Grieg was still very much contented with his life in Rungsted, Nordraak had insisted on going ahead to Berlin, where he thought he had at last found a sympathetic teacher of composition in Friedrich Kiel. He wrote from there on 12th September to thank Edvard for his review; and then, in October, soon after Grieg had at length reached Berlin, Nordraak was

[1] H. J. Hurum: *I Edvard Griegs verden* (Oslo, 1959,) pp. 52 fol.
[2] The review is reproduced in full in English translation in Schjelderup-Ebbe, op. cit., pp. 266–7.
[3] Hauch, 19 December 1906.

struck down by one of the dreaded diseases of the age, pulmonary consumption. Grieg seems to have had little idea at first of the seriousness of his friend's condition, but he promised to return to Berlin after spending a few days in Leipzig for performances of his Sonatas, Op. 7 and Op. 8. Eventually, however, he started on the nine days' journey to Rome, leaving Nordraak on his sickbed, a course of action for which Nordraak was to reproach him bitterly, and for which it is difficult to find an altogether creditable excuse. It is clear that Grieg was anxious to be out of Berlin, for he wrote to Hornbeck: 'Berlin is a miserable hole; I wish I were with you in Copenhagen. . . . Everything is different there, with poetry in the air, poetry in the people—that is Denmark.'[1] He may also have felt apprehensive about his own precarious health. He may even have been embarrassed by Nordraak's characteristic self-dramatization under the stress of illness: 'None of my doctors', the sick man wrote, 'has had such an extraordinary case'.[2] Grieg also maintained that Nordraak might not have fallen ill at all if he had gone directly from Denmark to Rome, as originally arranged.

Nordraak grew steadily worse and died, after six months' heroic struggle against the disease, on 20th March 1866. Grieg marked the date when he received the news (6th April) with a black cross in his Rome diary, and on the same day began one of his most moving and original works, the *Funeral March in Memory of Rikard Nordraak*. In other ways he tried to make amends for neglecting his friend. On his way home from Italy he visited Nordraak's grave in Berlin, and afterwards wrote to the dead man's father expressing both his grief and his determination to carry on the task they had planned together, and to keep his promise

that his cause should be my cause, his goal mine. Do not believe that

[1] Norsk Musikkgranskning Årbok 1937, p. 50.

[2] The word used is '*storartet*', literally 'grand'. See Monrad Johansen, p. 45.

what he aspired to will be forgotten; I have the great vocation of bringing his few but great works to the attention of the people, our people of Norway, of campaigning for their recognition, and of building further on that splendid foundation.[1]

Grieg's first winter in Italy was on the whole a stimulating and fruitful experience, darkened though it may have been by periods of anxiety and remorse. He did the usual round of sights—the Roman palaces, Naples, Capri, Sorrento and Pompeii; he listened critically to the singing in Italian churches (his diary notes under 17th December 1865: 'Appalling music in Chiesa Nova—Bellini, Donizetti, Rossini. Two castrati, unnatural, disgusting'); and he was mildly scandalized at the sight of Liszt making sheep's eyes at the ladies and of Ibsen in his cups. In more sober mood, that poet contributed a typically sardonic rhyme to Grieg's album (see Plate 1); it may be translated as follows:

Orpheus with his wondrous tones
Roused souls in beasts, struck fire from stones.

Of stones has Norway not a few,
And beasts she has in plenty too.

Play then, that sparks from rocks may leap!
Play then, and pierce the brutes' hides deep!

Apart from the Nordraak March, and some songs to texts by the Norwegian poet Andreas Munch (Op. 9), Grieg completed at this period only one important work, the Overture *In Autumn*

[1] Greni, op. cit., p. 132. Grieg's sense of guilt for not having returned to Nordraak's bedside during the winter of 1865–6, despite Nordraak's poignant letters, may lie behind a curious story told by John Paulsen (*Billeder fra Bergen*, 1911, pp. 131–3), of Paulsen's mother and Grieg watching over the deathbed of a friendless young musician, Lauritz Grimstad, during one of Grieg's later visits to his native town.

(*I Høst*), based on the song 'The Autumn Storm' composed at Rungsted in the previous year, and alluding in the coda (and less explicitly elsewhere) to a hardanger-fiddle tune that had been published in Bergen in February 1865. An uncertainty of aim is still evident. In spite of mildly nationalist colouring, the form chosen—that of a concert overture—suggests that Grieg could not yet see himself developing on any other than traditional German classical-Romantic lines. We must remember that his portfolio already contained two full-length sonatas and a symphony (not yet disowned). The Piano Concerto was soon to follow, and he may have wished to add a single-movement orchestral work that might win the approval of the still-influential Niels Gade, just as Gade's own Overture, *Echoes from Ossian*, had attracted the notice of the composer of *Fingal's Cave* a quarter of a century earlier. In this Grieg was to be disappointed, for Gade showed little enthusiasm for *In Autumn* when the composer brought him the score on returning to Copenhagen. No doubt his coolness was justified, for the reason that Grieg was still an inexperienced orchestrator. The original version of the Overture is not extant; it was, however, turned into a piano duet, entered for a competition sponsored by the Swedish Academy of Music, won the first prize (Gade being one of the judges), and was published in the four-hand version by the Academy. Not until 1888 was the Overture performed as an orchestral piece, after the composer had re-scored it for the Birmingham Festival.

Whether under the influence of Nordraak's patriotism, or from his own heightened sense of responsibility towards the future of Norwegian music, Grieg now decided to make his headquarters in Christiania. With a view to a possible church appointment there, he took organ lessons from his Danish friend Matthison-Hansen, reaching a standard that allowed him to perform Bach's G minor Fugue (presumably 'the Great') in Roskilde Cathedral. He wrote to Ibsen in Rome, asking him to use his influence with Bjørnson, who was now Director of the Christiania Theatre, in support of an application for the vacant post of music director there; Bjørnson, however, failed to respond to his appeal, whereupon Ibsen, with surprising insight—for he was no musician—consoled Grieg by saying that he was surely destined for a more interesting career than that of theatre conductor.

Grieg's first bid for recognition in Christiania was made on 15th October 1866, when he announced a public concert with an all-Norwegian programme—in itself an event of some historic importance. Nina Hagerup sang songs by Nordraak, Kjerulf and Grieg (the Andersen *Melodies of the Heart*); the violinist Wilhelmina Norman-Neruda played Grieg's F major Sonata with the composer at the piano; and Grieg performed three of the *Humoresques* and most of the Piano Sonata. This venture not only attracted favourable notices in the press but also left the composer with a cash balance of 150 specie-dollars, and brought, soon afterwards, an invitation to become conductor of the city's amateur orchestral society (*Det Philharmoniske Selskab*).

The way to these successes had been smoothed by a generous though not uncritical article appearing in the Christiania newspaper *Morgenbladet* a month earlier, entitled 'On Norwegian music and some compositions by Edvard Grieg'. The author was Otto Winter-Hjelm, a slightly older man than Grieg, like him a product of the Leipzig Conservatory, and composer in 1861 of what is believed to be the first Norwegian symphony. He was to become one of Grieg's staunchest allies. By the end of the year they had planned together a school of music in Christiania, which opened in a modest way on 14th January 1867. In the same season the Philharmonic Society began a series of concerts under Grieg's direction. The first programme played for safety with Beethoven's Fifth Symphony, but the two subsequent concerts were more adventurous. On 23rd March Grieg conducted three movements of his own Symphony, together with the first part of Gade's cantata *The Crusaders*. On 13th April the symphony was Winter-Hjelms's second, in B minor, and Grieg re-orchestrated for the occasion Nordraak's incidental music to *Sigurd Slembe*. At the beginning of the next season, in autumn 1867, came an all-Grieg concert without orchestra. The Overture *In Autumn* was performed as a piano duet, and the rest of the programme included two male-voice part-songs to words by Jørgen Moe ('The Bear Hunt' and 'Evening Mood'), a Gavotte and Minuet for Violin and Piano (later to be used in the incidental music to *Sigurd Jorsalfar*) and a new Sonata for Violin and Piano, in G major (Op. 13), which had been written during the past summer and was dedicated to Svendsen.

Between the concert seasons, Edvard and Nina had been married in Denmark, and had returned to Christiania to make their home in an apartment in Øvre Voldgate. At the same time Grieg severed one of his links with Denmark by resigning from *Euterpe*. He was now to become more closely involved with Norwegian musicians, and in particular Johan Severin Svendsen and Halfdan Kjerulf. Svendsen, who was three years older than Grieg, had (like Carl Nielsen after him) learnt in youth to be a sound practical musician by playing in military bands and dance and theatre orchestras, and only at the age of twenty-four had enrolled at the Leipzig Conservatory, where he wrote his first Symphony (in D), and also proved his abilities as violinist and conductor. In autumn 1867 he gave a concert in Christiania, conducting the Symphony and other works. It was a disappointing occasion; the hall was half empty, but Grieg did what he could to awaken his countrymen to the great merits of Svendsen's music, and particularly to his clear, brilliant orchestration, by writing an enthusiastic article in *Morgenbladet* beginning: 'Today Norwegian art celebrated one of its triumphs.' To Svendsen, however, the indifference of this small and culturally immature capital city represented a personal defeat, and for several years he turned his back on Christiania. Not until 1872, after winning greater fame in Germany and France, did he return to his native country for a period of ten years, during which he became Grieg's strongest supporter in raising the standards of orchestral music in Christiania. Eventually, in 1883, he was to settle in Copenhagen as permanent conductor of the Royal Theatre Orchestra.

In contrast to Svendsen, Halfdan Kjerulf was a shy, retiring man who had originally studied for a legal career, turning to music as a full-time occupation only when he was thirty. In 1857 he had organized subscription orchestral concerts, the first ever known in Christiania, but his reputation was mainly that of a reliable piano-teacher and a composer of solo and part-songs, salon pieces for the piano, and folk-music arrangements. The sensitive workmanship and attractive national colouring that distinguish Kjerulf's compositions at their best entitle him to be considered not only as the most significant Norwegian composer of his generation, but also a major source of influence on Grieg's style—a fact that has been overshadowed by the more glamorous personality of Nordraak.[1] Kjerulf's most individual songs are his settings of lyrics from Bjørnson's stories of peasant life written about 1860, among the finest of these being 'Young Venevil', 'Ingrid's Song', and 'Synnøve's Song': the last-named may well have been in Grieg's mind when writing 'Solveig's Song' in *Peer Gynt*, just as echoes of Kjerulf's short piano pieces and folk-tune settings can be heard in the keyboard music of the younger composer. When Kjerulf died, in 1868, Bjørnson commemorated in verse his slender but choice legacy:

> Late into the summer bloomed the flowers;
> Late into the autumn spread the ripeness;
> Few were the fruits, but of a fragrant sweetness.

[1] Kjerulf's dry comment on hearing of the meeting of Grieg and Nordraak was: 'I must say, *les extrêmes se touchent!*'

The loss of Kjerulf and Svendsen left Grieg more isolated than ever in the still-provincial atmosphere of Christiania. Writing to Matthison-Hansen[1] he refers to 'the total isolation and feeling of ineffectiveness over here', and to the jealousy and hostility that seemed to surround him: 'Everyone hates my music, even the professional musicians.' [2] But he held on with resolution. When the Philharmonic Society looked like foundering for want of regular support, he revived Kjerulf's idea of subscription concerts as a means of creating an élite of serious music-lovers. The first concert, on 12th December 1867, included Mozart's G minor Symphony, Beethoven's *Egmont* music, the Nordraak Funeral March arranged for wind band, and a group of Kjerulf's songs with Nina as soloist. In the second concert, on 1st February 1868, the pianist Agathe Backer Gröndahl, later to become widely known as an interpreter of Grieg's Concerto and herself a composer of distinction, played the solo part in Beethoven's 'Emperor' Concerto. The third concert, on 4th April, was devoted to Mendelssohn's 'Scottish' Symphony with, again, the popular Gade cantata *The Crusaders*. Grieg's later retirement from long-term conducting engagements doubtless caused his pioneer work for concert life in Christiania to be undervalued; but it was no small achievement to have drawn audiences to substantial programmes like those just mentioned, and the major works that were heard in subsequent seasons: Mozart's Requiem, Mendelssohn's *Elijah*, Schumann's *Paradise and the Peri* and concert selections from Wagner's *Lohengrin*.

If Grieg came to look back on these years in Christiania as 'entirely unproductive', he must have been referring to his reduced activity as a composer. Apart from the second Sonata for Violin and Piano, all he had to show for the year 1867 was the first of the long series of books of *Lyric Pieces* (Op. 12). Yet one of these unpretentious keyboard miniatures was to bring

[1] Hauch, 12 December 1866.

[2] Hauch, 30 July 1867.

him into closer touch with that giant of the new Norwegian literature and eloquent spokesman for the nation, Bjørnstjerne Bjørnson. The Griegs spent Christmas 1867 with the Bjørnsons. When Grieg gave his host a copy of the recently published Op. 12, playing to him the wordless *National Song* which stands at the end of the collection, Bjørnson was inspired to set to this tune a stirring call to Norwegian youth, beginning 'Fremad!' (Forward!). The song was heard for the first time in public one evening in November 1868, in a students' torchlight procession in honour of the poet Welhaven, who had been compelled through ill-health to relinquish his university post. On the same occasion the *Serenade to Welhaven*, beginning 'Listen, O weary singer', was sung by the students; this also was the joint work of Grieg and Bjørnson, and was later to be published in the second book of *Romances* (Op. 18).

Though hardly more knowledgeable about music than Ibsen was, Bjørnson had a passionate belief in the power of song to animate and unite a nation. His earlier collaborators Nordraak and Kjerulf no longer being available, he henceforward turned again and again to Grieg, whether for a full-scale theatre score or for such occasional commissions as a cantata for the twenty-fifth anniversary of the opening of the Hals Brothers' piano factory,[1] or a chorus, the *The Norse Seaman*, for a regatta at Stavanger.

[1] The Hals Cantata, together with those written for the unveiling of the Christie, Kjerulf, and Holberg monuments, has recently been critically described and analysed by Bjarne Kortsen in *Four Unknown Cantatas by Grieg* (Oslo, 1972). While concurring in Dr Kortsen's judgment that closer acquaintance with these occasional works is most unlikely to enhance Grieg's reputation, one must admit that in the case of the Hals tribute both Bjørnson and Grieg made the most of the humorous possibilities of their subject; the poet's text includes a description, in his liveliest manner, of the vicissitudes of the domestic piano which the Hals firm had done so much to popularize

On 10th April 1868 a daughter was born to the Griegs and christened Alexandra. A song, 'Margaret's Lullaby', to verses from Ibsen's *The Pretenders*, dates from this time, and may enshrine a memory of the child who was to live little more than a year. 'Margaret's Lullaby' was published as Op. 15, No. 1. Another song can with greater probability be associated with Alexandra—the setting of a short poem in *landsmål* by Kristoffer Janson, 'Millom Rosor' (Among Roses, Op. 39, No. 4), which mourns the loss of a much-loved child.

Unmindful of the sorrow that lay in store for them, the Griegs spent a halcyon summer in a rented cottage at Søllerød in Denmark. Here came into existence the most satisfying and successful of Grieg's attempts at composing in the larger traditional forms, and the one that is generally agreed to be the most complete musical embodiment of Norwegian national Romanticism. Grieg dedicated the Concerto in A minor for Piano and Orchestra (Op. 16) to Edmund Neupert, who seems to have first played it in Copenhagen in April 1869. Within three years a full score was published, mainly through Svendsen's warm advocacy, by Fritzsch of Leipzig; this has long been superseded by the Peters scores, products of successive revisions of orchestral and solo parts which were to be carried out at intervals during the rest of the composer's life.

---

in Norway, while Grieg not only caricatures the child-beginner's efforts and the progress of a cat, Scarlatti-wise, across the keyboard, but at one point involves all the pianos in the Hals showroom in a simultaneous fantasia.

3 'The great tone-poet' (1868-77)

The creative outburst that produced the Piano Concerto in A minor during the peaceful summer weeks at Søllerød was to cease with Grieg's return, in the autumn of 1869, to the uncongenial environment of Christiania and the routine work of teaching and rehearsal. Without the stimulus of his Danish friends and the cultural life of Copenhagen he felt isolated and barren. It seemed as if the hardness of the Norwegian winter had its counterpart in human indifference and philistinism. 'Just think', he wrote to Matthison-Hansen,[1] 'for the whole winter I have heard no music except what I have been involved in.' The prospect of a State travelling grant seemed as remote as ever. Then, during the first dark days of 1869, he received Liszt's gracious letter, beckoning him out of his obscurity:

Monsieur,
il m'est fort agréable de vous dire le sincère plaisir que m'a causé la lecture de votre sonate (œuvre 8).
Elle témoigne d'un talent de composition vigoureux, réfléchi, inventif, d'excellente étoffe—, lequel n'a qu'à suivre sa voie naturelle pour monter à un haut rang. Je me plais à croire, que vous trouvez dans votre pays les succès et les encouragements que vous méritez; ils ne vous manqueront pas ailleurs non plus; et si vous venez en Allemagne

[1] Hauch, 10 April 1869.

cet hiver, je vous invite cordialement à vous arrêter un peu à Weimar, pour que nous fassions tout à fait bonne connaissance. Veuillez bien recevoir, Monsieur, l'assurance de mes sentiments d'estime et de considération très distinguée.

29. Decbr. 68, Rome. F. Liszt.

This generous testimonial appears to have been quite unsolicited, though perhaps prompted by some well-wisher of Grieg's among the Scandinavian community in Rome, such as Niels Ravnkilde, who may also have brought the Sonata for Violin and Piano (Op. 8) to Liszt's attention. Whatever its origin, the letter quickly opened doors that the young composer had been knocking at in vain, and a renewed application for a State grant was successful. More than a year was to pass, however, before taking up Liszt's invitation. In the meantime, there was the new Concerto to be introduced to the public in Denmark and Norway, and Grieg loyally gave two concerts in memory of Kjerulf, playing among other piano works the *Peasant Idyll*, an extended piece by Kjerulf in the programmatic national style that Ole Bull had made popular with his *Visit to the Sæter*. The summer was spent at the old family home of Landås, where Gesine Grieg, knowing her son's composing habits, had an outhouse (the traditional *stabbur* raised on short pillars to keep out damp and rats) set aside as a studio. There Grieg finished some of his Op. 18 songs to texts by H. C. Andersen and Jørgen Moe.

It was at Landås also that Grieg made a discovery that may be said to have changed the direction of his career. This was the treasury of Norwegian folk music, entitled *Ældre og nyere Fjeldmelodier* (Mountain melodies old and new), collected by the organist Ludvig Mathias Lindeman, who for more than a quarter of a century had been listening to singers and fiddle and *langeleik*[1]

[1] The *langeleik* is an elongated plucked string instrument with a single or double melody string provided with frets, and several free-sounding accompaniment strings or drones. The instrument is related

players in the more isolated parts of the country, and noting down their tunes in piano score. For the first time Grieg was now able to realize fully the variety and wealth of the traditional music of his native land,[1] and also to learn how a skilled musician (Lindeman was an organist of international renown and a most learned contrapuntist) could apply both technique and imagination to the transcription of folk-music, thereby underlining rather than obscuring its distinctiveness of tonality, intervals, rhythm and primitive polyphony. Before long Grieg had made his own arrangements of twenty-five of Lindeman's tunes, dedicating the little collection (Op. 17) to Ole Bull; and from this time until the end of his life he was to return to Lindeman again and again for fresh material and inspiration. From now, also, he began to lose interest in handling the major classical forms; in fact, only three such works—a string quartet and two sonatas—were to be completed after this date. Henceforward Grieg's best creative work was to be in the areas of lyric song and piano miniature, interspersed with folk-music arrangements for keyboard, voices or orchestra.

In February 1870 the Griegs at last caught up with Liszt, not in Weimar but in Rome, and Edvard described in racy letters to his parents how generously he was welcomed and encouraged. At the first interview, on 17th February, Liszt eagerly seized upon Grieg's portfolio, which happened to contain the G major Sonata for violin and piano. After getting the composer to run through it on the piano, Liszt took it over himself, playing violin part and all, and brushing aside all compliments with

---

to the Swedish *hummel*, and both gained a fresh lease of life in the New World as the Appalachian or mountain dulcimer. Grieg is known to have visited a player of the *langeleik*.

[1] Part of Lindeman's collection had been published as far back as 1841, so that Nordraak and Kjerulf, among others, may very well have been familiar with much of the material and Lindeman's way of treating it.

'I'm an experienced old musician and ought to be able to play at sight.' On a later visit (9th April) Grieg found Liszt surrounded as usual by an adoring throng: 'Sgambati and Winding were there, and a German Lisztite whose name I do not know, but who goes so far in the aping of his idol that he even wears the gown of an abbé. Add to these a Chevalier de Concilium, and sundry young ladies of the kind that would like to eat Liszt, hide, hair and all.' This time it was Grieg's newly completed Piano Concerto that aroused Liszt's curiosity and again demonstrated his fabulous sight-reading powers. His appreciation of the work was unstinted:

I must not forget one delightful episode. Towards the end of the finale the second theme is, you will remember, repeated with a great fortissimo. In the very last bars, where the first note of the first triolet—G sharp—in the orchestral part is changed to G natural, while the piano runs through its entire compass in a powerful scale passage, he suddenly jumped up, stretched himself to his full height, strode with theatrical gait and uplifted arm through the great monastery hall, and literally bellowed out the theme. At that particular G natural he stretched out his arm with an imperious gesture and exclaimed: 'G, G, not G sharp! Splendid! That's the real thing!' And then, quite *pianissimo* and in parenthesis: 'I had something of the kind the other day from Smetana.' He went back to the piano and played the whole ending over again. Finally, he said in a strange, emotional way: 'Keep on, I tell you. You have what is needed, and don't let them frighten you'.

In a more formal report which Grieg made to the Norwegian Ministry of Church Affairs and Education on the results of his study-tour, he stressed the importance of travel in the development of a Norwegian artist:

A northerner has within his national character so much heaviness and introspection, which cannot make any real headway against the *exclusive* position of German art. In order to serve the nationalist cause, a well-balanced disposition is required, a healthiness of mind, such as can only be gained when one's eyes are opened to what is to be learnt in the South. It is there that a freer and more comprehensive view of the world and of art in its entirety begins to unfold.[1]

He enlarged on the influence of Italian scenery, of the pictorial arts so richly displayed in that country, and of the opportunities for meeting other Scandinavian artists visiting or resident in Rome. In his own case, Grieg added, there had been the additional and invaluable experience of meeting Liszt:

I brought him several of my compositions, which he played, and it was of greatest interest for me to observe that it was the national element in them that arrested his attention, and indeed excited him. Such a triumph for my efforts and national ideals was in itself worth the journey.

But it was not only the immense prestige of commendation from Liszt that brought Grieg into the forefront of Norwegian cultural life. He reached this position even more rapidly through his close association, during the 1870s, with two of the leading figures in a regenerated literature that was soon to extend its influence not merely throughout Scandinavia, but over the whole Western world. The name of Grieg was to be linked with those of Ibsen and Bjørnson until the deaths of all three of them in the first decade of the twentieth century. After the lapse of another fifty years, fame has treated them very differently. Bjørnson is now honoured chiefly in his own country, his prose writings, poems, and plays little read outside Norway, although in his lifetime they made a deep impression throughout Europe, and perhaps above all in France. Ibsen's world reputation, on the other hand, has steadily increased, until he is now universally recognized as one of the greatest dramatists since Shakespeare and the founder of a new concept of dramatic literature and theatrical production. Grieg, because of the immediate acces-

[1] Grieg, *Artikler og Taler*, ed. Ø. Gaukstad (Oslo, 1957), p. 236.

sibility of his art and the relatively few intellectual demands it imposed, was in his lifetime the best known of the three; his fame, however, though still international, has contracted in the perspective of twentieth-century musical developments. The modern student of Ibsen may find it almost incredible that in the stage history of *Peer Gynt* Grieg could have performed the service of mouse to Ibsen's lion, though for a considerable time the musician's contribution to that notable drama was often valued equally with, and even above, the playwright's.

Grieg's contacts with Ibsen, though friendly, were intermittent. He was on closer terms with Bjørnson, who called him, in verses written after a visit from Grieg in 1899, 'the great tone-poet':

> He walked here beside me,
> the great tone-poet;
> I heard the waters flow
> with a lovelier cadence.
> And never in the world before,
> no matter how often I had trod the same path,
> had I understood completely
> how dear Nature had become to me in this place.[1]

Much of Bjørnson's finest lyric poetry gains heightened expression from settings Grieg made between 1870 and 1872. One of the most elaborate and widely performed, 'From Monte Pincio' (Op. 39, No. 1), might have been written to support Grieg's statement on the need for Norwegian poets and musicians to absorb the spirit of Italy. Of the four songs from Bjørnson's

[1] Han gikk her ved min side,
den store toneskald,
jeg hørte elven glide
med et skjønnere fall.
Og aldri før i verden,
så ofte jeg gikk turen,
forsto jeg helt hvor kjær den
var blitt meg her, naturen.

story *The Fisher Lass* published as Grieg's Op. 21, the opening one, 'The First Meeting', is a marvellous example of the restrained but intense passion, both in verse, and music, that is characteristic of the highest Norwegian art. In 'The Princess' (composed in 1871, and published without opus number), Grieg set a Bjørnson poem that had already been effectively treated by Kjerulf and was also to be chosen as the text of a song by Delius under the title of 'Twilight Fancies'.

The words of a cantata *Before a Southern Convent* (Op. 20), for women's voices, orchestra, and organ, come from *Arnljot Gelline*, an extended poem by Bjørnson which is based on Norse saga-lore and has been called 'one of the lasting glories of the national literature'.[1] Grieg at first intended to dedicate the cantata to J. P. E. Hartmann, but on learning that the Danish composer had himself set the same passage from *Arnljot* he transferred the dedication to Liszt. From Bjørnson's *Poems and Songs*, published in 1870, Grieg took the text, based on an episode in the Heimskringla saga, for a melodrama, *Bergliot* (Op. 42, 1871), which he originally set for spoken declamation with piano; the accompaniment was orchestrated in 1885. In 1872 poet and musician collaborated in a short choral work for male voices with orchestra and organ, or organ only, on the subject of Olav Trygvason's return to Norway to claim his throne and establish the Christian faith; this composition, entitled *Landkjenning* ('Landsighting' or 'Recognition of Land'), was meant for a special occasion: the inauguration of a fund for the restoration of the ancient cathedral of Trondhjem on 17th May 1872, a project of symbolic importance in the growth of nationalist pride. On the same date (Norwegian Constitution Day) Bjørnson's historical drama, *Sigurd Jorsalfar* (Sigurd the Crusader), the plot of which also was taken from the Heimskringla saga, was performed in Christiania. Grieg had provided the

[1] Brian Downs, *Modern Norwegian Literature, 1860–1918* (Cambridge, 1966), p. 23.

incidental music—two songs with chorus and three orchestral interludes. Both author and composer were present, though without much satisfaction. Bjørnson was critical of the dramatic production, while Grieg became more and more dejected as the audience chattered through the orchestral pieces and the principal actor made a poor attempt at the straightforward song assigned to him.

The way seemed open, however, for the partnership of Bjørnson and Grieg to culminate in a full-scale operatic work. They discussed the possibilities of *Arnljot Gelline* from this point of view, and Grieg even made a few sketches, but eventually they agreed to return to the Olav Trygvason story, and Bjørnson promised to provide a libretto on that subject. We shall deal later with the unhappy outcome of these proposals.

A set of three of Grieg's longer piano pieces published in 1872 under the title *Folkelivsbilleder* ('Scenes of Folk Life', Op. 19) includes the spectacular *Bridal Procession*;[1] the composer played it one Saturday night to the University Students' Association, and described afterwards its powerful effect on the national sympathies of the young audience:

I explained to them first what my idea was, and then played, and they understood in a flash what it was all about. There were shouts of 'Encore!' I was delighted, for there was a feeling of warmth on both sides... Then I said a few words about Nordraak and asked the students to sing the National Hymn. I didn't have to speak twice. I sat down at the piano, and now enthusiasm broke out with a vengeance: 'Ja, vi elsker dette landet'.[2]

It was not often that he could count on such spontaneity and sincerity of response, least of all in Christiania, where philistinism was rampant, the press lukewarm, and the quality of much of the orchestral playing lamentable. In one season (1874) the full

[1] The MS. of this piece is dated Landås, 24 July 1871.
[2] Letter to Beyer, 18 April 1872

orchestra could not be used at all, as the two bassoonists went on strike and there were no others to be had in the capital; in this emergency Grieg was glad to come across Schubert's *Song of the Spirits over the Waters* for male voices (there never seemed to be any lack of willing choral singers) and string orchestra.

Yet the autumn of 1871 saw the establishment, largely through Grieg's dogged persistence, of a professionally stiffened Music Society, from which the present-day Oslo Philharmonic is descended; and further progress was made possible by the return of Johan Svendsen to share with Grieg the conducting of the orchestral programmes and eventually to take them over altogether for a period. These exertions on behalf of the growing artistic life of the nation did not go entirely unregarded by the State. In 1873, when the new King, Oscar II, was crowned in Stockholm and Trondhjem, official honours were bestowed with a liberal hand on prominent citizens, Ibsen and Grieg being among those created Knights of St Olav. In addition, both Svendsen and Grieg were at last awarded substantial grants for study-tours. The terms of their joint application for this financial aid, submitted to the Department for Church Affairs and Education in February 1874, are interesting: once again they emphasize the need for a Norwegian artist to gain more experience abroad, especially in view of 'the still developing state of our cultural life, with none of the fruitful influence on the creative artist's imagination that exists abroad; since we lack the fundamental support subsisting in a national opera, with an orchestra and choir equal to the artistic demands of our times'.[1] As the grant awarded even now seemed too small to cover Grieg's expenses abroad and loss of income from work at home, he made a further application to the Department, stressing his desire 'to study dramatic music and to hear performances of the works of modern composers'. The original grant, he argues, will not suffice 'if

[1] *Artikler og Taler*, pp. 237–8. From the autumn of 1874 the Government agreed to pay Grieg an annual stipend of 1,000 *kroner*.

at the same time and with any effect I am to engage in some actual creative work in the dramatic field'.

This obsession with the operatic stage is understandable in any young musician of the 1870s, not least one belonging to a nation whose ancestors had evolved much of the Germanic mythology that inspired the new music-drama. But even the swelling tide of Wagnerian domination does not entirely account for Grieg's insistence on the necessity for developing a national opera in Norway. A full explanation of his attitude in this respect lies, yet again, in his relationships with the two major dramatists who were his compatriots and, for longer or shorter periods, his close associates.

On 10th July 1873 Bjørnson sent Grieg the first three scenes of *Olav Trygvason*, with a not untypical non-musician's airy request that the whole opera should be ready by October. Grieg at once set to work on the three scenes, which have their setting in a Norse pagan temple, and soon finished them in piano score. Then a whole year went by, and he was still awaiting the rest of the libretto, or even an outline of the plot. An exchange of letters, increasing in acerbity, followed; and when Grieg divulged that while waiting for the complete *Olav Trygvason* text he had undertaken to compose music for Ibsen's *Peer Gynt*, Bjørnson exploded with indignation, imagining that *Peer Gynt* was another opera. The upshot was that although Grieg was still asking for the rest of *Olav Trygvason* as late as 1876, Bjørnson never wrote another line of it. The breach that widened between the two friends was healed only in 1889, when Grieg adapted the temple scenes as a choral cantata.[1]

[1] It was typical of Bjørnson to form close attachments with fellow-artists, break them off impulsively on some real or imagined pretext, and later renew them on an even warmer basis. A long-standing quarrel with Ibsen had been patched up two years earlier (1887), but almost simultaneously a breach had come about with Strindberg. See Michael Meyer, *Henrik Ibsen*, Vol. 3, pp. 39–40.

The real truth was probably that Bjørnson had exhausted his interest in Norwegian legend and history. Since about 1870 there had been a reorientation of social, political, and literary thought in Norway, with Bjørnson as one of its most energetic pioneers. The 'modern breakthrough', which is usually dated from lectures given by the Danish author and critic Georg Brandes at Copenhagen University in 1867, had led to a decline of national Romanticism, especially in Norway, and its replacement by a stronger concern for contemporary problems, both at home and in the world at large. This movement was reflected most clearly in the development of serious prose drama, which was virtually the creation of the two giants, Bjørnson and Ibsen (to be followed before long by the younger Swede, August Strindberg). Bjørnson's plays of modern life dating from 1874 (*A Bankrupt* and *The Editor*) show this change of direction. Grieg, on the other hand, was always to remain a national-Romantic at heart, never really at home with the realistic, psychological, and expressionist manifestations of contemporary art and literature.

Yet the Norwegian theatre owed much to Grieg, no inconsiderable part of whose music came into existence in response to commissions from the two great dramatists. To understand their reliance on what to a modern producer would seem an excessive use of incidental music, it is necessary to bear in mind not only techniques of production and the tastes of theatre audiences at that time, but also the earlier history of the Norwegian stage since its tentative beginnings in the 1840s. It has been noted that the first national theatre was the realization of the dream of a musician, Ole Bull, in 1849, and had attempted to build a repertory around folk-music and ballet and musical plays (*syngespil*) such as Bjerregaard's *Fjeldeventyret* (The Mountain Story) and Wergeland's *Fjeldstuen* (The Mountain Hut); even Bjørnson himself had, in his younger days, written such a piece, interspersed with songs and dances, for the Christiania

Theatre.[1] In fact, the whole of the theatrical repertory in Christiania, when Ibsen and Bjørnson first came into contact with it, and whether traditionally Danish or self-consciously 'Norse', was biased towards *syngespil*, vaudeville, musical comedy, and ballet, with an admixture of grand and light opera by such composers as Rossini, Auber, Bellini, and Donizetti. Only by slow degrees was a public educated to accept continuous spoken drama as a serious form of entertainment. This explains why, even in the 1870s, the greatest living playwright could not think of adapting his poetic drama *Peer Gynt* (originally written in 1867) for the Christiania stage without a liberal sugaring of incidental music.[2] Ibsen explained his intentions in a lengthy letter addressed to Grieg from Dresden on 23rd January 1874:

A third edition of *Peer Gynt* is to appear shortly, and I intend to arrange it for stage performance. Will you compose the music required for this? I will explain briefly how I am thinking of adapting the work.

The first act is to be kept in its present form, except for a few cuts in the dialogue. I want Peer Gynt's monologue (Act I, sc. ii, opening) treated either as melodrama or in part as recitative. The wedding scene is to be made more telling than in the text, with the help of ballet. A dance-tune should be composed for this, and should continue in a subdued manner until the end of the act.

In the second act the scene with the three *sæter*-girls must be treated musically according to the composer's discretion, but there must be devilry in it! I have imagined the monologue (Act II, sc. iv) as accompanied by harmonies, that is to say, as melodrama. The same applies to the scene between Peer and the green-clad woman. Similarly there should be a kind of accompaniment to the scene in the Hall of

[1] Øyvind Anker: 'Bjørnson's syngespil *Nissen.*' *Norsk Musikkgranskning Årbok 1951–3*, pp. 37 fol.

[2] According to Ludvig Josephson, the Swedish-born director of the Christiania Theatre, a score for *Peer Gynt* had already been composed by his compatriot August Söderman, but this disappeared without trace after Söderman's death in 1876. See Michael Meyer, *Henrik Ibsen*, Vol. 2 (London, 1971), p. 193.

the Old Man of the Dovre, but here the dialogue is to be considerably shortened. The scene with the Bøyg is to be given in full, and must also be provided with music. The bird voices are to be sung; bell ringing and psalm singing are heard in the distance.

In the third act I need a few chords for the scene between Peer, the woman, and the troll-child....

Practically the whole of the fourth act will be omitted in performance. In its place I have imagined a big musical tone-painting, depicting Peer Gynt's wanderings about the world: American, English and French tunes might be heard in the course of it, as themes succeeding one another and vanishing again.

The chorus of Anitra and the girls will be heard behind a curtain, with orchestra. The curtain is to rise while it is in progress, and in the distance is seen the tableau described in Act IV, sc. x, where Solveig as a middle-aged woman sits singing in the sun outside the house. After her song, the curtain falls slowly, while the music continues in the orchestra and goes on to depict the storm at sea, with which the fifth act begins.

The fifth act, which counts in performance as the fourth or as an epilogue, is to be considerably shortened.... The incident of the wreck and the churchyard scenes are omitted.... The scenes with the Button-moulder and the Old Man of the Dovre are shortened. In sc. x the church congregation sings on its way through the wood; bell-ringing and psalm-singing are heard through the music that follows, until Solveig's song closes the play; then the curtain falls, while psalm-singing again sounds nearer and stronger.

That is roughly my idea of the whole. I shall be grateful if you will let me know whether you are willing to undertake the task.... I intend to stipulate for a royalty of 400 specie-dollars to be divided equally between us. I regard it as certain that we shall also be able to rely on performances in Copenhagen and Stockholm. But I request you to treat the matter as confidential at present, and to send me a reply as soon as possible.

Yours very sincerely,
Henrik Ibsen.

Grieg was all the more disposed to accept this flattering and attractive invitation now that the *Olav Trygvason* project seemed to be in abeyance. He also believed that all Ibsen required was 'a few fragments' of music, especially as the dramatist's extraordinary idea of replacing Act IV by 'a big musical tone-painting' had been firmly discouraged by Josephson. Yet initially he could summon up little enthusiasm for the job. He admired *Peer Gynt* as a literary work, but considered it 'the most unmusical of all subjects'. He worked on it throughout the second half of 1874 and well into the following year, at first in an ivy-covered garden house or pavilion in Sandviken, near Bergen, lent him by a friend, and later at Fredensborg in Denmark. In a letter addressed 'from the Pavilion' on 27th August 1874 he told Frants Beyer:

Peer Gynt progresses very slowly, and there is no possibility of having it finished by autumn. It is a terribly unmanageable subject, except in a few places, as where Solveig sings; I have in fact finished that already. I've also done something about the Hall of the Old Man of the Dovre, and I literally can't bear to listen to it, it is so full of cow-turds, Norse-Norsehood, and Be-to-thyself-enoughness! But I am taking trouble to let the irony come through, especially where Peer Gynt is forced at last to say, against his will, 'May the cat scratch me, if both dancing and playing weren't very nice indeed'.

The play was first performed, with Grieg's music, on the Christiania stage on 28th February 1876, in the absence of both dramatist and composer; the former was still living abroad, the latter was in Bergen. The production was a success, running for thirty-seven performances, until a fire in the theatre destroyed the scenery and costumes. There was a revival in Copenhagen in 1885, another in Christiania in 1892, with Bjørn Bjørnson, the son of Bjørnstjerne and now Ibsen's son-in-law, in the title-role, and yet another Christiania production in 1902. On each of these occasions Grieg was asked to add to the music. The full score, published by Peters in 1908, contains over twenty numbers.

As the literary and dramatic greatness of Ibsen's work came to be more fully appreciated, and as techniques of stage production became more sophisticated, it was inevitable that much, if not all, of Grieg's incidental music should become outmoded and redundant, though Ibsen, who saw his play on the stage for the first time in 1892, had to admit that it was the music that helped *Peer Gynt* over the footlights. The Viennese critic Hanslick, the original of Wagner's Beckmesser, with his unfortunate proclivity for backing the wrong horse, expressed his opinion (in 1891) that 'perhaps in a few years Ibsen's *Peer Gynt* will live only through Grieg's music, which to my taste has more poetry and artistic intelligence than the whole five-act monstrosity of Ibsen.'[1]

The two orchestral suites Grieg put together from the longer *Peer Gynt* pieces did more than any of his works, except the Concerto, to spread his reputation through the world's concert halls; indeed, after a quarter of a century their incessant overexposure, hastened by a plethora of arrangements (some by Grieg himself) and by the development of the mechanical media, had almost destroyed the freshness that had been among their most appealing qualities. To the composer the two *Peer Gynt* suites brought not only fame and money but also a much-needed access of confidence; these were, after all, fairly sizeable works, useful programme-fillers, and an answer to the charge that he was nothing more than a purveyor of pretty trifles. He also felt, no doubt, that the experience of working with Ibsen had brought him several stages nearer to the creation of the true Norse opera which had been one of the chief ambitions of Norwegian composers from Ole Bull and Rikard Nordraak onwards.

Grieg's ties with the Norwegian capital became looser during

[1] Quoted by Henry T. Finck, *Grieg and his Music* (New York, 1929), p. 129.

the middle 1870s. He had never liked Christiania, preferring, as so many Norwegians still do, the Westland and above all the endearing town of Bergen and its mountain hinterland. Notwithstanding his growing international reputation, his works were neglected in Christiania. A detailed concert calendar for the year 1875[1] shows that scarcely anything of his was publicly performed in the capital during that year—only a handful of part-songs, occasionally a solo song, and two movements from the first Sonata for Violin and Piano. Several music teachers, however, were advertising themselves as having been pupils of Grieg, and a newspaper announces that 'Edvard Grieg will be returning home in late September and offers from 1 October tuition in piano-playing and harmony'.[2] Any lessons arranged must have been cancelled, as both of Grieg's parents died in the early autumn, and he remained for several weeks in the old family home in Strandgaten, Bergen, spending part of the time in composing one of his major piano works, the *Ballade in the form of Variations on a Norwegian folktune* (Op. 24), whose poignancy, inspired by the beautiful melody from Valdres, seems also to overflow into the songs written at this melancholy time. These include the settings of six poems by Ibsen (Op. 25), all of which belong to Grieg's highest achievements in lyric song. The first of the Ibsen settings, 'Fiddlers' (*Spillemænd*), was to be used later as the motto-theme of the String Quartet (Op. 27), and two of the others, 'A Swan' and 'With a Water-lily', were among those most often sung by Nina in her recitals. Grieg's

[1] W. P. Sommerfeldt, 'Musiklivet i Christiania . . . en Dagbok fra 1875', in *Festskrift til O. M. Sandvik* (Oslo, 1945), pp. 223–46.

[2] The demand for piano lessons must have increased perceptibly in Norway at this time. T. K. Derry, in *A Short History of Norway*, 2nd edition (London, 1968), describes the economic expansion of the country, and notes (p. 180) that in a four-year period (1869–73), 'Norway was able to double the consumption of sugar and coffee, silks and wines, and even of pianos.'

old friend from the early years in Bergen, John Paulsen, provided the texts for another set of songs (Op. 26), among them 'With a Primrose', which also became intimately associated with Nina Grieg.

In August 1876 Grieg and Paulsen set off together for Bayreuth to attend the first cycle of the complete *Ring* ever to be performed there. The newspaper *Bergensposten* commissioned Grieg to send home by instalments a detailed account of the Festival. The six lengthy despatches that resulted are excellent examples of his lively style of writing and of his independent but generally balanced judgment. Unlike many of his contemporaries, he was neither resistant to Wagner's genius nor subservient to it, but was able to make personal reservations against a background of sincere appreciation of the stupendous greatness of *The Ring* and of the ideal conditions of performance at Bayreuth. His critical integrity and gift for sharp-pointed observations are well illustrated in the following excerpt from his article on *Götterdämmerung*:

There is no doubt that *Götterdämmerung* is the foremost and in a dramatic sense the most effective of the four dramas. Here is enacted the great tragic conflict to which the other dramas lead up, here the fate of human beings and gods is fulfilled, here Wagner for the first time in the whole trilogy [*sic*] includes crowds (men and women of the Gibichungs); he knew what he was doing to keep these resources to the end. And then the rapid succession of events! And what an ending! Just as in the first drama the Rhine maidens appear as guardians of the gold, so in the fourth they finally come into possession of it again. Thus the poet forces us to look back and survey the whole cycle, whose main features now assert themselves with renewed force . . . I can hardly venture to write about the music of this last gigantic work. It presents such a world of greatness and beauty that one is almost dazzled. If I go rapidly through the score, I am brought up right at the outset by the song of the Norns. The dark colouring of this passage is noteworthy. Monotonous figuration sounds menacingly against ominous harmonies; the orchestra spins the thread of life as significantly as the Norns, who indeed only contribute subordinate parts to the texture. I have heard this scene under Wagner's own baton at a concert in Berlin. He had no Norns, let the orchestra play alone very quietly, and hummed with it himself. I mention this, because it helps to make my point when I maintain that the voice-parts in the work as a whole are not balanced with the orchestra, but seem as it were to be superimposed on it. The orchestra is used to the uttermost, so why not the voices also? . . . The voices should either be allowed the same freedom as the orchestra to express the deepest human emotions or they ought not to be there. But then we should have melodrama. Such a transitional style, between singing and non-singing, has no future, no intelligibility, even though defended in a whole literature of pamphlets. It is the feeling of untenability in Wagner's theories on the treatment of the voice which always puts a restraint on the immediate enjoyment that a great work of art should give. This of course has nothing to do with the great ideal worth that Wagner's music possesses, and which I do not hesitate to describe as unique in modern dramatic music.[1]

Writing as he was for a Norwegian paper, Grieg could hardly avoid reference to the relationship between Wagnerian mythology and the Edda, saga and ballad literature that formed part of the inheritance of his readers. For example, he discusses Hagen's horn-calls summoning the vassals:

Here we find, now and then, some trace of the old Scandinavian atmosphere, something one would naturally not expect in Wagner. But the fact that it is there shows the strength of his inspiration in this episode. It is of course not his fault, though it must be regretted, that the Scandinavian folk-element is not natural to him; here of all places one would wish for it, when he is portraying Scandinavian antiquity, of which our ballads are the most distinctive product. He wants his mediæval Teutonic hero to be 'primitive Germanic'; but I cannot help thinking that if a Scandinavian with Wagner's gifts were to work on the myth of Sigurd the Slayer of Fafnir, we should feel rather more of

[1] *Artikler og Taler*, pp. 75 fol.

the Edda-atmosphere. It is unfortunate that works like Hartmann's *Valkyrien* and *Thrymskviden* are presumably unknown to Wagner, for in them we have brilliant examples which could not fail to impress a man of Wagner's vision.

Grieg's reactions to Wagner's musical personality are perhaps best of all summed up in the notice he sent to *Bergensposten* a week earlier, after attending *Rheingold*:

I go home and say to myself that in spite of all reservations, in spite of the restlessness with which the gods are depicted, in spite of the many chromatic modulations, the ceaseless harmonic changes, which cause one to be overcome gradually by a nervous irritability and finally by complete exhaustion, despite the intricate detail, the total lack of points of repose, despite the way the whole work is poised on the extreme verge of beauty, despite everything,—this music-drama is the work of a giant, the like of whom the history of art can only have seen in Michelangelo.

When the Bayreuth Festival was over, Grieg and Paulsen resolved to travel by rail to Gossensass, where Ibsen was then living. Grieg got on extremely well with Ibsen, as he sometimes did with notoriously difficult people (including Brahms), and Ibsen always unbent in his company. Grieg wanted to discuss the recent production of *Peer Gynt*, and perhaps also to broach further plans for collaboration. Paulsen, who must have been present at much of their conversation, refers to this subject in his memoirs:

Grieg, who always dreamt of writing a lyric opera, was for ever hunting for a good text.

Regarding his youthful work, the lyrical, romantic, ballad-influenced *Olav Liljekrans*, Ibsen had once told me that if it was no more use for anything else it would at any rate do for an opera libretto. He had in fact at one time tried to adapt it as such, calling the new work *The Mountain Bird* (*Fjeldfuglen*) and invited the Trondhjem composer Udbye[1] to set it to music; but somehow the plan came to nothing.

I told Grieg about this, and he now consulted Ibsen, who mentioned his old play. But *Olav Liljekrans* could not satisfy Grieg. He wanted something new and fresh, something that would inspire him, and apparently he cherished the secret hope that Ibsen would write something specially for him.[2]

But Ibsen was too busy, and tried to put the composer off with other suggestions, like using Welhaven's ballad *Eivind Bolt.* '"You ought to do what the young Wagnerians do", Paulsen suggested to Grieg, "and write the libretto yourself. You have more of a literary flair than other composers, and you would do it extremely well." But Grieg only shook his head.' Paulsen continues: 'Many, many years after this memorable summer in Gossensass Grieg confided to me that his dearest wish had at last been gratified. Ibsen wanted to make an opera text for him out of *The Vikings of Helgeland.* Grieg was delighted. *The Vikings,* with its strongly dramatic scenes and resonant saga character, was eminently suitable.' But when Grieg eventually saw Ibsen's text he was disappointed to find that very little adaptation had been done: 'And so the collaboration between poet and composer came to a sudden halt, and we lost our chance of that irreplaceable thing, a national opera from the pen of Grieg.'

Did Grieg ever realize that his contemporary, Smetana, was at this very time achieving what he himself was never destined

[1] Martin Andreas Udbye (1820–89) is one of the least-known of Norwegian composers of the generation before Grieg's. Very little of his music has been published, and the score of his one completed opera, *Fredkulla,* was destroyed by fire in the theatre where it was about to be produced. An opera based on *Olav Liljekrans,* by Arne Eggen, was performed in Oslo in 1940.

[2] John Paulsen, *Samliv med Ibsen* (Anden Samling) (Copenhagen and Christiania, 1913), pp. 16 fol.

to do, either by talent or by opportunity—the foundation of a whole national operatic repertoire? If so, it must have heightened his disappointment that the fulfilment of a similar mission was denied to him. In a letter to Beyer, dated 27th August 1886, Grieg refers to Beyer's recent hearings of *Tristan* and *Parsifal* during a holiday in Germany:

Now you can realize why many a time I go and stare up at the clouds, as if I could find there the Norwegian drama in Norwegian music which I have dreamt of, which I have always believed I could create one day, but which I now begin to believe is fated to come from another. Yet come it will; and it will come with the depth and greatness of Wagner himself, perhaps after our time, and then only if there are souls like yours to recognize it. Then I shall lie as joyfully in the grave as if I had done it myself. It is human nature to strive to encompass everything, and I have, alas, to admit that the circumstances of my life have brought it about that I find my expression in the lyric. But apart from that, and taking everything into account, I have never yet set eyes on a text that could kindle my musical imagination. And if I do not find one, I would rather leave the drama unwritten than write it badly.

4 In Hardanger country 1877-87

The tour in Germany and immersion in Wagner's greatest music reinvigorated Grieg's own creative zest. But he still had little time for composition. The season 1876–7 was largely occupied with the Music Society and with a concert tour in Sweden, a country where, despite the political tensions then existing, the Griegs were always welcomed, and where Grieg's music was to have almost as strong an influence as in Norway itself; by the end of the century he was more frequently performed there than any other composer. Back in Christiania, he wrote to Max Abraham, of the Leipzig publishing firm of Peters: 'You speak of composition, and here I sit and give lessons and hold rehearsals, choir-practices, and the rest of it. I shall be glad of the summer, when I can get into the country and work.'[1] A curious by-product of his piano-teaching was the set of second-piano parts to four of Mozart's sonatas, an act of sheer vandalism in the view of many critics, though perhaps to be condoned in an age such as our own, when the 'recomposing' of older works, far from being treated as impertinence, may attract commendation in the highest quarters.

With the arrival of summer, the Griegs began their long stay in the beautiful Hardanger country,[2] at first on a farm at Upper

[1] Zschinsky-Troxler, 31 January 1877.

[2] The romantic beauty of the Norwegian mountains was a comparatively recent discovery. It had begun in the 1830s with scientific and artistic tours by geologists, naturalists and painter. It was a geologist, B. M. Keilhau, who gave the name 'Jotunfjellene' ('The giant moun-

Børve, and then at Lofthus, in a guest-house kept by Hans and Brita Utne, who had a family of twelve children and habitually wore their traditional Hardanger costumes. For a time Grieg used the village school room as a study, but soon acquired a log hut on the edge of the Sørfjord, just large enough to hold a piano, a chair, and a table, and with an uninterrupted view of the Folgefonn Glacier. When passers-by, attracted by the sound of the piano, began to eavesdrop outside what was locally called 'the tune-house', Grieg availed himself of the custom known as the *dugnad*, enlisting the help of about fifty men, liberally supplied with food and drink, to manhandle the structure to a more sequestered position: a day's work the composer described amusingly in words—not forgetting his playing of the folk-dance *Stabbe-Låten* (Op. 17, no. 18) to the festive peasants—and the painter Wilhelm Peters illustrated in a spirited series of sketches. Peters, who was a fellow-guest of the Griegs' at this time, has given us a glimpse of Edvard's methods of work:

On stormy days, when the wind shook our house, rattling doors and windows like spirits playing an immense orchestra, Grieg sat in a corner, listening. I have known composers who, in writing a little song, would use up a cart-load of paper. Not so with Grieg: he would use only a single sheet. He wrote his music with a lead-pencil, rubbed out, and substituted and changed again, until he was satisfied. Then he wrote it over in ink, and sent to the publisher the same sheet with which he began.[1]

This first stay in Hardanger country, from summer 1877 to

---

tains') to the great range between Sogne and Valdres, and mapped and sketched it for the first time. Well after the middle of the century a tour in the mountains was still regarded as a bold and strenuous venture.

[1] Wilhelm Peters, 'Grieg the man: reminiscences of a friend', in *Illustrated Monthly Magazine* (New York), November 1907. The artist's sketches of the *dugnad* are included in this article in half-tone reproductions.

autumn 1878, was among the happiest and most fruitful of Grieg's career. He had quiet and solitude in which to work, but was not too far from Bergen to receive an occasional visitor, or even to travel there and give a concert. At first he was troubled by uncertainty of aims, and wrote to Matthison-Hansen in Denmark:

Day by day I become more dissatisfied with myself. Nothing I do pleases me, and even if I seem to have ideas, there is neither fluency nor form when I proceed to the working out of anything on a large scale.... It is due to lack of practice, and also to lack of technique, because I have never managed to get beyond composing by fits and starts. But there must be an end of that now. I want to battle through the larger forms, cost what it will.[1]

But he wrote to Paulsen a few days later in more relaxed mood:

It is a beautiful Sunday morning. I am sitting in the school house, where I have made myself a little study, and watching the people rowing by to church on the Sognefjord.[2]

Such a scene, with a fiddle being played in one of the boats, is said to have inspired the middle section of the *Album Leaf* (Op. 28, no. 4).[3]

Only one of the Hardanger works really comes within the category of 'the larger forms' Grieg was so anxious to master. This is the String Quartet (Op. 27):

It is in G minor [he wrote to Matthison-Hansen],[4] and is not intended to deal in trivialities. It aims at breadth, movement, and above all at bringing out the sound of the instruments for which it is written. I needed to write this as a study. Now I want to tackle another chamber music work. I believe that in this way I shall find myself again. You have no idea what trouble the forms have given me, but that is because

[1] Hauch, 13 August 1877.
[2] Hauch, 19 August 1877.
[3] Röntgen, p. 19.
[4] Hauch, 10 September 1878.

I was coming to a standstill, and that in its turn was partly due to a number of occasional works (*Peer Gynt*, *Sigurd Jorsalfar*, 'and other horrors'), and partly to an overdose of 'folkiness'.

The Quartet follows a cyclic pattern, with the first of the Ibsen songs, 'Fiddlers' (Op. 25, no. 1), used as a motto theme. Grieg took endless pains with this work, dwelling on its revolutionary structure, and sending numerous amendments to Robert Heckmann, the violinist to whom it was dedicated, and whose quartet gave the first performance in Cologne in October 1878. The composer's plan for producing another chamber work was not to be realized; he seems to have begun a Piano Trio at Lofthus, but only an Andante movement survives. The second String Quartet, begun in 1891, was published in fragmentary form after the composer's death.

Grieg hoped to find a series of texts for a large-scale choral work by drawing upon the collection of words of old Scandinavian ballads published by M. B. Landstad in 1853 under the title of *Norske Folkeviser* (though not all of them are Norwegian, and philologically the work suffers from an uncritical outlook). Only one ballad offered Grieg what he wanted—*The Mountain-Thrall* ('Den Bergtekne')—but his setting of this for solo baritone, two horns, and strings (Op. 32), is among his strongest national-Romantic works, written, as he said, 'with his heart's blood'.

He also drew again on Lindeman's great treasury of folk music, making free arrangements for male voice ensemble of twelve of the songs (Op. 30), ranging from the broadly humorous 'Røtnams Knut' from Valdres, to the ecstatic hymn 'The Great White Host'; from the children's jingle 'Bådn-Låt' to the satirical 'It is the greatest foolishness'. A whole virile peasant culture is mirrored in this notable collection.

Again the composer's imagination was being concentrated into miniature forms, but with a compensating enhancement of expressive power, principally through the intensified use of what had always been, from his student days, a leading feature of his style, namely his fondness for chromaticism, especially in combination with diatonic melody. Whether in original compositions or in arrangements of folk music, this tendency asserts itself most strongly in the works of the Hardanger period.

Perhaps the finest of these are the two books of settings of *Melodier* (Op. 33) by Aasmund Olavsson Vinje, a journalist and poet of peasant stock who had struggled to gain a higher education but had died in distressful circumstances in 1870. His verse was written in the dialectal Norwegian first studied and formulated in 1848 by the grammarian Ivar Aasen, who called it the rural language (*landsmål*) as distinct from the Dano-Norwegian (*riksmål*) of the urban educated classes. *Landsmål* has rich sonority and is capable of a rugged vigour of expression. In his journal *The Dalesman* (*Dølen*), where most of the poems first appeared, Vinje calls it 'the old tongue':

> Old tongue and fiddle-tune,
> rhyme and halling-dance:
> these four go with one another,
> bound together in a circlet
> placed around the people's brow
> like a bridal crown.[1]

[1] *Dølen*, 5 June 1859: Gamalt mål og felelåt,
dikt og hallingdans:
desse fire fylgjast åt,
bundne saman i ein ring
lagde folkepanna kring
som ein brure-krans.

Norway's most influential writers, Bjørnson and Ibsen, never supported *landsmål*, Ibsen making it an object of ridicule in *Peer Gynt*. These authors preferred a gradual transformation of the language through the widening of its vocabulary from colloquial and dialect sources and the re-spelling of Dano-Norwegian to bring it into conformity with spoken usage.

The second of the Vinje songs, 'The Spring' (*Våren*), is perhaps the most moving of all Grieg's compositions; together with 'The Wounded Heart' (*Den Sårede*) it was later transcribed for strings under the title of *Elegiac Melodies* (Op. 34).

His repeated visits to the Hardanger region brought Grieg into direct contact with the still-living traditions of folk music. He became acquainted with several of the local hardanger-fiddle players, and even tried to write down their elaborately ornamented dance tunes and bridal marches. He spent his thirty-fifth birthday at Lofthus, and gave a party at which Ole Bull was among the guests. Perhaps it was at Bull's suggestion that a renowned local fiddler, Ola Mosafinn, was sent for to entertain the company. Another *spelmann*,[1] Lars Kinsarvik, recalled Grieg's interest in the 'Norwegian scale, following one rule ascending and another descending!'.[2]

The periods of rest and tranquillity spent at Lofthus alternated with an increasingly busy public life. Grieg's fame was growing rapidly, especially in Germany, and the autumn and winter months were usually filled with extended concert tours. He was in Leipzig more than once in the season 1878–9; on 30th November there was an all-Grieg programme at the Gewandhaus, with the composer playing piano pieces from Ops. 6, 19 and 28, the piano part in a performance of the Violin Sonata in G (Op. 13), and accompaniments to a group of songs. The String Quartet also was performed in the same programme by the Heckmanns. The *Signale* notice of this work, from the pen of the critic Bernsdorf, can have done little to sweeten Grieg's old associations with Leipzig:

We have experienced nothing but distaste for the absurdities here

[1] *Spelmann* (plural *spelmenn*), 'musician, fiddler', is an alternative way of writing *spillemand* (plural *spillemænd*, as in the Ibsen song, Op. 25, No. 1).

[2] Arne Bjørndal, *Norsk Folkemusikk* (Bergen, 1952), pp. 285 fol.

brought together under the cloak of nationalism, which scarcely conceals with the style and colour of Norwegian costume (which in any case the non-Norwegian must take on trust) the insignificance of the invention, and above all the want of any power of organization and development, any ability to fill out the design appropriate to an extended movement (particularly in the Sonata and the Quartet) without letting the seams show.[1]

Bernsdorf added ruefully that the entire concert was received with rapturous applause. How little Grieg's popularity suffered from adverse press criticism was evident from his recall to Leipzig the following March, when the Violin Sonata in F was performed, attracting another acid notice from *Signale*, and yet again in October 1879, when he played the solo part in his Piano Concerto. The Griegs seem to have enjoyed themselves socially in Leipzig, forgathering with other Norwegian musicians —Christian Sinding, Iver Holter, and Ole Olsen—and the Finnish conductor and composer Robert Kajanus, who may have been behind the offer, made to Grieg a few years later, of the directorship of the newly founded Helsingfors conservatory (now the Sibelius Academy). Between his Leipzig seasons he had a particularly heartening reception in Copenhagen on 30th April 1879. The royal family was present, and the hall was sold out; again, the only dissentient voice came from a local critic who found the F major Sonata 'bizarre and formless'. He must, Grieg said drily, have been reading the Leipzig *Signale*.

On his return to Norway, Grieg accepted, out of loyalty to his birthplace, the appointment of conductor to the Bergen *Harmonien*. He found the duties no easier than those he had so gladly relinquished in Christiania. His choral singers were responsive enough, but the orchestral resources, especially the wind, were lamentable, and he had trouble with the administra-

[1] The German original of Bernsdorf's notice is quoted in the English edition of Monrad Johansen's biography, pp. 217–18.

tors. 'I was up to the neck', he wrote, 'in stupidity, anonymous abuse, and all the rest of it.' It was neither the first nor the last time that his artistic integrity, combined with an inherited toughness, brought him into conflict with regional complacency. But he had set himself an objective and meant to achieve it, as he told Matthison-Hansen:

I said to myself, once I had agreed to give up a winter to my native town, that I would work with all my energies to advance artistic taste a step forward in that time. And I do not think the work has been wasted. But I cannot go on with it any longer. Someone else must now carry on the task. I have not given a lesson this winter, or composed a single note.[1]

The first *Harmonien* concert of the 1880–1 season began with Ole Bull's well-loved melody 'The Sæter-girl's Sunday', in memory of the grand old man of Norwegian music, who had died on his estate at Lysøya the previous August, mourned by the whole nation. Among the works the Society performed in the course of the season were the Mozart *Requiem*, Beethoven's Fantasia (Op. 80) with Erika Lie as soloist, Svendsen's Norwegian Rhaposdy (Op. 21), and Gade's *Agnete and the Merman*, in which Nina Grieg sang the soprano solo part. Grieg was persuaded to stay with *Harmonien* for another year, during which he conducted Beethoven's Seventh and Svendsen's B♭ Symphonies, Mendelssohn's *Elijah*, and his own Piano Concerto.

As for original composition, Grieg was in one of his periodic troughs of nonproductivity. Even Lofthus seemed to have lost its magic: 'The mountains no longer have anything to say to me', he lamented. The only new work since the Vinje Songs was the set of *Norwegian Dances* for piano duet (Op. 35), based on folk-tunes taken from the inexhaustible Lindeman collection. Grieg dreaded these barren stretches, which he attributed variously to chronic bad health, to the distractions of travel and

[1] Hauch, 29 April 1881.

concert-giving, and to what he still insisted was a deficiency of technical equipment, to be laid at the door of the Leipzig Conservatory. He realized, too, the problems of reconciling his devotion to folk-music with the principles of sophisticated art-forms.

But these factors do not make up a completely satisfactory explanation of the spasmodic and uneven character of Grieg's creativity. A more comprehensive analysis has been offered by the historian, Wilhelm Keilhau:

> The causes lay rather in certain idiosyncrasies of his inner nature. In the first place, he was extremely self-critical, and for this reason he did not always have the heart to follow his inspirations; he was also afraid to realize anything that was not complete in every detail. But in addition there was some lack of initiative in his personality. He needed an impetus from outside to set him going, or to meet people who could give him his head. Many of his compositions owed their origin to commissions and to the influence of others—of his Leipzig teachers, of Nina Hagerup, Nordraak, Bjørnson, Ibsen, the management of the Christiania Theatre, the Holberg Festival committee of Bergen, and so on. For this reason there is something fortuitous about his work; he was not able to pursue a self-chosen path towards distant goals. And finally, Grieg did not have the good fortune to be in harmony with his own time. He was a romantic through and through—at first early-romantic, then national-romantic—and he was at the height of his creative powers in the anti-romantic 1880s. And when the new-romantic movement dawned, he blazed up again and set to music Vilhelm Krag's poems and *Haugtussa*. But it was in the 1890s that his health was particularly weak. Then came the twentieth century, with music representing technological and sensational tendencies. Grieg could not endure the contemporary age.[1]

Grieg's relationship to artistic tendencies in the early twentieth century is perhaps more complex than Keilhau suggests; but

[1] Wilhelm Keilhau, *Det norske folks liv og historie gjennem tidene*, Vol. 10, 1875–1920 (Oslo, 1935), pp. 296–7.

much of his diagnosis of Grieg's need for the stimulation of other personalities is convincing enough. Yet his Romantic outlook in itself often prevented Grieg from appreciating the value of outside commissions in setting in motion his creative impulses. He was prone to underestimate the quality of such works as the *Peer Gynt* music and the *Holberg* suite for the very reason that they were produced under circumstances not of his choosing, until their continued popularity at length convinced him that they must have some intrinsic value.

In 1881, however, he took a step which was to impose some kind of regular pattern on his output, even if not to increase it materially. Half in earnest, he wrote from Bergen to Max Abraham:

The *Norwegian Dances* are ready and will follow in the next few days. ... I notice to my surprise that composing is good for my constitution, providing that I am, so to speak, forced into it. I believe that if someone offered to pay me 1000 *Thaler* a year, my conscience would give me no rest until I had finished the agreed quantum. But I cannot compose just now, though I feel at this moment the impulse to do so, since I have again taken on the conducting of the winter concerts and must begin preparations as soon as possible.[1]

Abraham replied almost by return of post, offering 3000 Marks, with the request that within twelve months Grieg would write another piano concerto, several piano pieces, and a concert overture, or a piano trio or violin sonata or some shorter pieces for violin and piano. From the first it was understood on both sides that the terms of the contract would be flexible, the dimensions and types of work being largely at the composer's discretion.

It was not until the spring of 1883 that the first of the promised new compositions was sent off from Bergen. This was the Sonata for Cello and Piano (Op. 36); it was dedicated to the

[1] Zschinsky-Troxler, 22 August 1881.

composer's brother John Grieg, but the first public performance on 27th October 1883 in Leipzig was given by Grieg with Julius Klengel, the Conservatory professor who had been John Grieg's teacher. Abraham's hopes of a second piano concerto were not to be fulfilled; in the composer's words, 'Pegasus wouldn't budge', and only a few sketches for it remain. The piano miniatures, however, which from now onwards appeared almost annually in the form of sets of half a dozen *Lyric Pieces*, must have given the publishers no little satisfaction with their side of the bargain. The popularity of the domestic piano reached its height in the fifty years straddling the turn of the century, and the *Lyric Pieces* were to carry the composer's name into parlours and schoolrooms on both sides of the Atlantic. Their familiar pink covers almost certainly prompted Debussy's notorious description of Grieg's style (though written *à propos* the *Elegiac Melodies*): 'On a dans la bouche le goût bizarre et charmant d'un bonbon rose qui serait fourré de neige.'

Although he had resigned his conductorship of *Harmonien*, Grieg must have found the year 1883 a gruelling one for his frail physique. He visited Bayreuth again in the summer, this time to attend the production of *Parsifal*; spent two months at Rudolstadt in Thuringia, where he tried to polish up his French in view of a forthcoming series of concerts in Paris; and then started on a concert tour that took in Weimar (where he found Liszt 'incredibly old . . . it was pitiful to see him'), Dresden, Leipzig, Breslau, the Rhineland, and some of the larger Dutch towns—Arnhem, The Hague, Rotterdam, and finally Amsterdam, where he spent Christmas with Julius Röntgen, henceforth to become one of his firmest friends and most faithful biographers.

After more concerts in Amsterdam in the New Year Grieg was too exhausted to accept Edouard Colonne's invitation to Paris. Instead he went about for a month making social visits, telegraphed for Nina to join him, and set off with her to Italy to recuperate. In Rome one evening in March 1884 they attended a party in the house of the Norwegian painter Kristian Ross, and found Ibsen among the guests. Nina sang nearly all her husband's settings of Ibsen poems,

> and after 'Margaret's Lullaby', and especially after 'I called thee my messenger of joy' and 'A Swan' the ice-crust melted, and he came over to the piano . . . with tears in his eyes, and pressed our hands, almost without being able to say a word. He muttered something to the effect that this was 'understanding', and I need not tell you that on this occasion Nina sang no less understandingly than she always does.[1]

The Italian holiday, with its visits to the show-places of Sorrento, Naples and Pompeii, varied with an occasional recital, allowed the Griegs to escape altogether the long winter and tardy spring of the North, and even to celebrate Constitution Day (17th May) beside Lake Maggiore, with red, white and blue flowers to represent the Norwegian colours, and a toast of the day drunk in wine of the country. The sight of the fjord-like Lake Como with its Alpine background brought a not unpleasing sense of nostalgia for the Sørfjord and Hardanger, and already plans were being discussed for a settled home near Bergen, and perhaps even for buying back the old Grieg estate of Landås, which had passed into other hands.

In December 1884 the citizens of Bergen celebrated the bicentenary of Ludvig Holberg, philosopher, historian, satirist and playwright, who was born in the town in 1684 and died in Copenhagen in 1754. Although most of his comedies were written and performed in Denmark, and are regarded as being among the foundations of Danish literature, the Norwegians, and especially the Bergensers, felt that he belonged very much to them. He had been one of the first men of letters to emphasize the distinction between the Danish farmer and peasant and the

[1] Letter to Beyer, 19 March 1884.

unique Norwegian *bonde* or peasant-proprietor, and he had described the sights and sounds of Bergen in his liveliest prose. That the Holberg celebrations should include musical tributes was no more than justice, since his plays provide many occasions for song and dance; indeed, this is among the many features of his dramatic work that earned him the title of 'the Molière of the North'. Grieg was invited to write two compositions for the festival—a cantata for male voices, to be performed in Bergen market place at the unveiling of a statue to Holberg, and a new instrumental work. Grieg wrote from Lofthus to Frants Beyer on 9th October: 'I have the boring job of writing a male voice piece for the Holberg Festival. But though I am writing bad music I am on the other hand catching good fish. Yesterday I caught seventy. The fjord is so full of herring that the boys take them in their caps, and we others in balers.'

He refers to the cantata again in writing to Röntgen on 30th October:

> I can see it coming—snow, hail, storm, and tempest; a huge choir of men with rain streaming into their open mouths, conducted by a raincoat, galoshes, and umbrella. And, of course, a cold to follow with goodness knows what ailments thereafter. Well, that is one way of dying for the Fatherland.

But the performance (with Grieg duly attired in fur coat, hat and boots) went off well, and was repeated indoors four nights later. On the same evening the composer played for the first time his five piano pieces written in imitation of the eighteenth century suite and later to be published under the title *From Holberg's Time* (Op. 40). The arrangement made for string orchestra a few months later has tended to overshadow the keyboard version, which seems to be the original one and which, like the Brahms *St Antoni* Variations, many prefer in keyboard form. Two other instrumental works by Grieg are connected with the Holberg Festival: the proceeds of the

Album Leaves (Op. 28) and the *Improvisations on Norwegian folk-tunes* (Op. 29) were donated to the fund for the Holberg statue in Bergen.[1]

During the early spring of 1885 Grieg was supervising the building of Troldhaugen, his villa situated above the fjord a short distance from Bergen. It was ready for occupation in April—the only settled home the Griegs had known since their engagement, and from now onward the centre of their social and professional life, though they usually lived there only in the summer months. Frants Beyer had already built a house (now no longer standing) on the opposite promontory, Næsset, and the friends were in almost daily communication by boat. The novelty of living at Troldhaugen encouraged the Griegs to give themselves a year's respite from the roving life that had been the pattern of the last few years. The only concerts undertaken at this time were either in Copenhagen or in Christiania. At last Grieg's music was beginning to find due recognition in the Norwegian capital, where two concerts took place in October. At the first John and Edvard Grieg played the Cello Sonata, Erika Lie Nissen and the composer played the four-hand Norwegian Dances, and groups of songs were contributed by Nina Grieg and Thorvald Lammers. At the second concert Grieg conducted a large orchestra in some of the Peer Gynt music, the *Holberg Suite*, the cantata *Landkjenning* with a male choir of a hundred voices, and the work for which he had so strong an affection, *The Mountain-Thrall*,

> which sounded much better than I have ever heard it before. The ensemble was so well unified, with beautiful *pianos* and climaxes. The legend of the giants had such a vividly demonic effect that I was quite carried away myself. There were curtain calls and much applause,

[1] A full account of the Holberg Cantata, with excerpts reproduced from the published vocal score, is contained in Bjarne Kortsen's *Four Unknown Grieg Cantatas*, pp. 28 fol.

though in moderation, for this is fortunately not a work anyone can grasp. . . . It is possible that in this work I have done one of the few good deeds of my life.[1]

After the concert Grieg was invited to a dinner by the Society of Artists, and found the hall surrounded by a giant frieze, executed by Gerhard Munthe and Andreas Bloch, which displayed the whole voice-part of *The Mountain-Thrall*, together with drawings of the pairs of creatures mentioned in the ballad, while Grieg himself knelt before the giant's daughter, and the giant, portrayed as the sculptor Bergslien, arrived in pursuit. The party went on until one o'clock the next morning, with Grieg playing folk-dance arrangements and Lammers singing the Vinje songs.

The success of *The Mountain-Thrall* was repeated in Copenhagen in December, at a concert where Gade, Horneman, and Grieg shared the rostrum. Then Grieg settled down to rehearsals for a new and more elaborate production of *Peer Gynt* for which he had re-orchestrated some of the original numbers, added others, and arranged music for a full-scale ballet in the Hall of the Old Man of the Dovre, using Frank van der Stucken's orchestration of the Norwegian Dances (Op. 35).[2] By this time the work had become almost more Grieg than Ibsen, as the composer himself was only too well aware:

Peer Gynt is not a drama [he wrote to Max Abraham] but a dramatic poem of the same order as Goethe's *Faust*. In the production here more than a third has been cut and a great deal of ballet substituted, so that Ibsen's noble conception has become a kind of fairy-tale 'Round the world in eighty days', or something of the kind. But the public fills the theatre, and is pleased with a work which it does not in the least understand.[3]

[1] Letter to Beyer, 25 October 1885.
[2] Or that of Hans Sitt (cf. p. 128, n. 1).
[3] Zschinsky-Troxler, 12 February 1886.

The Griegs stayed on in Copenhagen until well into the spring of 1886, Edvard having promised Nina that she should see the Danish beech-woods in leaf before they returned to their new villa in the still wintry Norwegian Westland. She was always more at home in Denmark, but Edvard was longing to be in Troldhaugen again:

What would you say [he asked Beyer in a letter on 26 April] to a quiet morning in the boat, or out between the skerries and cliffs? The other day I was so full of this longing that it turned itself into a gentle song of thanksgiving. There is nothing new in it, but it is genuine and as it is really nothing other than a message to you, I enclose it here.

The two dozen bars that follow are the very simple and beautiful piano miniature published soon afterwards in Book 3 of *Lyric Pieces* (Op. 43, No. 3) under the title *In my homeland* (*I Hjemmet*).

Before leaving Denmark, Grieg gave a series of recitals in the principal towns of Jutland—Aarhus, Vejle, Aalborg, Horsens and Ribe. He found a new friend in the prolific Danish writer Holger Drachmann (1846–1908), one of whose biographers writes: 'He is the most ingenious versifier Scandinavian poetry has known, only slightly influenced by other poets and then fortuitously, but profoundly by music.'[1]

Grieg's opinion of him, expressed to August Winding,[2] is interesting:

He is a strange fellow, your Drachmann; there is something of the troubadour or minnesinger about him. . . , and he cuts such an odd figure in this material age. In the poems he wrote for me I persuaded him to be brief, which, as everyone knows, is not his usual habit.

Whatever Drachmann gained from Grieg as a musician he repaid by stimulating Grieg to start composing again. The two

[1] C. F. Bricka, in *Dansk Biografisk Lexikon.*

[2] Hauch, 3 September 1886.

of them holidayed in the Jotunheim mountains in the summer of 1886, making their centre for three weeks at Eidfjord, an arm of the Hardanger fjord. They called several times on Nils Bergslien (the 'giant' of the *Mountain-Thrall* caricatures), who had a studio there, and the susceptible Drachmann wrote poems to his wife, Johanna, and his daughter, Ragna. Two other girls, Ragnhild and Ingebjorg, a peasant girl with a fund of traditional songs, completed a little portrait gallery in verse, and the outcome was the song-cycle *Travel Memories from Mountain and Fjord* (*Rejseminder fra Fjeld og Fjord*), Op. 44.[1] Grieg had not set Danish poetry for about twenty years, and Drachmann's slight album-verses failed to touch his heart as Andersen's more imaginative lyrics had done then; still less have these Drachmann songs the passionate depth of the Vinje settings. But at least Grieg had broken another period of silence.

It was also a visitor from overseas who set him to work on what was to prove his last completed chamber composition. A twenty-year old Italian violinist, Teresina Tua, was a guest at Troldhaugen in the autumn of 1886; Grieg called her 'the little fiddle-fairy on my troll-hill',[2] and said that it would be entirely due to her if he were 'again to perpetrate something for the violin'. His third Sonata for Violin and Piano, in C minor (Op. 45), was published the following year, with a dedication not after all to Teresina but to the painter Franz von Lenbach. Its first performance, in Leipzig with Adolf Brodsky as violinist, drew another sour notice from Bernsdorf, who found in it 'a lack of organic development, a laborious talent barely concealed by all manner of affectations, especially in harmony, a want of invention, faults of taste and absence of seriousness, under the cloak of Norwegian nationalism'.

[1] Drachmann originally proposed the title *From Troldhaugen to Tvindehaugen.*

[2] No doubt a pun here: *tue* means hillock.

On the other hand, when it was heard in Paris, at the beginning of 1890, the critic of *Le Matin* found it a brilliant work, giving the lie to the accusation sometimes brought against the composer that he was essentially a miniaturist, incapable of writing anything on an extended scale (*de longue haleine*).[1]

[1] These opposing views are quoted in D. Monrad Johansen, *Edvard Grieg*, English translation (New York, 2nd edition, 1945), pp. 278 fol. In fairness to Bernsdorf it must be admitted that later critics have upheld his judgment in most respects: see Gerald Abraham, *A Hundred Years of Music* (3rd edition, London, 1964), p. 158.

5 The climax of international fame (1887-97)

By this time Grieg was being overwhelmed with invitations to play and conduct in European centres from St Petersburg to Madrid, from Edinburgh to Vienna. Offers from the American continent he ruled out altogether, if only through dread of the long ocean voyage, deliberately setting his terms so high that the wealthiest transatlantic communities would find him too expensive. Yet although he knew only too well the aftermath of nervous exhaustion, he could not resist the lure of the concert platform, the acclamation of the public, meetings with other artists of international standing, and above all, in those days before the mechanical reproduction of music, regular opportunities of hearing his works performed with skill and sympathy.

He began one of his longest and most arduous tours in the autumn of 1887, in a mood of physical euphoria and with a glow of patriotism. He wrote to Beyer from Carlsbad, where he had been taking the cure:

> It is a long time since life has seemed so pleasant and good to me as it does now. I am well again . . . and many friendly letters, full of kindness and understanding, make it easier than for many a day to look towards the future. . . . Yes, Norway! Norway! Let Ibsen say a hundred times over, that it is best to belong to a big nation; I can perhaps agree with him on practical grounds, but not a step further. Ideally I would not want to belong to any other nation on earth![1]

He spent almost the whole winter in Leipzig, forming another life-long friendship there with the violinist Adolf Brodsky, who was a few years later to become a teacher at the Manchester

[1] 8 October 1887.

College of Music and, for a short time, its Principal.[1] Grieg played the C minor Sonata with him, and Brodsky's quartet performed the G minor Quartet. The Griegs were often in company with two other Norwegian musicians, Christian Sinding and Johan Halvorsen, and sometimes their circle was joined by the young Englishman, Frederick Delius, who had been sent to Sweden in 1882 as a representative for his father's woollen business, had learnt to speak Swedish and Norwegian fluently and had set several Norwegian poems. In 1886 Delius entered the Leipzig Conservatory, returning to Norway for the vacation, and was now setting Ibsen's poem *On the Heights* (*Paa Vidderne*).[2] Grieg called him 'the Hardangerviddeman', and gave him both encouragement and practical advice.

Other memorable encounters took place in Leipzig. On New Year's Day, January 1888, at the home of the Brodskys, Tchaikovsky arrived in time to find Brahms seated at the piano rehearsing his C minor Trio, Op. 101. Shortly afterwards, the Griegs were announced. Tchaikovsky has given us the most exact word-portrait we have of Grieg in his forties:

> There entered the room a very short middle-aged man, exceedingly fragile in appearance, shoulders of unequal height, fair hair brushed back from his forehead, a very light, almost boyish, beard and moustache. He had an uncommon charm, blue eyes, not very large, but irresistibly fascinating, recalling the glance of a charming and candid child.[3]

[1] The Grieg-Brodsky correspondence is now in the keeping of the Royal Northern College of Music, whose Principal and Council kindly granted permission for passages from the letters to be quoted.

[2] Delius set the poem first for tenor voice with orchestra, but later turned it into a melodrama.

[3] P. I. Tchaikovsky: *Diary of my tour in 1888*, trans. Rosa Newmarch (London, pp. 191 fol.). Tchaikovsky gives a companion picture of Brahms, and adds for good measure a description of another guest at this historic luncheon-party—Ethel Smyth. Tchaikovsky's account is corroborated and supplemented by Florence May in her Life of Johannes Brahms, pp. 602 fol.

Of Nina, Tchaikovsky wrote:

In the first place she proved to be an excellent, though not very finished, singer; secondly, I have never met a better-informed or more highly cultivated woman, and she is, among other things, an excellent judge of our literature, in which Grieg himself was also deeply interested; and thirdly, I was soon convinced that Madame Grieg was as amiable, as gentle, as childishly simple and without guile as her celebrated husband.[1]

Grieg wrote after a subsequent meeting: 'In Tchaikovsky I have gained a warm friend of my art. He has as much sympathy for me as I for him, both as an artist and as a man.'[2]

Ironically, Grieg had to re-enter the doors of the hated Leipzig Conservatory in order to practise the piano, for he had agreed to play his Concerto with the Philharmonic Society in London in the spring. By a coincidence, he followed Tchaikovsky as guest conductor with that orchestra. On 3rd May, in the St James's Hall, he performed the Concerto under the baton of Frederick Cowen (who, in the same programme, gave the first performance in England of Bizet's *Jeux d'enfants*), and then conducted the strings in his *Two Elegiac Melodies*. He was enchanted by the quality and responsiveness of English string-playing, the like of which he had not heard even in Germany; how deeply it moved him is evident from the account of this concert he sent to Beyer on 4th May:

Then I stood and conducted *The Last Spring* (*Våren*), and it sounded as if the whole of Nature was calling to me from home; yes, I was proud and glad to be Norwegian. I truly believe that the sympathy the English show for my art must come from their feeling for Norway, since in no other way can I account for the ovations I received yesterday. It reminded me of when Ole Bull, in former days, used to appear with his instrument before a Bergen audience, except that here it

[1] ibid.
[2] Letter to Beyer, 29 January 1888.

lasted much longer. When I showed myself at the orchestra doorway, the whole of the vast St. James's Hall, completely filled, broke into an uproar, so intense and so continuous (I think for over three minutes) that I did not know what to do. . . . Is it not wonderful, and in a foreign land? Art is indeed a mystery: 'More than my merit to me has been given . . .'[1]—that is true enough.

A fortnight later the Griegs gave a joint recital with the aid of their old colleague, Wilhelmina Norman-Neruda, who in this year became Lady Hallé. The programme, which *The Times* found one of the most interesting of the season, included the F major Sonata and two movements of the G major.

It was during the earlier London visit that Frederick Delius contrived a meeting between his father, the Bradford wool-merchant, and Grieg, who was able to induce the elder Delius to let his son give up wool-dealing and orange-planting and devote himself to composition.[2]

Within a few months, in August 1888, Grieg was back in England, this time for the Birmingham Festival, for which he had re-scored the Concert Overture *In Autumn*,[3] and at which he also gave the string version of the Holberg Suite. Grieg's conducting excited no less admiration than his compositions: Sir George Grove, then aged sixty-eight and full of memories, was present at the Birmingham concert and wrote:

A very interesting thing was Grieg's Overture last night and his conducting of it. How he managed to inspire the band as he did and

[1] '*Meire eg fekk, enn eg hadde fortent*': one of Grieg's favourite quotations, from Vinje's *Våren* (*The Spring*).

[2] For a full account of this episode see Alan Jefferson, *Delius* (London, 1972), pp. 22–4.

[3] The Overture was performed, in a programme that also included Sullivan's *Golden Legend*, on 29 August; the Suite, quaintly described in the Birmingham programme book as an 'Orchestral Fantasie', was performed on the following evening along with Schumann's Piano Concerto and Frederick Bridge's cantata *Callirhoë*.

get such nervous thrilling bursts and such charming sentiment out of them I don't know. He looks very much like Beethoven in face, I thought, and though he is not so extravagant in his ways of conducting yet it is not unlike.[1]

Grove enlarged on the same subject in his notes made at a rehearsal:

Such men cannot be judged by the standard of ordinary men—of Englishmen particularly. They are free from conventions which bind us, they are all nerves, they indulge in strange gestures and utter odd noises and say strange words, and make everyone laugh till we find that the gestures and looks and words are the absolute expression of their inmost feeling . . . And they get what they want. Those who have seen Grieg conduct will know what I am attempting to describe.

His next tour in England, in the spring of 1889, took Grieg as far as Manchester, where again he revelled in the sound of his *Elegiac Melodies*, played this time by the Hallé strings. He was also the soloist in the Piano Concerto, afterwards describing the performance as 'mediocre, but what else could be expected of the old man?'. Before leaving the country, he took part in a notable series of performances of all three of the Violin Sonatas—Op. 8 with Lady Hallé, Op. 13 with Joachim, and Op. 45 with the Belgian violinist Johannes Wolff. The newly founded newspaper *The Star* sent its self-appointed music critic, 'Corno di Bassetto', to the third of these events, but he found nothing more illuminating to say than that the music reminded him 'of the style of Grieg's great countryman, the late Ole Bull'.

Heartened by his successes in England, Grieg was prepared to face the more temperamental audiences of Paris. But first he had to arrange in Christiania a first performance of his scenes from *Olav Trygvason*, a choral and orchestral cantata salvaged from the ill-starred Bjørnson opera. The warmth of its reception

[1] C. L. Graves, *Life of Sir George Grove* (London, 1903), p. 337.

exceeded all his hopes, though he was modest enough to realize that much was due to the timing of the performance; patriotic fervour was mounting with the increase of strained political relations with Sweden, and Bjørnson, who generously shared his ovation with the composer, was approaching the height of his popularity as a representative of national idealism.

After giving three concerts in Brussels, Grieg finally reached Paris in mid-December 1889. Norwegian painters, authors and musicians were no rare phenomenon in the French capital. Ole Bull had been well known there, and the pianist Thomas Tellefsen, a pupil of Chopin, had lived in Paris from 1842 to 1874 as the doyen of the Scandinavian colony; his Piano Concerto (published in 1852) was not only the first known to have been composed by a Norwegian, but was probably also the first Norwegian orchestral work to use a folksong quotation.[1] Grieg certainly knew Tellefsen by reputation, and may possibly have met him in the 1860s.

Norwegian men of letters were even more numerous in Paris at this time. From 1882 Jonas Lie, the great novelist of the Norwegian golden age, had made his home there, and another distinguished novelist and playwright, Alexander Kielland, lived near Paris during the eighties, while Bjørnson had spent much of his time there between 1882 and 1887, becoming a warm admirer of Victor Hugo, in many respects his French counterpart.

Grieg and the Parisians soon adjusted to each other's concert deportment. When the platform attendant offered the diminutive northerner a baton 'almost as long as himself, but luckily as thin as a reed', he broke off a piece and threw the rest into a corner. French audiences, he soon learnt, were more volatile

[1] For accounts of Tellefsen's contributions to Norwegian national-Romanticism see Schjelderup-Ebbe, *op. cit.*, pp. 96 fol. and Huldt-Nystrøm, *Thomas Dyke Acland Tellefsen*, in *Norsk Musikkgransk-ning Årbok 1956–8*, pp. 80 fol.

than the English, applauding not only between items but also now and then in the middle of them. Among the orchestral works performed were the predictable *Peer Gynt* suites and the Concerto, together with the melodrama *Bergliot*, which enjoyed particular success through its double associations with Bjørnson and with the fashionable cult of nordic mythology. The critics, from the judicious Bellaigue[1] to the insufferable Bigeon (of whom more later), devoted much of their space to discussing and praising this now little-heard work:

> Il suffirait d'un tel sujet [wrote Bellaigue] pour intéresser les *dilettanti* du jour, car rien n'est plus en vogue aujourd'hui que les Sagas, les Eddas, toute la cosmogonie allemande ou scandinave. L'Olympe est démodé, et le Walhalla le remplace dans la faveur des musiciens sérieux. Wagner a donné l'exemple . . .

But, he adds, one's appreciation of *Bergliot* need not depend on a thorough knowledge of its literary background; it is simply and profoundly a human experience.

Like so many other contemporary artists and writers from Scandinavian lands, Grieg found in the atmosphere of Paris a wonderful stimulus, compensating for much that had been lacking from his German and Danish education. The clarity of French orchestral writing especially appealed to him, in contrast to the growing density of many late-romantic German scores. He admired above all the textures of Bizet's *Carmen*, and he expressed a wish that Édouard Lalo could be commissioned to orchestrate the four-handed *Norwegian Dances* (Op. 35).[2] French influences show themselves in Grieg's piano music from the time of his first Paris concerts, as in the fifth book of *Lyric Pieces* (Op. 54) containing the impressionistic 'Shepherd Boy'

[1] Camille Bellaigue: 'M. Edvard Grieg', in *Revue des deux mondes*, 97 (1890), pp. 672–81.

[2] Lalo's *Rapsodie norvégienne* and *Fantaisie norvégienne* show that he shared the contemporary Parisian interest in Scandinavian colour.

and 'Bell-ringing'; in the five subsequent sets; and in the *Stemninger* (*Moods*), Op. 73. More speculative is the extent to which he in his turn made a contribution to contemporary French musical idioms and styles, particularly through his harmonic originality. We shall return to this question, but apart from the possibility of more subtle and far-reaching cross-influences there are curious and apparently unconscious echoes of Grieg in Parisian music of the early 1890s, as when, for example, Debussy's salon-piece *Rêverie* (1890) seems to mimic the chord-progression of *Morning Mood* from the first *Peer Gynt* suite:

The enthusiasm for his work shown in London and Paris, and the success of his recent concerts in Germany, only confirmed Grieg in his resolve to husband his energies and restrict his acceptance of the invitations that continued to pour in. Thus in September 1890 he wrote from Bergen refusing offers from places as wide apart as Vienna, Prague, London, Edinburgh, St Petersburg and Munich. Composition was again almost at a standstill; he had produced, during the past year, nothing more than two books of songs—one of them (Op. 48) to German texts and the other (Op. 49) to Danish poems by Drachmann. He still hoped to write something on a larger scale, and proposed, in a letter of 10th December 1890[1] that he and Bjørnson should write an oratorio together:

What do you say to the thought of taking the concepts of peace, which music can explain and deepen, and putting them into a poem by Bjørnson—a kind of cantata form, which could be set for solo voices, choir and orchestra?

In recent years I have felt that nothing could be finer than to write a Requiem—a modern Requiem, free from dogmatic belief. But I have not found the text, though I have searched both in poetry and in the Bible. But when I read your oration on Peace, given to the Workers' Union, it was at once clear in my mind—an apotheosis of Peace, that

[1] Hauch, 10 December 1890.

is to say, a Requiem in a very special sense! There are obvious contrasts: the great light of Peace beside the horrors of War! I have faith in this idea. Think it over, and let me know if it interests you.

[Postscript] The old Latin Requiem text contains important matters within its formal framework.

Bjørnson took up the proposal with enthusiasm, and within a week had sent a sketch of how he intended to treat the subject. Grieg was delighted with this immediate response (the idea of a modern Requiem could, he thought, be treated as a separate project, independently of Bjørnson), but closer inspection of Bjørnson's draft for *Peace* aroused misgivings. Bjørnson obviously intended to handle the theme from the standpoint of political and social realism, with references to topics like factories, barracks, banks and telegraphs, for which there could be no possible counterparts in Grieg's romantic musical vocabulary. The whole enterprise thus foundered, like the abortive *Olav Trygvason* collaboration, on radical differences in the personal development of the two creative artists. Grieg got no further in composing *Peace* than a single song 'I loved' (published without opus number), while Bjørnson, with his usual impetuosity, published the whole of his text without waiting for Grieg to make up his mind.

Fortunately Grieg was on the brink of a fresh period of composition, brought about mainly by a revival of poetry in Norway in the 1890s, but also by his own passionate love of Norwegian nature and folklore, which his cosmopolitan professional life seemed only to intensify as he grew older. This Indian summer of his creative powers, interrupted though it frequently was by recurrent illness and by the everlasting round of concert engagements, was to produce some of his most original and important work.

The summer tour in the Jotunheim region had now become almost a fixed event in Grieg's calendar. He never penetrated further north than Trondhjem (that ancient cathedral town being still the terminus of the railway), but he went on exploring the picturesque tracts of wild country east of Bergen, with the various arms of the Hardanger fjord and the mountains to the north and south of it. Here he had long become almost a part of the scenery, as Werenskiold painted him, and as tourists like the Rev. W. A. Gray described him:

Scarcely had I taken my place in the hotel porch . . . when Grieg stood beside me alone, and lit his cigar. His figure, even shorter and slighter than I first imagined it to be, was encased in a tight-fitting ulster and gaiters; his thick hair, just turning white, fell down on his collar from beneath a grey felt hat; and ulster, gaiters, and hat alike bore traces of mountain walks and mountain weather, during repeated visits to Jotunheim, the wild Alpine region where Grieg caught his passion for mountain scenery when a boy [*sic*], and which is still, in his later days, a source of musical inspiration as well as a favourite health resort.[1]

His companions on these mountain expeditions included at various times his neighbour Frants Beyer, the composers Christian Sinding, Frederick Delius and Percy Grainger, and the Dutch musician Julius Röntgen, who has given the most detailed and lively account of a tour he made with Grieg and Beyer in 1891; this includes valuable notes on what was a still living tradition of folk music:

Grieg and I travelled from Lofthus by *stolkjerre* [a small two-wheeled carriage, holding three people] to the Sognefjord, whence we reached Skjolden by rowing-boat. From there the road leads uphill to Turtegrø. On the way we picked up a *spillemand*, that is a player on the hardanger-fiddle, and he played us his tunes during the whole of the glorious drive. . . . Grieg listened rapt, his head nodding in time to the music, and in his hand a glass of wine which he kept offering the player. 'This is Norway', he said with gleaming eyes.

[1] W. A. Gray: 'Among the fjords with Edvard Grieg', in *Woman at Home*, January 1894. Röntgen mentions 'an English lady' who said epigrammatically: 'Now I'm happy. I have seen the North Cape and Mr. Grieg.'

It was a warm August afternoon, the fjord lay dark green and we, stretched out on sacks of hay, let the splendid mountain landscape slip slowly past our eyes like a tapestry. We made the journey up to Turtegrø on horseback, but before we started Grieg drank with me in token of brotherhood. ... The Jotunheim range now appeared gradually before our eyes: Fanaraak, Ringstindene, and finally the great Skagastølstind, the Matterhorn of Norway. The dark rock was tinted reddish-brown by the evening sun. At last we reached the hut of Ole Berge, the well-known guide, and received a hearty welcome from him.

Suddenly we heard from outside the yodel that was Frants Beyer's signal, and presently he was with us in radiant Jotunheim mood. Beside Ole Berge's cottage were two more hillside huts where the *jenter* [*sæter*-girls] live. Of course we made our way to these two on the first evening, and Frants Beyer persuaded the girls, after some hesitation, to sing. For the first time I heard Norwegian folksongs in their proper surroundings; what a fine effect they had there! Frants Beyer told us how in the morning, when the cows were being milked, he laid his music-paper on the cow's back while the girls sang, and so got his songs 'fresh from the cow'. Early the next morning I heard Ole Berge's sister calling the goats and singing. There was singing everywhere! Among Grieg's manuscripts left behind at his death I found a sheet dated *Turtegrø 1893*, with various motives from the Jotunheim. [Here Röntgen quotes half a dozen folk-tunes] ...

After some days we journeyed from Turtegrø over the Kaiser Pass to Skogadalsbøen, a tourist hut, the central point of the Jotunheim. ... Passes and dales lead from it in every direction. ... It lies on a spur of the mountain from which one looks down far into the wooded Skogadal, with its rushing *elv* (mountain stream), a striking contrast to the otherwise treeless Jotunheim. In Skogadalsbø we had an unforgettable evening. At that time the tourist hut was in charge of Tollef and Brit Holmestad. The wife had recently had a child, and her sister, Gjendine Slaalien, was staying with her to help her. ... When first we saw her she was rocking her sister's child in her arms, singing it to sleep with the following song: [Here Röntgen gives the melody and words of the lullaby which Grieg later arranged for piano as op. 66, No. 19]. ... Gjendine could also play on the goat-horn, an instrument on which only the first three notes of the minor scale can be sounded. With these three notes she could produce the most original melodies.

So passed the evening in this pleasant hut with song and gaiety, and when we came out there lay the mountains in the fantastic light of the moon, while from the depths sounded the rushing of the stream. Gjendine stood on a rock and sang us the lullaby again. How overwhelmingly beautiful it all was! Grieg said to me: 'You are certainly in luck; one doesn't hear this kind of thing very often in Norway nowadays!'

The next morning we left Skogadalsbø. We had already gone some distance on our way when we heard the notes of the goat-horn. Gjendine was bidding us farewell by playing the following tune, which became ever softer and died away in long notes:

Grieg's Lyric Piece entitled 'Longing for Home' [Op. 57, No. 6] makes use of this same motive of three notes.[1]

In November 1891 Christiania celebrated the twenty-fifth anniversary of Grieg's début as conductor and recitalist in the capital. A commemoration concert was followed by a banquet at which the whole cultural life of the country was represented; even Ibsen, who was at that time living alone in Christiania, attended and made a gracious speech. Afterwards several

[1] Röntgen, pp. 33–7. Röntgen used some of the folksong motives heard on this tour in a Suite for Violin and Piano, *Aus Jotunheim*, which he gave Edvard and Nina as a silver-wedding gift the following year.

thousand people watched a torchlight procession of university students in Grieg's honour.

The Griegs' wedding jubilee took place at Troldhaugen on 11th June 1892. A military band roused them at dawn with the chorale 'Ein' feste Burg'. Then came lavish presents from home and abroad: a new Steinway grand from Bergen, the Werenskiold portrait from Christiania, a silver sugar-bowl filled with gold pieces from Peters in Leipzig, a silver writing-set from 'a music school in London'. Over a hundred guests came by rail during the day to offer their congratulations, and in a rash moment Grieg invited everyone to supper, thus precipitating a domestic crisis that was too much for Nina but was resolved by the efficiency of Fru Beyer. Nina sang to the guests 'the songs she sang twenty-five years, ago, and sang them as well as ever', and Edvard played the Steinway, having already prepared, as a gift for Nina, 'Wedding Day at Troldhaugen' (*Lyric Pieces* Op. 65, No. 6).[1] Ingolf Schiøtt, accompanied by Beyer, sang a specially composed setting by Christian Sinding of words by Jonas Lie. The night was further enlivened by fireworks, bonfires and cannon salvoes, the fjord swarmed with boats, and every vantage point around Troldhaugen was occupied by a detachment of the five thousand or so people who had come out by excursion trains, so that the occasion became, as Grieg said, a kind of popular festival.

Monrad Johansen heads one of the later chapters of his Grieg biography *The Monotonous Nineties*, since this decade becomes mainly a chronicle of journeys and platform appearances before audiences that were content to keep on accepting and applauding Grieg as the composer of the Piano Concerto, the *Peer Gynt* suites and the earlier songs, works which he himself often felt he had outgrown:

[1] The original manuscript bore the title *Gratulanterne kommer*. It is reproduced between pp. 112 and 113 of Schjelderup and Niemann, *Ed. Grieg: Biographie und Würdigung seiner Werke* (Leipzig, 1908).

It is a long time [he wrote] since I composed the *Peer Gynt* music and the Ibsen songs—so long that I conduct and play these works as if they were not my own. I want to develop further, and have done so inasmuch as I now feel differently. How glad I would have been to give expression in sound to my mental development at the present time! Bodily ailments have been insuperable impediments, and now the end is near. I am resigned, however.[1]

It was not only the majority of the general public, but also many of the professional critics who seemed to assume that Grieg's earlier works represented the essence of his personality and the norm of his style. The repetitive chorus of flattery was disturbed by comparatively few dissentient voices, among them that of Bernard Shaw who, in writing about a now forgotten Overture, *Richard III*, by Edward German, added:

It is far surpassed by Grieg's Peer Gynt music, which consists of two or three catchpenny phrases served up with plenty of orchestral sugar, at a cost in technical workmanship much smaller than that lavished on Mr. German's overture. But the catchpenny phrases are sufficiently to the point of the scenes they introduce, and develop—if Grieg's repetitions can be called development—according to the logic of those scenes and not according to that of Haydn's symphonies. In fact, Grieg proceeded as Wagner proceeded in his great preludes, except that, being only a musical grasshopper in comparison with the musical giant of Bayreuth, he could only catch a few superficial points in the play instead of getting to the very heart and brain of it.[2]

As a devoted Wagnerian and as a reforming dramatist, Shaw felt little but scorn for the rest of Grieg's theatre music, alluding to the *Olav Trygvason* temple scenes as 'these Simon Tappertit solemnities and turnip-ghost terrors', and dismissing the *Sigurd Jorsalfar* suite as

[1] Letter to M. Monastier-Schroeder, 22 August 1903, quoted in Finck, p. 136.
[2] In *The World*, 27 January 1892; reproduced in *Music in London 1890–94* (London, 1932 etc.), Vol. 2, p. 617.

trumpery stuff enough, except for a fanciful and delicate movement for muted violins pianissimo, with starts and shudders on the drum, representing somebody's uneasy dreams.

Shaw was fair enough, however, to pay tribute to Grieg's conducting of the Philharmonic orchestra, saying that he was 'so successful in getting fine work out of the band that if the directors were wise they would make him a handsome offer to take it in hand permanently'.[1]

Yet Grieg's intellect and imagination were far from being at a standstill during his fifth decade. His patriotism was now more often openly expressed than at any time in his life, probably under the influence of his restored friendship with Bjørnson. The status of Norway in the increasingly uneasy union with Sweden caused him personal distress and anxiety; in a letter to Max Abraham[2] he declared that if Sweden carried out her threat to suspend the Norwegian constitution, he would shake off his illness and either seize a pistol ('a rifle being unfortunately too heavy'), or, as a less desirable alternative, let himself be carried off to prison. 'Truly, Ibsen was right in saying what he did in his pessimistic masterpiece, if the Norwegian people has sunk so low that it will not stand together as one man to drive the enemy out of the land.'

This active concern with the political situation recurs in Grieg's correspondence right up to the final separation of the crowns in 1905. His involvement in another question of principle, the Dreyfus case, will be described later. His sturdy republicanism (again, perhaps, reinforced if not inspired by Bjørnson's) showed itself in his dealings with royalty when they deigned to notice him: Queen Victoria, Edward VII (who talked through his music), the Danish royal family, the German Kaiser, all met with cool, humorous assessment on personal and artistic grounds,

[1] *Music in London*, Vol. 1, p. 158, and Vol. 3, pp. 239–40.
[2] Zschinsky-Troxler, 3 May 1893.

while the orders, medals and academic distinctions that came his way were treated with half-amused indifference.

Those whom he could meet as fellow-artists, however, were immediately won over by his unassuming charm and frankness. There is a delightful account of a reunion with Ibsen, contributed to an American magazine[1] by Bolette Sontum, whose father had been Ibsen's physician and personal friend and practised at Bad Grefsen, where Grieg was a patient at the time:

In the summer of 1893 Ibsen and Grieg met at our home at Grefsen, and were together for the first time for many years. Grieg had come back to Norway from a sojourn in Germany, tired and utterly worn out. His physician had ordered the air at Grefsen instead of his own delightful place, Troldhaugen near Bergen.

The 15th of June, Grieg celebrated his fiftieth birthday with us. Ibsen was not present that day, but later, one Sunday in July, while he sat on our little porch, Grieg walked over to see him. I can never forget that meeting. Ibsen sitting on our veranda looking at the glorious panorama—the black Asker mountains brushing their firs against the intense blue sky, the broad lapped fjord holding its islands like jewels flashing their fires to colour the broad white sails as they skimmed over the water.

Ibsen sat brooding, solemn and melancholy. But suddenly his face lighted up radiantly as Grieg, light-hearted and buoyant as a sunbeam, tripped up the steps. The two masters clasped hands. They had not met for years and there was a shot of questions and answers as between two boys, Ibsen's deep basso vibrating thunders to Grieg's piping Bergen soprano. Half serious, half jesting, they discussed the plan of Grieg's setting *The Vikings of Helgeland* to music.

But we already know the fate of that project.

Grieg was no less successful in gaining the confidence of that other notorious grizzly bear of the European cultural scene, Johannes Brahms. They had first met in Leipzig in 1885, at the

[1] 'Personal recollections of Ibsen', in *The Bookman* (New York) Vol. 37 (1913), pp. 247–51.

home of the Herzogenbergs, and had played to each other, Grieg choosing his *Norwegian Bridal Procession* and Brahms his G minor Rhapsody;[1] and, as we have seen, they were together at Brodskys' historic luncheon party in 1888. Their final meetings took place towards the end of 1896 and the beginning of 1897, in Vienna. Though in failing health, Brahms treated Grieg and his companion, Röntgen, with the greatest consideration, entertaining them at his favourite 'Red Hedgehog' and, when Edvard was laid up with influenza, calling on him three times. Grieg heard Brahms's Fourth Symphony conducted by Nikisch, and Brahms stayed for the whole of Grieg's own concert, when Busoni played the Piano Concerto. Grieg was also present, on 2nd January, at the Joachim quartet recital, when Beethoven's Op. 135 and Brahms's Quintet (Op. 111) were performed, and witnessed the ovation given to the ailing master.

Another giant among Grieg's contemporaries was Verdi, whom by mischance he never met, but who called on him in Paris and left his visiting card, which Grieg ever afterwards kept with pride. In some ways he felt that his own career had run parallel with Verdi's; this emerges clearly from an article Grieg wrote on the Italian composer for the magazine *The Nineteenth Century* in March 1901. After discussing Verdi as a national composer, recognized as such by the whole Italian people, Grieg continues: 'Then came to pass the remarkable thing that Verdi as a fully matured man greatly widened his horizon, though retaining at the same time what was national in his art: he became cosmopolitan.' This echoes almost exactly what Grieg was saying at the time about his own development. His essay goes on to mention, with his usual bitterness when reflecting on his student days, the lack of concern at the Leipzig Conservatory in the 1850s and '60s for any music outside the

[1] 'I got the impression', notes Röntgen (p. 25), 'that neither of them liked the other's piece. On the other hand, Brahms spoke very warmly to me of Grieg's *Ballade* (Op. 24).'

German classical-romantic main stream; only Wagner's admission of how much he had learnt from the Italians, especially Bellini, had persuaded the Germans that Italian music, Verdi's included, was worth serious attention. He then turns to Verdi's development as shown in *Aïda*, written in 1871, which

stands upon the shoulders of the art of all time. The newer masters of both France and Germany gave him impulses, but nothing more: *Aïda* is a masterpiece in which his own originality is combined with a wide and sympathetic view of what is best in musical contemporaneity. Verdi the Italian and Verdi the European hold out a hand to one another: the language he here speaks is the language of the world, and we need not go to the country of the composer to understand it.

Grieg singles out for special praise the Egyptian local colour and the orchestral means Verdi used to produce it. He can hardly have helped thinking of his own attempts, soon after the composition of *Aïda*, to create an oriental atmosphere in his music to *Peer Gynt*.

He now arrives at the late Verdi operas, and above all *Otello*, to compose which 'it was necessary for Verdi to undergo his long uninterrupted process of transformation', and once again he refers to Verdi's instrumentation, with

the use made . . . of the entire collective orchestral apparatus for the production of a pianissimo, and a fear-inspiring pianissimo it is. This effect, is, I think, new, at any rate I do not remember to have met with it in the works of any other master.

Grieg had himself, however, used the orchestral strings for impressive pianissimos in such pieces as *The Death of Åse* and *The Last Spring*, and we know that as a conductor he took pains to realize the full effect of a concentrated pianissimo from a large body of strings. In connection with *Otello*, he mentions the absurd suggestion that Verdi was alluding to a Norwegian folksong in the instrumental introduction to the 'Willow Song', where the familiar Griegian formula of minor tonic-leading-note-dominant happens to occur—a notion that caused questioning eyes to be turned in Grieg's direction during the performance of *Otello* in the Copenhagen Royal Theatre.

Finally, after a mention of Verdi's String Quartet, he comes to the *Requiem* and 'his *Swan Song*: sacred pieces for choir and orchestra. . . . It is a curious fact that both Verdi and Rossini concluded their lengthy dramatic careers by writing sacred music'. It was even stranger, though perhaps not accidental, that Grieg rounded off his own career five years later with a set of sacred pieces—the *Four Psalms* (Op. 74).

The article on Verdi was not the only excursion Grieg made at this period into musical journalism. In January 1894 he had written a long article on Robert Schumann for the American *Century Illustrated Monthly Magazine* and in November 1897 another for the same journal on Mozart. The Mozart essay he wrote at Tinhølen, on the Hardangervidda: he was staying with Beyer and another friend in a stone-built mountain hut, and wrote most of his article wrapped up in a reindeer-skin sleeping bag for warmth. Though discursive and sometimes a little perverse, these essays throw light on his attitudes towards the two composers who, perhaps more than any others, had influenced his own style.

At the outset of the Mozart article it is made clear that the writer is concerned above all with Mozart's significance to contemporary music, and this at a time when there were some musicians 'who are so advanced that they care no longer to hear Mozart's music, and reluctantly give it a place in their programmes'. The testimony of Wagner, who had 'engraved Mozart's name on his shield', should be enough to dispel such arrogance. Grieg links Mozart with Wagner in other ways, and especially through their common admiration for J. S. Bach and the technical strength they both drew from his polyphony. He is scathing on the perfunctory treatment of Mozart by 'one-sided Wagnerians':

> How often have I heard in Germany perfect performances of Wagner's music-dramas under the direction of the same conductors who huddle a Mozart opera in a workaday manner. Nay, here and there these operas are even entrusted to second-rate conductors, the chief being reserved for Wagner.

He makes an honourable exception of Nikisch, to whom 'the great is great, whether its name is Wagner or Mozart'. In attempting to account for the neglect of Mozart by some younger musicians, Grieg confesses that he too turned away from his early allegiance, seduced by the brilliance of modern technical resources and colouring: 'I loved Mozart for a time, lost him, but found him again, never more to lose him.' The writer looks forward to a time, not far in the future, when the importance of *line* will be relearnt from Mozart, and 'this new art will . . . unite lines and colours in marriage, and show that it has roots in all the past, that it draws sustenance from old as well as from new masters'.

Turning to Mozart's instrumental works, Grieg inserts an apology for certain attempts to make Mozart more accessible by presenting him in modern dress; he refers to Tchaikovsky's suite *Mozartiana*, where, he thinks, the process of modernization has been carried out 'with admirable discretion and taste', and to his own use of a second piano 'to impart to several of Mozart's pianoforte sonatas a tonal effect appealing to our modern ears'. He defends his own action on the ground that he has not changed a single note of Mozart's, and maintains that

> provided one does not follow the example of Gounod, who transformed a Bach prelude into a modern sentimental and trivial show piece . . . but seeks to preserve the unity of style, there is surely no reason for raising an outcry over a desire to attempt a modernization as one way of showing admiration for an old master.

Of greater interest than this ingenuous special pleading, and more relevant to Grieg's own harmonic idiom, are his observations on Mozart's G minor Symphony (K. 550):

It is worth noticing what astonishing effects he gets here by the use of chromatic progressions. Excepting Bach, who here, as everywhere, is the fundamental pillar on which all modern music rests, no one has understood as well as Mozart how to use the chromatic scale to express the highest effect in music. We must go as far as Wagner before we find chromatic harmonies used for the expression of ardent feeling (*Innigkeit*). In the case of Spohr, who made extensive use of them, and who in so many respects followed Mozart, they remain without any deep significance.

His remarks on Mozart's fondness for the key of G minor, citing not only the Symphony but also the String Quintet (misprinted 'Quartet'), 'note the wonderful chromatics of the first theme', and the Piano Quartet in that key, are particularly interesting in view of Grieg's own use of G minor in such works as the String Quartet, the lamentation in *Bergliot*, the *Ballade* (Op. 24), the *Air* in the Holberg Suite, the *Olav Trygvason* temple scenes and the transcription of *Gjendine's Lullaby* in Op. 66.

The article ends with a plea for more careful production of Mozart's dramatic works in the opera house, and with an affirmation of belief that 'neo-romanticism' will eventually add Mozart to 'the trinity of Bach, Beethoven and Wagner'. His prophecy of a Mozart revival was hardly to be realized in his lifetime, nor could he have foreseen the impact of the neo-classical movement which, within two decades of Grieg's death, was to lead to an apotheosis of Mozart alike in the theatre and the concert hall.

The Schumann article is even lengthier, spreading itself over eight large octavo pages in double-column print. Here Grieg's enthusiasm for his subject, his burning indignation against Schumann's detractors past and present, and his desire to cover every aspect of the composer's production lead him into diffuseness. He is chiefly concerned to defend Schumann against the venomous attacks of Wagner and the coldness of Mendelssohn, and to emphasize the virtues of Schumann's orchestral music, despite its technical blemishes. He also devotes considerable space to the piano music, the chamber works and the songs. His remarks are illuminated by personal reminiscences of his old Leipzig teacher, Wenzel, who remembered Schumann's own piano-playing, of Clara Schumann and her bitterness at the tardy recognition of her husband's genius, of Schröder-Devrient's singing of 'Ich grolle nicht' and other songs, and of his own performances of *Paradise and the Peri* in Christiania.

Grieg's song-writing underwent change and renewal in the 1890s. By that time Nina seldom sang in public, but Grieg still addressed his songs ideally to her. In the winter of 1893 she had to spend a few weeks in a nursing home in Copenhagen, though she was well enough when Edvard visited her on her birthday on 24th November to share a meal of oysters and hare and to drink to the health of their absent neighbours, the Beyers.[1] Grieg took away from the nursing home some of the new songs he had been showing her—'Homecoming' (Op. 58, No. 1) to words by Paulsen and 'The Mother Sings' (Op. 60, No. 1) to words by Vilhelm Krag. These, he told Max Abraham, were part of the 'Song-Spring' (*Liederfrühling*) he and his wife were enjoying: 'It is incredible how much younger I have felt in the last few months. I have become so lyrical, that the songs pour out of my heart, better, I think, than ever before. But for heaven's sake, no self-flattery!'[2] A few days later he told Röntgen: 'While my wife was in the nursing home I wrote a mass of songs for her. I shall divide them into three books, one of which I should like to dedicate to Messchaert.'[3] The three books are Op. 58 (*Norway:* five songs to texts by Paulsen), Op. 59 (*Elegiac Poems*, also by Paulsen), and Op. 60 (*Poems by Vilhelm Krag*). The texts, it will be noted, are all Norwegian. John Paulsen was his old Bergen friend; Vilhelm Krag, a young poet still in his early twenties, came from the southern coastal

[1] Letter to Beyer, 24 November 1893.
[2] Zschinsky-Troxler, 7 January 1894.
[3] Letter to Röntgen, 12 January 1894, p. 44.

region of Norway, and had been much influenced by Danish writers, especially Drachmann. Yet another song-collection belongs to the years 1894–5; this also is Norwegian, but of a more specialized intention, being a set of seven *Children's Songs* (Op. 61), to verses from a school reading book edited by Nordahl Rolfsen, another Bergenser and a distant relative of Grieg's.

Within another year or so he was to produce what is probably his most original set of songs, the *Haugtussa* cycle (Op. 67) to poems by Arne Garborg, one of the major figures in Norwegian literature in the second half of the nineteenth century, and one of the strongest supporters of the *landsmål* movement. The background of *Haugtussa*, which Garborg published on 1st May 1895, was the desolate farming country of Jæren, south of Stavanger,

> as [Garborg] could just recollect it from the time before pietistic revivalism had invaded the neighbourhood. That life was both earthy and exuberant, hardly touched by Christian conceptions or morbid broodings over the soul, sin, and damnation.[1]

In a series of lyric poems, with much variety of form and metre, Garborg traces the story of the young girl (*Veslemøy*) who has the gift of insight into the supernatural world, and through sorrow and spiritual dangers attains a state of wisdom and peace: in Jungian terms, one might find in it a poetic account of the integration of a personality. Grieg seems to have got hold of a copy almost as soon as it appeared, and was immediately impressed by its 'deep philosophy of life', describing it as 'a most original book, to which the music is really composed already, and only needs to be written down'.[2] Not since the Vinje songs of Op. 33 (also to *landsmål* texts) had Grieg become so profoundly moved by lyric poetry. The language of *Haugtussa* almost defeats translators, and the cycle is still comparatively little known outside the Scandinavian

[1] Downs, op. cit., p. 108.

[2] Letter to Röntgen, quoted in *Grieg*, p. 48.

countries. It was to be Grieg's last set of songs, with the exception of those written in 1900 (Op. 69 and Op. 70) to words by a minor Danish poet, Otto Benzon.

The instrumental compositions of the nineties are all (at least in their original form) for piano. The earliest, and also the longest, is the *Old Norwegian Melody with Variations*, for two pianos (Op. 51), one of the composer's few large-scale keyboard works; its form owes much to Schumann's *Andante and Variations* (Op. 46) and to Saint-Saëns's *Variations on a theme of Beethoven* (both for two pianos). Grieg orchestrated the work in 1900, making some reduction in length. Another work for four hands (on one keyboard), the *Symphonic Dances* (Op. 64), is also based on folk-tunes. The compositions for solo piano from this period include four more sets of *Lyric Pieces*, of which Book 5 (Op. 54) is noteworthy not only for the variety and high quality of its contents, but also because four of its items, orchestrated by Anton Seidl, form the popular *Lyric Suite*.

The most important piano work of the decade, however, is the collection of *Nineteen Norwegian Folk-tunes* (Op. 66), which are the gleanings of Jotunheim tours with Beyer and Röntgen. The latter supplements his earlier account with another, describing a holiday at Fosli, above the Vøringfoss, in the summer of 1896:

Frants Beyer's brother-in-law, Börre Gjortsen, had built a hut on a site a day's journey from Fosli . . . by a small lake, Tinhølen, far from any human habitation. We made our way there, Grieg, Beyer, Gjertsen with his two sons and I, well provisioned, and spent some wonderful days amid grand scenery and solitude. We lived chiefly on trout, which we caught ourselves in great numbers. . . . Frants Beyer had brought with him from Jotunheim many new melodies, which Grieg harmonized immediately and arranged for piano. They appeared shortly afterwards in a collection, *Norwegian Folk-tunes*,

Op. 66, dedicated to Beyer. Besides this, Grieg was occupied with his essay on Mozart.[1]

Grieg wrote to Röntgen from Bergen on 22nd August, quoting his setting of the folksong, *It is the greatest foolishness* (Op. 66, No. 2), and adding: 'I have certainly put some hair-raising chromatic chords on paper. The excuse is that they originated not on the piano, but in my brain. If one has the Vøringfoss beneath one's feet, one feels more independent and daring than down in the valley.' The melodies in this collection were taken from the singing of Gjendine Slaalien and others, and had not been previously recorded by Lindeman or other collectors. One of them (No. 14) is well known as the source of a theme in Delius's *On hearing the first cuckoo in spring*,[2] and others clearly served Percy Grainger as models for his folk-music transcriptions.

[1] Röntgen, pp. 55 fol.

[2] There are other echoes of Grieg in the same piece, including the triplet figure in the second bar which is reminiscent of 'En Svane', and the theme beginning two bars later which is remarkably like 'The Students' Serenade' (Op. 73, No. 6):

6 The final decade (1897-1907)

Notwithstanding the welcome the English had always given Grieg and his music, he was persuaded only with difficulty to repeat his visits in later years. The hazards of the sea-crossing and of the big towns with their pall of nineteenth-century industrial smoke always had to be balanced against the blandishments of friends and admirers and memories of the excellence of English orchestral playing at its best. Thus he wrote to Brodsky, who was now established in Manchester, to support Hermann Kretzschmar's application for the post of conductor in succession to Hallé: 'I myself once conducted the Manchester orchestra and was enthralled by the achievement of the strings. It was, I think, in the year 1889. Who knows, perhaps your presence there may yet hypnotize me there again?'[1] When he finally decided to accept Brodsky's invitation (two years later) he makes his conditions, requesting 'that during our stay in Manchester you give the cursed "Fog" its passports. From what I hear you have such standing that you only need to command! So—please!'[2] By the middle of November the Griegs are in London, and Edvard sends one of his microscopically written postcards:

We arrive Wednesday 24th at 2.30 and will go direct to 41 Acomb Street. And may I ask straight away, Frau Brodsky, if I can have at *4 o'clock* a beefsteak (underdone!). I know this is impudent, and you see for yourself that you should have let us stay in a hotel. But before

[1] Brodsky letters, 6 November 1895.
[2] ibid., 3 September 1897.

a concert you *must* not be offended if I am very strict about my food. It is absolutely necessary. The concert is at 7.30 and I must rest beforehand. And there is one more thing you must permit: Bechsteins are sending a pianino; will you please have it put into my room. . . . [Written across the card]: As soon as I arrive I intend to exercise my fingers a little in my room, so I should be grateful for a fairly warm room. And now I will leave you in peace!

In fact he withstood the rigours of an uncommonly heavy tour; two days after the Manchester concert he conducted in Birmingham, four days after that in Edinburgh, and returned to London, where the 'cursed Fog' was doubtless awaiting him: at least, he caught cold a few days before he was due to conduct the Philharmonic Orchestra in his Piano Concerto. Before leaving the country he gave further concerts in Cheltenham and Brighton and again in London.

Of all the countries he visited, none gave him more pleasure than the Netherlands. He was made much of by the Dutch, from royalty down to the shop assistants, he enjoyed unlimited supplies of oysters, and the second of his three tours in the country (in 1897) was filled with agreeable surprises. At a chamber concert in Amsterdam, Nina was called on at short notice to deputize for Messchaert, and sang ten songs to triumphant acclaim. After a concert in The Hague a royal messenger conferred on Edvard the Order of Orange-Nassau, another of those decorations which, strategically placed inside the lid of his travelling-trunk, made their due impression on customs officials. Above all, Grieg was enthralled by the sound of the Concertgebouw Orchestra under Mengelberg, so much so that he took a decision that was to have far-reaching consequences for the future of orchestral music in Norway.

An international fisheries congress, combined with an exhibition of Norwegian trade, industry, arts and crafts, had been planned for the summer of 1898 in Bergen, and the general secretary of the exhibition, Johan Bøgh, one day button-holed Grieg with the suggestion that a music festival should be held at the same time. It would be the first attempt to review the achievements of Norwegian music since Kjerulf, with meagre resources, had attempted something of the kind forty years earlier in Christiania, when Grieg was still a schoolboy. Bøgh's proposal was taken up without hesitation by Grieg, Svendsen and other prominent musicians, and a special committee was set up under the chairmanship of John Grieg, the Bergen publisher, to arrange programmes and select composers and performers. Into this smoothly running machinery Grieg now threw the heaviest of spanners; while still in Amsterdam, and without consulting the Bergen committee, he telegraphed home that he had engaged the Concertgebouw Orchestra, with Mengelberg, for the entire festival.

Local and national interests were affronted, the committee resigned in a body, and only the tactful influence of John Grieg and Iver Holter, who as conductor of the Christiania *Musikforeningen* (the only professional orchestra in Norway at that time) was an interested party, saved the situation. It was agreed to accept the engagement of the Dutch orchestra as a *fait accompli*, and to recruit an amateur Festival Choir of 400 and engage Norwegian professional soloists. Grieg now learnt, as he said, the true meaning of Ibsen's play-title *An Enemy of the People*, since he had to answer not only for preferring a first-class foreign orchestra to an indifferent native one, but also for making invidious selections from the programme material offered to the committee. He wrote to Röntgen:

> The Music Festival is making my hair whiter than ever. The most incredible composers are arising out of the dark abyss and demanding in peremptory tones to be considered. . . . I will die, I will give my body to be burned, but I will rise for the Festival like the phoenix from its ashes, to the confusion of my enemies.[1]

[1] Letters dated 8 April 1898 and 25 May 1898.

To the composer Gerhard Schjelderup he confided the principles on which he was working:

I have had to concentrate chiefly on some of the works that have gained a certain reputation in our literature and on the composers whose contribution in their own country to the advancement of Norwegian musical life seems to entitle them to be represented on this occasion.[1]

As for performers, his idea of a national Music Festival was that it should allow Norwegian music to be performed under the best possible conditions, 'and it is all the same to me whether this involves Norwegians, Germans, Japanese or Dutchmen'.[2]

In the event, the first Bergen Festival proved a complete vindication of Grieg's anti-chauvinism and artistic integrity. He did not allow his own works too much prominence: only the Piano Concerto, the choral suite from *Olav Trygvason*, and three songs with orchestra were included. Svendsen was generously represented by his first (D major) Symphony, the tone poem *Zorahayda*, the *Norwegian Rhapsody* (Op. 32), the *Romance for Violin and Orchestra*, and two folksong arrangements for strings; Selmer by his *Scandinavian Festival March* (with Nordraak's 'Ja, vi elsker' as its peroration) and *La Marche des Turcs sur Athènes* for baritone, male choir and orchestra, to words by Victor Hugo; Sinding by his Piano Concerto; and Holter, Schjelderup, Elling and Ole Olsen by various orchestral items. There was no chamber concert as such, but piano pieces and songs were interspersed among the orchestral works, and included piano compositions by Tellefsen, Neupert, and Agathe Backer Gröndahl and songs by Kjerulf, Nordraak, Sinding, Winter-Hjelm, Alnæs and others. The leading critic Aimar Grønvold, in his account of the Festival in the Bergan periodical *Samtiden*, wrote with moderate but justifiable pride:

[1] *Artikler og Taler*, pp. 163, 167.
[2] ibid., p. 167.

A small nation of two million people has succeeded in producing a musical art which may have its limitations, but also has its distinctive stamp in melody, harmony, and rhythm, together with a certain universal character, facing out towards the rest of the world.

Grieg himself was jubilant, writing to Brodsky in Manchester:

I have been victorious, marvellously victorious. There were performances such as no one in Scandinavia has ever experienced, and will not experience again in our time; *nowhere else* have I heard better. . . . And then the enjoyment and enthusiasm of the public, about three thousand of them, who for seven days on end listened to these splendid performances. You should have seen the countryfolk, who had come from afar and stood there during the wonderful pianissimos of the string orchestra, as reverently as if in church, while the tears ran unchecked down their faces. It was most moving—and who, under such circumstances, can estimate the cultural importance of these days?[1]

In short, as he said, 'a lucky star reigned over the Festival'. Local factions had made up their differences, and the visiting Dutchmen had been received with true Norwegian hospitality, Grieg setting the example by entertaining the orchestra and other participants, to the number of some two hundred guests, in the Exhibition restaurant after the first concert. At the end of the Festival, at one o'clock in the morning, more than ten thousand people headed by a military band escorted the departing Concertgebouw Orchestra through the streets of Bergen to the quay, whence the steamboat *Olav Kyrre* was to take them on the first lap of their journey back to Amsterdam.[2] Grieg and Svendsen both agreed that they felt ten years younger. Best of all, it was

[1] Brodsky letters, 27 July 1898.

[2] The voyage to Bergen must have been in itself a memorable experience for the visiting orchestra. The Festival Committee chartered a special boat to meet the regular Rotterdam–Stavanger service, and this took them up the Hardanger fjord as far as Eide, whence a fleet of horse-carriages transported the orchestra to Vossevangen, the journey being completed by rail to Bergen (Röntgen, p. 74).

already being said both in Bergen and in Christiania that Norway must aim at having a first-class orchestra of her own.

In the following year a definite step forward in this direction was marked by the opening of the new National Theatre in the capital, with an orchestra of symphonic dimensions subsidized by the municipality. The Theatre was inaugurated with performances of Holberg's comedy *The Lying-in Room*, Ibsen's *An Enemy of the People* and Bjørnson's *Sigurd Jorsalfar* with Grieg's incidental music, on successive evenings and in that order. *Sigurd*, as a national-Romantic drama, was to have been given on the opening night, but Bjørn Bjørnson, the Theatre director, had been stopped in the street by Ibsen, who pointed out that he was senior to Bjørn's father: to which the spirited young man retorted that if it was simply a question of age, Holberg was certainly older still. A day or so later he got a letter from his father, addressed from Venice, saying that both he and Grieg had come to the conclusion that *Sigurd* was too immature a work to begin the festival, whereupon Bjørn telegraphed back to Venice: 'Thank Heaven, Holberg is dead.'[1] Grieg, however, was delighted to conduct the newly formed orchestra in his *Sigurd* music, and even more intrigued by the novel mechanism that allowed him to signal from the orchestra pit for the curtain to be raised. After the performance, the Griegs went to stay with the Bjørnsons on their estate at Aulestad, a visit that was to set in train events involving the composer in another public controversy.

The large Bjørnson household, made up of members of the family and numerous guests, was seething with liberal-minded indignation over the notorious Dreyfus case, and, as it chanced, the news of Dreyfus's conviction had arrived on the same day as Grieg received an invitation from Colonne to conduct in Paris at the Châtelet Theatre concerts. Grieg immediately sat

[1] Frances Bull, *Tradisjoner og minner*, 3rd ed. (Oslo, 1963), p. 70.

down and wrote a letter of refusal, expressing his unwillingness to appear in public in a country where such a miscarriage of justice could occur. Bjørnson's son-in-law, a journalist named Albert Langen, helped him to put this into French, and then asked whether Grieg would object to having the letter published also in the *Frankfurter Zeitung*. Grieg consented, being assured that such wider publicity would be for the benefit of international justice and freedom. Soon his letter appeared in the press of most European countries, and the composer was almost universally praised for his gesture. Only from France came anger and derision; one journal, addressing itself 'au compositeur de musique juive, E. G.,' threatened, if he were to show himself in Paris at any future time, 'de le recevoir dans notre ville par coups de pied dans la partie le moins noble de son individu'.[1]

It was not until April 1903 that Grieg felt that he could accept a renewed invitation from Colonne, by which time it was hoped that the personal opposition to him would have cooled down; but this was not the case, and demonstrators tried to wreck the first concert with whistles and cat-calls. Grieg mounted the rostrum, however, and plunged the orchestra into his *Autumn* Overture, while the interrupters were ejected. Ellen Gulbranson sang with orchestra 'Solveig's Lullaby', 'From Monte Pincio' and 'A Swan'. Raoul Pugno was the soloist in the Piano Concerto, the orchestral strings played the two *Elegiac Melodies*, the dramatic cantata *Before a Southern Convent* was performed (complete with a '*chœur de nonnes*'), the inevitable first *Peer Gynt* Suite followed, and Ellen Gulbranson, as Brünnhilde, sang the closing scene from *Götterdämmerung*.

After the concert the Griegs, not without a sense of drama, were escorted back to their hotel by a police guard. The fact that Grieg was a compatriot and friend of Bjørnson, who in his

[1] For complete texts, in English translation, of the exchange of letters between Grieg and Colonne, see Finck: *Grieg and his Music* (London, 1929), pp. 79–81.

uncompromising way had recently told the French nation that they were the Chinese of Europe shut away inside their protective walls, may have added to his unpopularity with the Parisian minority who still cherished resentment of his Dreyfus letter of four years earlier. But there was no question about the general goodwill; the hall had been sold out and the audience had been almost beside itself with enthusiasm. The press was more variable in its reactions: Gabriel Fauré wrote generously in *Le Figaro*, Pierre Lalo (son of the composer) exasperatedly in *Le Temps*, alleging that Grieg merely took his songs from folk-music, and Debussy quite waspishly in a lengthy article in *Gil Blas*.[1]

Debussy's notice begins with a sardonic reference to Grieg's former refusal to appear in Paris, continues with an amusing account of the disturbances at the beginning of the concert, and describes Grieg's person as that of a clever photographer seen from the front, and a sunflower from behind.[2] He does not deny Grieg's effectiveness as a conductor: 'Malgré son âge, il est allègre et sec, et conduit l'orchestre avec une minutie nerveuse qui s'inquiète, souligne toutes les nuances, distribue l'émotion avec un infatigable soin.' The three songs with orchestra, including 'A Swan', are dealt with in non-committal though highly ornate language, with several lines reproduced word for word from Debussy's own notice of Delius's *Danish Poems* for voice and orchestra, which had been heard in Paris two years earlier. As for the Piano Concerto, Debussy is of the opinion

[1] See *Monsieur Croche et autres écrits*, ed. François Lesure (Paris, 1971), pp. 123 and 149–53.

[2] The odd comparison to 'un photographe génial' may conceivably have arisen out of an unconscious association with Hjalmar Ekdal, the self-deluded ambitious photographer in *The Wild Duck*. Ibsen's play had been presented in Paris in April 1891. Debussy was in any case not the only French journalist unable to resist caricaturing Grieg's appearance. On one of his earlier visits Grieg had fallen a victim to a

that the soloist, Raoul Pugno, disguises his antipathy to the work, so that

> on ne s'aperçoit plus que ce concerto, qui commence par du Schumann et finit par une apothéose digne d'*Excelsior* n'est pas un œuvre d'art très personnelle. La façon d'y traiter le piano est toute traditionelle, et je n'ai jamais compris pourquoi il était traversé çà et là par des souvenirs de trompettes guerrières, celles-ci annonçant généralement qu'un petit 'cantabile', où l'on se pâme, va commencer . . .

—a description that is in some respects cruelly accurate.

Debussy's next paragraph, devoted to the *Elegiac Melodies*

---

precious literary figure who wrote under the name of Maurice Bigeon a collection of essays entitled *Les Révoltés scandinaves* (Paris, 1894). The essay on Grieg, cryptically headed '*Pour Mme. Réjane, la Nora désirée*' (Gabrielle Réjane had played Nora in *A Doll's House* with much success in Paris earlier that year), contains this passage:

> Petit, fluet, pâle, l'air suffreteux, Grieg est à peu près l'homme de son œuvre. On dirait à le voir avec sa mise tres simple, ses gestes menus et débonnaires, un de ces vieux professeurs de piano comme en peignait Balzac et qui s'en vont pauvres bohèmes de l'idéal, à travers les rues boueuses des cités, donner pour cinq francs d'art à des demoiselles de bonne maison. Mais une crinière frissonante, indomptable et fougueuse, accentue fortement le profil, donne à la physiognomie je ne sais quel déconcertant héroïsme, et l'œil vert, où semble dormir la couleur changeant des vagues, l'œil profond et doux, laisse plonger jusqu'au fond obscur où dort la poésie—

with much else in similar strain. Grieg was so furious that he accepted an invitation to Jonas Lie's home only on the understanding that Bigeon would not be among the guests.

Louis Laloy, writing in 1928 (*La Musique retrouvée 1902–1927*, p.19,) recalls his parents' accounts of rehearsals of the *concerts Colonne*, with 'Saint-Saëns grincheux, Massenet agité, César Franck engourdi en sa béatitude, Grieg escaladant les gradins pour vérifier une partie de trombone, agile comme un kobold à tête grise.'

for string orchestra, ends with the often-quoted words about 'pink sweets filled with snow':

L'on a dans la bouche le goût bizarre et charmant d'un bonbon rose qui serait fourré de neige.

Towards the *Peer Gynt* music he is, rather unexpectedly, more generous:

Les idées en sont charmantes et les rythmes adroits; l'émotion en est plus véridiquement norvégienne. L'agencement orchestral y est aussi plus pondéré; des effets trop faciles sont remplacés là par d'ingénieuses trouvailles.

He finds it inexplicable, however, that the Wagnerian soprano Ellen Gulbranson should have been asked to round off the Grieg programme with the closing scene from *Götterdämmerung*, and says that he left before this item, since

on ne mange pas de rosbif après les petits fours.

The notice ends with an attempt to sum up Grieg's art on which, in Debussy's view, this concert has thrown no fresh light, though he realizes that the composer's later works are still unknown in France. He compares him unfavourably as a nationalist with Balakirev and Rimsky-Korsakov, and concludes that

il n'est plus qu'un musicien adroit plus soucieux d'effets que d'art véritable.

In the course of his article Debussy digresses on the subject of Grieg's debt to Nordraak, a matter on which he has obviously taken little trouble to inform himself. As to his own indebtedness to Grieg, he seems to have avoided mentioning or even thinking about it, unlike Ravel, who openly admitted that Grieg had influenced his work. But one cannot deny that the astringency of Monsieur Croche, like that of Corno di Bassetto, comes as a welcome relief to the indiscriminate chorus of praise that Grieg and his music generally aroused at the height of his fame.

We do not know whether the middle-aged Debussy agreed with the younger musicians of Paris who, a few years later in 1906, were said to be discussing excitedly what they termed 'le nouveau Grieg'. The object of their interest was the set of folk-dance tunes Grieg transcribed for piano under the title of *Slåtter* (Op. 72). Except for the collection of short original pieces entitled *Stemninger (Moods)* (Op. 73)—in effect an additional book of Lyric Pieces—the *Slåtter* was his last keyboard work, and in some ways his most original one. Even now it is comparatively little known, and its importance in relation both to Grieg's development and to early twentieth-century music has been underestimated.

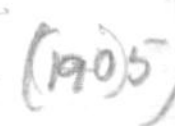

The originals of the *Slåtter* were part of the repertory of a hardanger-fiddle player named Knut Dale, of Telemark, who had learnt some of his tunes and manner of performing them from the still more renowned Møllergutten or Myllarguten ('The Miller's Boy'),[1] whose recitals had been among the opening attractions of Bull's National Theatre in Bergen in 1850. Beginning in April 1888, Dale wrote several letters to Grieg,[2] enquiring if he would be interested in noting down some of the fiddle tunes, so that they could be saved for posterity. Grieg's reply seems to have been at first half-hearted, perhaps because experience had already shown that the subtleties of the traditional style were almost impossible to transcribe in conventional notation. Yet Grieg was well aware of the need to record the *slåtter* in some way or other before they faded entirely from popular memory, as he feared they would in face of the increasing use of the *trekkspill* or accordion; he was

[1] His real name was Torgeir Augundsson. He died in 1872 at the age of 71.

[2] The Dale-Grieg-Halvorsen correspondence has been published by Øyvind Anker in *Norsk Musikkgranskning Årbok 1943–6*, pp. 71–90.

particularly distressed by the sound of this mechanized instrument wafted up from boats passing by Troldhaugen, and lamented: 'These hand-organs are destroying all good and true national music.'

He realized that if the fiddle music were to be faithfully noted down this could only be done by the intermediation of an expert string-player, and accordingly he wrote two letters on 18th October 1901, one to Knut Dale promising to do what he could to arrange an audition for Dale with a professional violinist in Christiania, and to defray his expenses; and the other to Johan Halvorsen, a former pupil of Brodsky and now conductor of the orchestra of the National Theatre, enclosing Dale's latest letter and proposing that Halvorsen should undertake to note down a selection of the *slåtter* from Dale's playing, and that Grieg himself should subsequently arrange the results for solo piano. He emphasized that

> *only a violinist with a feeling for the Norwegian spirit, who is able to write from dictation,* can carry out this task. It is completely nonsensical that the Storting pays people who are not violinists to collect folk-music, as they cannot take down what is at least the equally important half of it—the folk-dances!

Halvorsen agreed to the plan, and the sixty-seven year old *spelmann*, provided with a remittance of 100 *kroner*, made the difficult journey from Tinn in Telemark to the capital in the middle of November. On the 17th of that month Halvorsen wrote:

> Knut Dale has arrived. Today I rescued two *slåtter* from oblivion. They are not too easy to write down. There are small turns and shakes like a little trout in a rapid. If you try to catch them they're gone. Knut Dale is an intelligent and sound musician. Now and then he had certain tricks, a mixture of 2/4 and 6/8 time which made me want to laugh aloud with pleasure. . . . I must keep him here for a fortnight or three weeks. He asks me to send you his regards and thanks for the money.

> A man from Telemark who was with him gave me to understand that he did not expect any payment for his work, and also that there were times when he took a drop too much. For this reason I shall keep an eye on him and see that he doesn't go on the spree but travels straight home again. I am taking down the *slåtter* in the tuning he plays them in, e.g.
>
> or

Grieg replied that it was certainly important to keep a watch on Knut's fellowship with Bacchus, though he would be no true *spelmann* if he were not fond of his glass. At intervals during the next three weeks Halvorsen reported further progress, with seventeen of Dale's best tunes safely fixed in notation. Halvorsen had taken to the modest old folk-fiddler, who was delighted that his repertory was being thus preserved, and whose eyes 'shone with a musician's pleasure' when Halvorsen played a tune back to him. Money-matters became more confused, however; by the end of a fortnight Dale had only 3 kroner 75 øre left out of the 100 kroner, had not paid his hotel bill, and had nothing left for the return journey. In the end, Halvorsen settled the bill, gave him 10 kroner, and put him on the train.

A letter from Halvorsen, dated 3rd December, encloses the completed violin transcriptions, and gives Grieg some technical details:

> With regard to the scale, it is noteworthy that G sharp is nearly always used (at the beginning of D major tunes); G natural only occurs near the close, on the lower strings. I find the G sharp fresh and attractive, whereas G would seem insipid. It's the same with the shakes and other grace notes. These shakes are the life and soul of the *slåtter*; they are produced by a vibration of the hand, and have the effect of a kind of 'quivering'.... I notice that even the most intricate appoggiature and trills do not detract in the least from the rhythmic flow of the *slåtter*. I practise the hardanger-fiddle every day, and have mastered not a little of the 'real thing'...

Grieg replied from Troldhaugen three days later:

> This is something like a Saturday night, my dear Halvorsen. A southerly gale rages outside and is shaking the house. But it is cosy indoors. I have just got your *slåtter* and have read them through, chuckling with delight the while. But all the same I am furious at not being a string-player. How I still hate the Leipzig Conservatory!—But to the matter in hand. The 'noteworthy' point you make about G sharp in D major is just what made me as mad as a hatter in the year 1871. Of course I immediately stole it for *Pictures of Folk Life*. The note is worth investigating. The augmented fourth can also be heard in the peasants' songs. It is a ghost from some old scale or other: but which? It is incredible that none of us applies himself to research into national music, since we have in our folk-tunes so many new sounds for those with ears to hear with, hearts to feel with, and understanding to write down.

Not until the end of 1902 was Grieg satisfied with his re-transcription of the tunes in pianistic terms. He insisted that the publishers should bring out Halvorsen's solo violin version simultaneously with his own piano settings, and that they should make it clear that Halvorsen's was not only equally important, but also the source of Grieg's work. With their annotations on the folklore background of the tunes, Halvorsen's directions to violinists, and Grieg's notes on his aims in making the keyboard adaptations, this pair of publications is a landmark in musicology comparable to Bartók's early folk-music transcriptions, which they antedate by several years.

The year 1903 was to be busy. Besides the publication of the *Slåtter* and the stormy visit to Paris already described, there were journeys as far afield as Warsaw and Prague, where Grieg was loaded with 'wreaths of silver laurel and palm as big as mill wheels', and where the Piano Concerto was played by

> a little witch named Teresita Carreño Tagliapietra, a daughter of Madame Carreño's first marriage. She runs about the keyboard like a

clever wild-cat and is damned talented. Everything she does has poetry in it. And one can hardly say that about her mother, despite her tremendous technique. I also had a little singer named Magda Dvořák, a daughter of the composer. She sang with feeling, but in Czech, which was a bit hard for me to follow. It was amusing to make contact with Dvořák. He is a character, to put it mildly; but he was very likeable. (Letter to Beyer, 1 April 1903.)

The same year there were elaborate celebrations of Grieg's sixtieth birthday. These began with a reception at Troldhaugen and a concert in Bergen on 15th June. On the following day a banquet was held at the Grand Hotel, at which Bjørnson made one of his extravagantly rhetorical speeches, comparing Grieg's career to the romantic course of the river Rauma. Grieg replied less formally but in his best after-dinner style, speaking wittily and touchingly of his debt to his native city. The same evening the orchestra of the National Theatre gave another concert, and on the 17th Grieg arranged for the whole orchestra to be taken up in horse-carriages to Fløyen, the most popular of Bergen's seven mountains, and entertained them all to luncheon, the day ending with an *al fresco* concert.

Though the letters of these later years are often filled with complaints of ill-health and failing powers, Grieg managed to keep up to a remarkable degree his interest in people and public affairs, as well as in artistic matters. Like a true Norwegian, he was no man's servant and his democratic outlook gave additional point and humour to his accounts of meetings with the German Kaiser in the summer of 1904. William II had become fond of the northern fjords, and all this summer had his yacht *Hohenzollern* moored in Bergen harbour. He kept his private orchestra on board with him, for he was a keen amateur musician, with ambitions as composer and conductor. Grieg received an invitation to breakfast with the Kaiser at the German Consul's, which he accepted reluctantly, not being, as he said, of a courtly disposition (*hoffähig*). The occasion, however, could hardly have been less restricted by protocol. They discussed music during breakfast, and afterwards for nearly an hour 'everything between heaven and earth: poetry, painting, religion, socialism, and God knows what else. Luckily he was a human being and not an Emperor. For that reason I was able to express my views fully, though of course with some discretion'.[1]

The Kaiser's orchestra of forty players was then called in, and the Kaiser took two chairs, placed them in front of the rest, and said, 'Front stalls, please'. The orchestra then began a programme of Grieg's works—*Sigurd Jorsalfar*, *Peer Gynt* and similar selections, while the imperial host invited his guest to correct any points of tempo or interpretation. 'He then illustrated the effect of the music by movements of the head and body. *Anitra's Dance* quite electrified him, and it was marvellous to see his serpentine convolutions in the manner of an oriental maiden.' Grieg then played on the piano the minuet from his early Piano Sonata, which the Kaiser found 'sehr germanisch und mächtig aufgebaut', and his *Wedding Day at Troldhaugen*.

The next evening was spent on the Kaiser's yacht, with the orchestra playing on deck after dinner, hundreds of rowing and steamboats swarming around within earshot, and the Kaiser protectively wrapping Grieg in his own cloak. Grieg's summing-up of his host was: 'A very unusual man—a strange mixture of great energy, great self-confidence, and great kindness of heart.' (The Norwegians had not forgotten the prompt help sent from Germany earlier in the year for the fire-ravaged town of Ålesund, north of Bergen.)

Grieg suspended judgment on whether the Kaiser was genuinely musical, but at least he respected music and gave it his attention. It was otherwise with King Edward VII of England, who during a command performance by Grieg, in

[1] Letter of 21 July 1904 to Max Hinrichsen (Zschinsky-Troxler, pp. 104 fol.).

Til

Edvard Grieg!

Orpheus slog med Toner rene
Sjæl i Vilddyr, Ild af Stene.

Stene har vort Norden nok af;
Vilddyr har det og en Flok af.

Spil saa Stenene spruder Gnister;
spil saa Dyrehammen brister!

Rom 30/3. 66

Henrik Ibsen

Verses written by Henrik Ibsen in Grieg's album, March 1866

Grieg's pen and ink sketch of Troldhaugen

Title page of the second part of L. M. Lindeman's *Ældre og nyere norske Fjeldmelodier*, 1867

Langsomt og tilbageholdt.
En Svane.
(Henrik Ibsen.)
Edvard Grieg
p
Min hvide Svane du stumme, du stille,
p
più p
pp sempre e molto tranq
hverken Slag eller Trille lod Sang-röst ane.
molto legato
pp sempre e molto tranq
pp
Angst beskyttende Alfen, som sover,
dolce
poco animato
Ped.
cresc.
altid lyttende gled du henover:
cresc.
Ped.
Ped.

Autograph of Grieg's setting of Ibsen's *En Svane*

Detail from the portrait of Grieg by Eilif Petersson

The Griegs in Leipzig during the winter of 1887–8. *Left to right*: Nina, Edvard, Johan Halvorsen, Frederick Delius, Christian Sinding

Poster by Edvard Munch for the Paris production of *Peer Gynt* in 1896

May 1906, followed the outrageous English custom of the time by carrying on so loud a conversation that Grieg twice had to stop playing.

But the best of the story [added Grieg[1]] is the sequel. The English King and Queen had asked us to bear their greetings to the King and Queen of Norway and we were therefore obliged to pay the latter a visit. As you know, our King [Haakon VII] is quite approachable, and when we came to speak of the King of England I told him good-humouredly about his talkativeness. 'Yes', said the King, who apparently wanted to defend his father-in-law, 'but I must tell you that the King of England can talk and listen at the same time!' But I had my reply, and retorted: 'That may well be possible' (which it isn't), 'but all the same it is not permissible, even for the King of England, and in justice to my art I cannot overlook it.' Whereupon the King shrugged his shoulders humorously and smiled amiably. In short, he is a most kindly man. All the more's the pity that he seems to have no feeling for music at all.

The year 1905 had brought to a head the crisis in Scandinavian internal politics, with the Norwegians intensifying their pressure for a 'pure' Norwegian flag (without the emblem of union with Sweden), for a separate consular service for their nationals, and for their own Foreign Minister. Among the leading figures in opposition to the régime were the Bergen ship-owner Christian Michelsen, the explorer Fridtjof Nansen and Bjørnstjerne Bjørnson. Relations during the earlier part of 1905 became so strained that the Swedish government threatened to suspend the Norwegian Constitution of 1814, and both sides even talked of mobilization for war. Grieg's letters are filled with earnest arguments and speculations on the outcome of events:

In Sweden, as in Norway, it is hoped that everything will be solved without bloodshed. The contrary would be a crime unparalleled. We

[1] Zschinsky-Troxler, 29 June 1906.

are fortunately prepared, however, and for this reason Sweden will probably take care not to attack us.[1]

The nations are horrified at the idea of war. Only a small party in the Swedish Government is egging the King on, and seems to be possessed by megalomania. Well, we hope for the best. Our Government is splendid and has the confidence of the whole people.[2]

The worst and greatest misfortune is that the Norwegian nation is a young one, whereas the Swedish is a middle-aged one. Conflict is thus unavoidable. With us, it is the nation itself that rules, in Sweden a few behind-the-scenes aristocrats with antediluvian attitudes. Everything depends on whether the King is forced to abdicate. If he stands his ground, peace will probably be saved, but if not—? All may be well, if Germany follows events without taking sides with one country or the other. We are also inspired with the wish that *both* may come well out of it.[3]

I have had to give up the concerts in Finland, where I was invited, since I cannot travel through Sweden. It sounds incredible, but chauvinism has gone so far in that country that they are driving out Norwegians who have been living there, and reject my compositions with hissing and other forms of demonstration, whereas we treat the Swedes with the utmost courtesy. You may judge which nation represents the healthier attitude in this respect. But more—you see in this an indication of which side is in the right. People only behave as the Swedes are now behaving if they are in the wrong.[4]

The treaty of Karlstadt signed on 23rd September brought only partial relief, for Norway resented having to agree, as a condition for attaining her full independence, to yielding up her fortifications along the eastern frontier and the creation of a neutral zone; fear of Russian penetration towards the North Sea was very real at this time. Two days after the signing of the treaty, Grieg wrote to Michelsen, who as Secretary of State was res-

[1] Zschinsky-Troxler, 29 May 1905.
[2] ibid., 14 June 1905.
[3] ibid., 25 June 1905.
[4] Ibid. 28 August 1905.

ponsible for the negotiations with Sweden, assuring him that 'the spirit of progress shone over his work', but the question of what form the new Norwegian Government should take had still to be settled. A letter to Max Hinrichsen enlarges on this subject:

In these days we live in a state of great tension. The big question is whether, in eight days' time, we are to have a new King, or not; and in the latter event, is it to be a republic? A widespread faction wants a plebiscite, but the rest of us wish the Storthing to proceed as quickly as possible to the election of a King (Prince Carl of Denmark).[1]

When a plebiscite was after all decided on, it gave the Storthing by an overwhelming majority a mandate to offer the throne to Prince Carl and thereby defeat the republican opposition. (Grieg, in the circumstances, was personally against the republican solution). The new King of Norway, with the title Haakon VII, was elected on 18th November; he was to reign until his death more than half a century later. Grieg declined an invitation to compose a coronation cantata, but he took part in a festival performance of *Sigurd Jorsalfar* on 6th December, and in company with Bjørnson was summoned to the royal box, where he found the King and his consort, Queen Maud, 'two unpretentious and amiable people, who are winning all hearts'.[2]

With the abatement of all this political excitement, Grieg was able to concentrate once again on his concert life, and even to complete a handful of new compositions. The piano *Moods* (Op. 73) have already been mentioned. In September 1906 he finished the *Four Psalms* (Op. 74) for solo voices and chorus, based on old Norwegian church melodies from Lindeman's collection. Among the concert tours undertaken, the happiest was in the Netherlands in April 1906, where Grieg conducted the Amsterdam Concertgebouw Orchestra, having beforehand participated in a feast of oysters that left him unscathed but

[1] ibid., 19 October 1905. [2] ibid., 3 December 1905.

caused Röntgen to take to his bed. The programme consisted of the *Lyric Suite* (apparently the first performance of Grieg's revision of Seidl's orchestral transcriptions), *Bergliot* with the declamation spoken by Marie Brema, the Piano Concerto with Fridtjof Backer-Grøndahl as soloist, and *Land-sighting* with a male voice choir. A few days later, at a chamber concert which was sold out and from which Grieg gave the profits to the Concertgebouw Orchestra's pension fund, the composer played a set of his *Lyric Pieces*[1] and, with Pablo Casals, the Cello Sonata. At the Röntgens' home afterwards Grieg was thrilled by Casals's playing of the Bach C minor Suite and gave him his portrait with the inscription 'To the incomparable Casals'.

From Holland he went on to England—his last visit there, as it was to prove. He was still in good spirits and able, as described above, to indulge his sense of the absurd at the court of Edward VII and at Oxford, where he received an honorary degree.[2] ('On the 22nd I became a Doctor . . . , so now I shall be able to cure myself and all my friends.') He valued much more highly the honour of being asked to address two hundred of his compatriots, including Nansen, at the Norwegian Club in London on the first Constitution Day (17th May) after the dissolution of the union with Sweden. But he was already growing weary of being a celebrity; from London he wrote to Röntgen:

How one is bothered here by letters of all sorts. This popularity is all very fine, or rather seems to be, but it is dearly bought. My reputation as an artist suffers thereby, and criticism becomes unfavourable. Those artists who did not gain so-called popularity in their lifetime were more fortunate. I can't help it that my music is played in third-rate hotels and by schoolgirls: so I feel just as warmly towards my music without considering the public. . . . If only time were to be granted me

[1] Specified incorrectly as 'Op. 46' in Röntgen, p. 107.

[2] Cambridge had already, in 1893, conferred an honorary doctorate on Grieg, together with Saint-Saëns, Tchaikovsky, and Boïto.

when I could be forgotten by the world and could live for myself and my art.[1]

But time was running out. In the summer of 1907 Julius Röntgen again came to stay at Troldhaugen, and found Grieg in better health than he had hoped. The party was soon joined by Percy Grainger, bringing with him some of his English folk-tune arrangements. Grainger was to play the Piano Concerto under Grieg at the Leeds Festival in the autumn, and the two spent much time in going over the work and making minute emendations in the solo part. At the end of the visit, when Röntgen was about to take the boat for Copenhagen, Grieg walked a little way in front, and as Röntgen caught up with him said: 'I feel and know for certain that we shall not see one another again. My strength is at an end and cannot hold out any longer. We must say farewell for ever.' Then, Röntgen added: 'I saw Grieg get into his carriage and I went, deeply moved, down to my cabin. I was aroused from my sad thoughts by the thunder of cannon from the neighbouring fort—a salute to the German Kaiser, who was in Bergen harbour in the *Hohenzollern*.'[2]

On 2nd September, notwithstanding his weakness, Grieg set out from Troldhaugen to stay at a hotel in Bergen and be ready to start the following morning for England. But his doctor had to be called, and ordered him at once into Bergen Hospital. As he arrived there, Grieg said: '*Saa dette skulde bli min bane*' ('This must be the end of me, then').[3] After a restless night he sank into a coma and died quietly in the early morning of 4th September 1907.

For years he had carried with him, on all his journeys, the military band parts of the Funeral March in memory of Rikard Nordraak, and had asked his Bergen friend and concert agent, Carl Rabe, to see that he was buried in his native place and had

[1] Röntgen, 25 May 1906.
[2] ibid., pp. 118–19.
[3] ibid., p. 120.

the Nordraak March played beside his grave '*muligst godt*' ('as well as possible'). No adequate military band being available, Johan Halvorsen orchestrated the March and conducted it with a special orchestra assembled for the occasion; among the violinists was Adolph Brodsky, who had hastened over from England. The orchestra also played *The Last Spring*, and a male-voice choir, with Ingolf Schiøtt at their head, sang 'The Great White Host', a traditional religious song from Hitterdal which Grieg had arranged in his Op. 30. Brodsky estimated that between forty and fifty thousand people watched the cortège pass through the streets of Bergen on 9th September.

The composer's ashes now rest in a grotto in the cliff face at Troldhaugen, overlooking the fjord. In 1919 they were temporarily removed to St James's churchyard, Troldhaugen having been sold; but in 1923, when the villa and grounds passed into the ownership of the parish of Fana and became a place of pilgrimage, the urn was replaced in the grotto.

Nina lived, chiefly in Denmark, until the age of almost ninety. In 1923, when she was seventy-five, she wrote to Anna Brodsky in England, describing a holiday she was spending in Lofthus with a relative. Her words may most fittingly bring the biographical section of this book to a close:

We are ensconced in a tiny cottage, where nature is overwhelmingly vast and picturesque. At our feet, the fjord with its green waves, and opposite—the fjord is quite narrow—the huge mountain range covered with glaciers and perpetual snow. Then we climb up and walk in lonely valleys where no one dwells and where the white waterfalls plunge down with deafening roar. And there in the grass flowers smile, more numerous and with brighter colours than are seen anywhere else, and with every step Edvard's music sounds in my heart and in my ears. We lived here a long time, Edvard and I, and the little house where we stayed is in the very same place. So many memories are buried here: I cannot believe that I am walking over their graves.[1]

[1] Brodsky letters, 15 July 1923. Original in German.

7 Grieg and Norwegian folk-music

In some notes sent in 1900 to his American biographer Finck, Grieg attempts to define the extent of folk-music influence on his work. Although, he says, certain critics have treated him as 'nothing more than a copying-machine of Norwegian folksong', the truth is that when he wrote his earlier works, including the piano pieces *Poetic Tone-pictures* (Op. 3) and the *Humoresques* (Op. 6), where 'a nationalist element frequently appears', he had practically no first-hand acquaintance with his native folk-song. In the light of our fuller knowledge of Grieg's career as a whole, we can now trace the stages by which he grew closer to Norwegian folk-music. First came the discovery of Lindeman's great collection in 1869; then followed his contacts with traditional singers and players in the Hardanger district from about 1877; and lastly, in the 1890s, he collected and arranged previously unpublished folk material with the help of Beyer, Röntgen and Halvorsen. These phases of developing interest can be linked with the various folk-music settings that form a substantial part of Grieg's total output, beginning with the *Norwegian Dances and Songs* (Op. 17), where the piano arrangements are seldom more ambitious than Lindeman's in keyboard technique and harmonic resource, and where the tunes are very little altered from the versions taken down by Lindeman. In the *Album for Male Voices* (Op. 30) the tunes and words are again borrowed from Lindeman but are handled more boldly (the subtitle reads 'freely arranged after Norwegian folksongs'). The *Ballade* (Op. 24), the *Improvisata* (Op. 29) and the *Old*

Norwegian Melody with Variations for two pianos (Op. 51), apply more extended and inventive treatment to themes from Lindeman's collection. When we arrive at the *Norwegian Folk-tunes* of 1896 (Op. 66), the *Slåtter* of 1902 (Op. 72) and the *Four Psalms* of 1906 (Op. 74) we feel that the composer has at last completely absorbed the borrowed material into his personal style.

Before discussing these works in more detail, however, it may be worth while to take a closer look at the composer's remarks to Finck, which seem on the face of them to imply that folk-music influenced his original work only remotely, if at all, during the first half of his life. We must not forget that he made these statements in response to an enquiry from Finck that dealt primarily with his songs, and we know from other evidence that Grieg was always sensitive on this point, denying categorically that his solo songs were imitations or adaptations of folksongs; the only exception he allowed was 'Solveig's Song' in *Peer Gynt*, and even then he did not specify its source, though this may be 'I lay down late' (*Jeg lagde mig saa sildig*), which appears as No. 300 in Lindeman, and which Grieg was later to use in his *Album for Male Voices*:

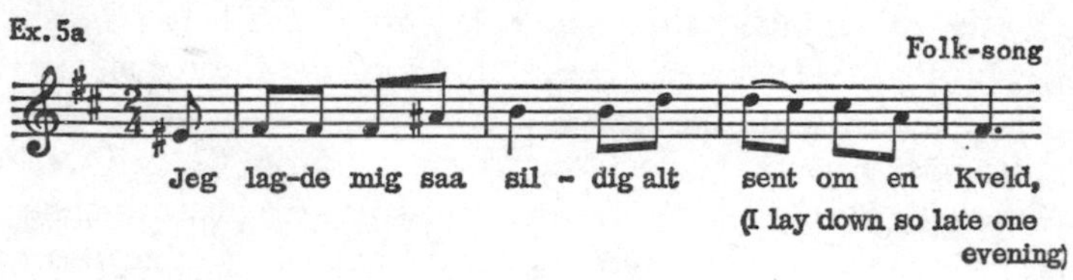

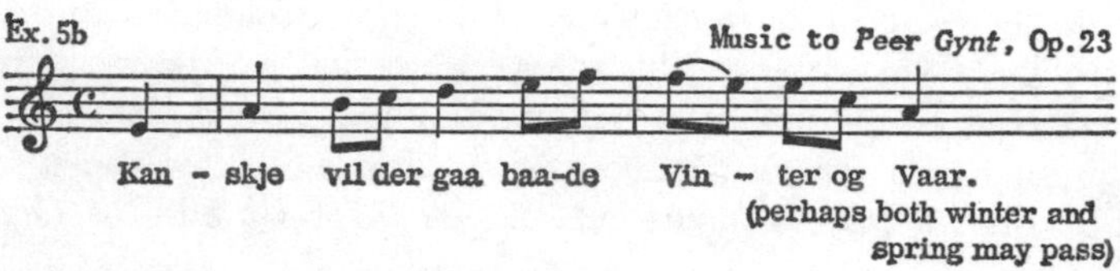

Even this apparently straightforward borrowing is complicated by the probability that the *Peer Gynt* song was unconsciously influenced by Kjerulf's setting of 'Synnøve's Song' from Bjørnson's *Synnøve Solbakken*, in which the hummed introduction and postlude correspond closely to the instrumental introduction and ritornello of 'Solveig's Song'.

But Grieg's statement does not exclude the possibility that instrumental music of traditional origin had been known to him from quite an early age. Players of folk-dance tunes on the hardanger fiddle were to be met with in his youth, not only in the more remote parts of Hardanger and Valdres but even in the neighbourhood of Bergen, and the Griegs would of all people be most likely to come in contact with them through their friendship with Ole Bull. It is hard to believe that members of the family, including perhaps the seven-year-old Edvard himself, did not hear the famous 'Miller's Boy' (Torgeir Augundsson) when he performed at Ole Bull's Norwegian Theatre in Bergen in 1850. In that year also the Theatre staged Wergeland's ballad opera *The Mountain Hut*, which contained a folk-dance ballet. Two years later Bull published a small selection of fiddle-tunes in simple piano arrangements, and other printed collections were in circulation in the next few years both in Norway and Denmark, those of Lindeman and the Danish collector, A. P. Berggreen, being the most influential.

Few Scandinavian composers could help being caught up in the prevailing fashion for 'Norse' colour to be obtained either by direct quotation or adaptation of folk-tunes, or more generally by the imitation of such common features of traditional music as dotted rhythms, varied or sequential repetition of phrases, sharpened fourths and flattened sevenths, primitive harmonization by means of open fourths and fifths and drone basses, and often a profusion of melodic ornament. All these characteristics, and others like the cadential 'Grieg' formula—upper tonic-leading note-dominant—appear in the music of Kjerulf and

Nordraak. These two men, together with L. M. Lindeman, were the chief agents in creating a national idiom for Norwegian art-music, an idiom for which Grieg was indebted to all three of them. With the advantages of greater talent, a sounder musical training, and—despite chronic ill-health—a longer life than either Kjerulf or Nordraak, Grieg was able to extend and enrich the national tradition and create within it a personal style compounded of German Romanticism, his own special flair for harmonic colour, his sensitiveness to literary values, and the folk-music to which he was increasingly attracted, and in which he discovered the 'hidden harmonies' that seemed to be those he had intuitively sought out from his earliest years.

Grieg's three most important sets of keyboard arrangements of folk-tunes represent different types of source and different approaches to the process of transcription. In the *Twenty-Five Norwegian Dances and Songs* (Op. 17), dedicated to Ole Bull, he takes many hints from Lindeman's settings, though he usually extends the shorter pieces by means of a brief introduction, a repeat of the melody with varied harmonies and perhaps a few bars of coda; even so, most of the pieces fill not more than half a page. Some mildly chromatic harmony is admitted, though in one or two instances Grieg is less venturesome than Lindeman, as when he adds a coda to 'Niels Tallefjorn' (No. 4) to bring it to a close on the conventional tonic, whereas Lindeman recognizes its modal character by ending on the dominant without a defining chord. Two of the Op. 17 settings were later transcribed for string orchestra: the 'Cow-call' (No. 22, *So lokka me over den myra*) and 'Stabbe-Låten' (No. 18, a boisterous dance traditionally played on the third day of wedding feasts). Two others, No. 23 (*Saag du nokke kjæringa mi*) and No. 24, again a wedding tune, were to be used in the *Symphonic Dances* (Op. 64, No. 4).

The *Norwegian Folk-tunes* (Op. 66: the original title, *Norske Folkeviser*, implies songs, not instrumental tunes) belongs to a much later period. They were published in 1897, and dedicated to Frants Beyer, who collected most of the songs from traditional singers in the Gudbrandsdal region. These melodies had not for the most part been published in any earlier collection, though variants of a few are found in Lindeman. Grieg now handles his material with much greater freedom and imagination; they are more adventurous in harmonization and more effective as piano music. Some of them, like No. 1 ('Cow-call'), use mere fragments of melody as a point of departure for an impressionistic miniature, with carefully spaced seventh and ninth chords. In others the folk-tune is enriched by intensely chromatic counter-themes, as in No. 2, 'It is the greatest foolishness', one of Grieg's favourite settings, which he quotes in its entirety in a letter to Röntgen. In some of the pieces motives from more than one song are linked together, giving opportunities for melodic and rhythmic variety and alteration of tempo. There are several lullabies, including the one noted down from the singing of Gjendine Slaalien and bearing her name. Two settings are of exceptional interest on account of their extended scale, their fully developed pianistic style, their outstanding beauty and their later influence on other composers. The first of these, 'I Ola-Dalom, i Ola-Kjønn' (No. 14), is now well known as the source from which Delius borrowed the Norwegian melody for *On hearing the first cuckoo in Spring*, and there can be little doubt that he was inspired also by Grieg's wonderful harmonies and figures of accompaniment. The love song 'Jeg går i tusind Tanker' (No. 18) is one of the most moving of all Grieg's piano works, and must have served as a model for several of Percy Grainger's settings of British folk-music.

Before discussing the *Slåtter* (Op. 72), whose origins in the playing of Knut Dale and the violin transcriptions of Johan Halvorsen have already been described, a little more must be said about the hardanger-fiddle itself. The instrument belongs chiefly to the western and southern districts of Norway, the ordinary violin or *flatfele* being traditionally commoner in the east. The *hardingfele* may have developed as a regional branch of the *viola d'amore* family, and reached the height of its popularity in the eighteenth and early nineteenth centuries. Although threatened in turn by the clarinet, the violin and the accordion, it has never become extinct; it survived longest in Hardanger, Voss, Telemark and Hallingdal, where instruments were made as well as played with great skill, and there are not a few modern exponents. The four playing strings are tuned in various ways, the most usual being E–A–D–A or E–A–E–A or E–A–C–G,[1] any of which facilitates the playing of three- or four-note chords. Beneath the playing strings are stretched the four sympathetic strings, vibrating to the notes (reckoning upwards) D–E–F♯–A or C–E–G–A,[1] series which suggest some ancient pentatonic origin. The under-strings impart to the instrument its characteristic penetrating tone-quality; the upper strings, combined with a flattish bridge, give it the basis for a polyphonic technique, with the constant occurrence of drone basses, inverted pedal notes, consonant intervals (3rd, 6ths, 5ths and octaves) and also dissonant ones (4ths, 2nds, 7ths and 9ths). The fourth degree of the scale is often raised (approximately to G sharp in the scale of D, though in untempered tuning). The traditional style of performance involves intricate conventions of ornamentation, with variations from player to player, the intermingling of triplet and duplet groupings, and hemiola effects. All these features appear in the quotation from one of Halvorsen's transcriptions (see Example 6, page 125).

In his preface to the piano version of the *Slåtter*[2] Grieg adopts

[1] Sounding a minor third higher.

[2] A *slått* or *slaat* is an instrumental tune, originally march-like and commonly played at weddings, but it may also be in one of the dance forms (*halling*, *springdans* or *springar*, *gangar*), or it may (as in several of the Knut Dale tunes) become a character-piece.

the point of view of a creative artist rather than a scholar, stating that his aim has been to 'raise these folk-tunes to an artistic level through what may be called conventional harmonization'. He recognizes that the piano could not reproduce all the subtler ornaments of the hardanger-fiddle style, but on the other hand it is able to increase the harmonic interest at each repetition of the melody and to weld the whole piece into an organic unity. He has occasionally taken the liberty of extending a movement by developing some motive or phrase from the original. Grieg's reference to his use of conventional harmony must be taken in a relative sense. It is true that he supplies a basis of functional harmony, but this is combined in a remarkably daring way with the non-functional dissonances of the traditional style, producing an entirely new harmonic perspective, unique of its kind until the appearance of Bartók's folk-music arrangements and improvisations. At times he keeps close to Halvorsen's violin versions, as in the opening of No. 4 (*Haugelåt*),[1] where the right hand of the pianist plays the violin notes unchanged, while the left has an *ostinato* of open fifths. But more often some detail of the original is developed freely until it dominates the whole movement, as in 'Gibøens Bridal March' (No. 1), where the

[1] Recorded, with the hardanger-fiddle original, in *The History of Music in Sound*, Vol. 9.

trills characteristic of the *hardingfele* are transferred to a low register of the piano to produce an effect of deliberate roughness:

Frequently the dissonant two-string intervals of the original become more aggressively prominent in the transcription, as in 'Knut Luråsens Halling II' (No. 11):

The above example illustrates two other stylistic features, also derived from the original: the combination of 6/8 and 3/4 metres and the Lydian tonality imparted by the sharpened fourth of the scale.

In two settings, No. 4 ('Haugelåt') and No. 7 ('Røtnamsknut') Grieg writes a free middle section developed out of a transformation of a motive from the first presentation of the tune—a device he may have learnt from Brahms (as in the *Intermezzo*, Op. 119, No. 2). Here the harmonic style reverts to the less dissonant chromaticism of the Op. 66 arrangements, though with some attractive modal colouring:

The neglect of the *Slåtter* is easier to account for than that of the less revolutionary Op. 66 settings. At the time of their composition, new sonorities were being extracted from the piano by Debussy, Ravel and Scriabin, but no one had yet explored its percussive and harshly dissonant potentialities in such an uncompromising way; least of all could such barbaric sounds be reconciled with the salon prettiness of the earlier *Lyric Pieces* and similar trifles with which the composer's name was by now irrevocably associated. And within a very few years Grieg's bold but belated excursions into the unexplored territories of keyboard writing were fated to be eclipsed by the still greater originality and audacity of Bartók and Stravinsky.

A number of other keyboard works based on folk-music call for briefer comment. The *Norwegian Dances* for piano duet (Op. 35, composed in 1881) and the *Symphonic Dances* (Op. 64, 1898) again draw upon Lindeman's inexhaustible treasury. Op.

35, No. 1 uses the tune known as 'Sinclair's March' which, in Lindeman's version from Vågå, has a central section in the dominant major, though Grieg chooses to keep to the same tonic. The other three dances are all *hallings*; No. 2 alternates gentle and violent moods in major and minor respectively, in No. 3 Grieg makes a middle section by changing the jaunty Lindeman tune into a minor version, *legato*, while No. 4 is more elaborately constructed, with an introductory motive, not apparently connected with the main *halling* tune but later developed along with it in a movement of considerable length and sustained interest. The *Norwegian Dances* were arranged for orchestra by Hans Sitt, the violist of the Brodsky quartet, and were included in the 1885 Copenhagen revival of *Peer Gynt* as a *ballet-divertissement* in the scene in the Hall of the Mountain King.[1]

The *Symphonic Dances* also were published for piano duet, though, as the title suggests, their orchestral version—in this case, the composer's—may be the original form. They may well have been intended [2] for the first Bergen Festival in 1898, when Grieg had an exceptionally large orchestra at his disposal: the score includes trombones, tuba and harp. Some of the folk-tunes used here have already been mentioned; the rest are of the *halling* and *springdans* types. The third dance may be taken as typical. It begins by inflecting the opening figure of the *springdans* into the characteristic Grieg motive of a descending minor second followed by a major third, and later the sequential patterns of the folk-tune are allowed to give rise to chord-progressions very much in the contemporary French taste.

The charm of these two sets of dances, apart from the fresh-

[1] It is not certain, however, that Sitt's arrangement was used on this occasion; for the same production the 'Bridal Procession' (Op. 19, No. 2) was orchestrated by van der Stucken.

[2] As far as can be discovered, however, the work was not performed during the Festival.

ness of the tunes themselves, lies in the scope they give for Grieg to display one of his strongest resources—his facility in continuously harmonizing and re-harmonizing a simple diatonic phrase, which, as so often in folk-music, is repeated incessantly, thus giving it a kaleidoscopic background. It is a device he may have borrowed from the Slav nationalists, by way of Tchaikovsky, though it originates with Glinka; Dvořák also has frequent recourse to it in his *Slavonic Dances* (likewise for piano duet) which first appeared in 1878.

The technically undemanding set of *Six Norwegian Mountain Melodies* for solo piano was published without opus number, having been extracted from the first volume of the anthology of songs and instrumental pieces entitled *Norges Melodier*, which appeared in 1875;[1] the editor is not named, but is now known to have been Grieg. Two of the *Six Melodies* only need be mentioned here, both of them borrowed from Lindeman. No. 6, 'The boy and girl in the cow-shed' (*Guten å gjenten på fjöshellen*) is given a more elaborate setting in the *Improvisata over norske folkeviser* (Op. 29, No. 1), where its companion piece is a ballad from Valdres, 'There was once a King'. No. 4 of the *Six Melodies*, 'Sigurd and the Troll-bride', reappears as the theme of a more substantial work, the *Old Norwegian Melody with Variations* (Op. 51) for two pianos. The tune is one of rare distinction, with a variable third (A or A♭) in its scale, and a change of metre at the end, corresponding to the *omkvæd* or refrain of the ballad to which it belongs. It is not, however, the best of material for variations, as by the very nature of its form the same melodic and rhythmic features are bound to recur and force themselves on the attention. This drawback is all the greater as neither Lindeman nor Grieg could resist the temptation to harmonize the prominent flattened third with chromatic chords which are enchanting when first met with, but do not bear repetition at regular intervals:

[1] Published by Hansen of Copenhagen and still in print.

Ex. 8a (Transposed down one tone) — *Sjugur aa Troldbrura*, arr. L. M. Lindeman

(O, the King he stood on the balcony high and gazed out afar.)

Ex. 8b — Grieg, *Old Norwegian Melody with Variations*, Op. 51

The *Variations* are one of Grieg's few virtuoso keyboard works, paying tribute in turn to the styles of Schumann (whose *Andante and Variations*, Op. 46, may well have suggested the general plan), Brahms, Liszt, Mendelssohn and Saint-Saëns.[1] There are fourteen variations in all, plus a finale which is undeniably over-lengthy and rather emptily rhetorical. When, in 1901, the composer transcribed the work for orchestra, he wisely omitted Variations 10 and 12, both of them essentially pianistic, and made cuts in the finale. The most attractive of the lighter sections is Variation 13—in the *Tempo di valse* which Grieg always carries off with unerring charm. Here the flattened chromatic chords of the theme give occasion for harmonic side-slips of Gallic wittiness; the work was dedicated to Benjamin Godard.

The remaining keyboard work based on a folk theme, and the only large-scale work for solo piano apart from the early Sonata, is the *Ballade in the form of variations on a Norwegian folk-tune* (Op. 24). The theme is *The Norland Peasantry*, a song from Valders, and again it is questionable whether Grieg chose it judiciously, for despite its beauty the tune is rather monotonously repetitive in construction. Lindeman adds a good deal of harmonic colour to it, chiefly through the use of augmented-sixth chords, and Grieg goes further, covering the melodic repetitions with glowing harmonies over a chromatically descending bass.[2] He thereby sets himself a problem similar to the one already described in connection with the

[1] Grieg came across Saint-Saëns's *Variations on a Theme of Beethoven* early in 1885, as he mentioned in a letter to Röntgen dated 1 February of that year (Röntgen, p. 24): 'A few weeks ago my wife and I played Saint-Saëns's Variations and I enjoy recalling the experience as much as the actual occasion; that fellow certainly knows how to write for two keyboards so that they sound well together.'

[2] Part of the Grieg harmonization is quoted in Alan Jefferson, *Delius*, Ex. 8, p. 94.

two-piano Variations, namely the difficulty of avoiding anti-climax in handling a theme so distinctively coloured and so highly charged with emotion.

As if aware of this, Grieg lightens the texture of the first variation while retaining much of his original harmony. The second and third variations are contrasted in tempo—*allegro agitato* and *adagio* respectively, exploiting in their different ways some Schumannesque figuration around the theme, which is outlined in the inner parts. Variation 4 (*allegro capriccioso*) is in the rhythm of the *springdans*, with chromatic semiquavers producing dissonant collisions reminiscent of the first movement of the Piano Concerto. Variation 5 brings another marked change of tempo; phrases in quasi-recitative alternate with harmonized responses, somewhat in the manner of Chopin's first *Ballade*. Variations 6 and 7 together form a *scherzando* episode, the former with alternating hands in *acciaccatura*-like figures, the latter with close canonic imitation in staccato semiquavers between the two hands—another idea borrowed from Schumann. Variation 8 (*lento*) uses densely packed chords, below and above which bells seem to toll and chime. Variation 9 (*un poco andante*) is once again indebted to Schumann; the keyboard writing here indeed actually suggests the theme of Schumann's *Andante and Variations* rather than the Norwegian folk-tune, whose outlines are only faintly discernible. In Variation 10 a carnival spirit seems to take over (the tempo is marked *un poco allegro e alla burla*), reaching its climax in a sequence of key-disrupting seventh chords. Now follows an interlude with a series of modulations leading to the key of G major, in which Variation 11 presents the theme in augmentation with the 'carnival' motive combined with it. A cadenza (*crescendo molto e strepitoso*) prefaces the final section of the work, where the folk-tune (in its original G minor) is transformed into a barbaric dance, a remarkably adventurous piece of writing for its time (1875) in respect alike of harmony, rhythm and keyboard idiom. This breaks off with a crashing low octave E flat, subsiding quietly on to the dominant (D), over which the theme returns, without its central (major mode) section but with a few subtle changes in the original harmonies. The *Ballade* has been described in some detail, as it remains little known, probably because Grieg found it physically too demanding to include in his own recitals. It deserves a place in the literature of Romantic piano music, as a not unworthy successor to the *Ballades* of Chopin and Brahms.

Two choral works, the *Album for Male Voices* (Op. 30) and the *Four Psalms* (Op. 74), are sets of folk-music arrangements. The idea of the male-voice settings was not new; Kjerulf, among others, had arranged Norwegian folk-tunes in this way. But the variety and resourcefulness of Grieg's set of twelve songs put it into a class by itself. Broad humour enters into the treatment of the nursery song ('Bådn-låt', No. 2) with its cat-calls, of 'Kvaalin's Halling' (No. 4)—an early example of the nowadays much-exploited choral 'mouth music' to meaningless syllables—of the bibulous 'When I go out of an evening' (No. 6) and of 'Røtnams-Knut' (No. 12). In contrast, there is pathos tempered by astringent harmonies in 'I laid me down so late' (No. 1), in 'It is the greatest foolishness' (No. 5—the tune is different from the one used in Op. 66, No. 5), and in 'Little Thora' (No. 3). In most of the settings a solo baritone is combined with male chorus in four parts. A useful selection (eight out of the twelve settings), edited and translated by Percy Grainger, is available for English-speaking choirs.

The *Psalms*, Grieg's last work, are based on traditional tunes which may be entirely of popular Norwegian origin, though the religious folk-music of Norway also includes melodies from German Lutheran sources, and even older pre-Reformation hymns, moulded into florid and often beautiful shapes by the congregations of remote country churches without organs but with individualist parish-clerks. These chorale-variants, which occur also in Sweden, are full of the modal inflections, untempered intervals and ornate turns of phrase characteristic of much of the secular community music, and lend themselves particularly well to Grieg's harmonic treatment. One is reminded of the composer's whimsical observation, made in a letter of condolence to a friend: 'Life is like folk-music—you sometimes can't tell whether it is major or minor.' This ambiguity appears in its most extreme form in the second of the four settings, 'God's Son hath set me free', where the solo baritone part is written in the tonic major against the minor harmonies of the mixed-voice chorus; granted that the appearance of the score, with its two simultaneous key-signatures, is more startling than the aural effect, the device is exceptional enough in the field of choral writing in the early years of the present century.

Edmund Rubbra[1] has no hesitation in placing the *Four Psalms* 'among the finest choral music of the . . . century', while Percy Grainger, who again has edited this work and supplied English singing versions, claims that (with the *Album for Male Voices*) the *Psalms* for the first time make 'the harmonic innovations of the latter nineteenth century available for choral music. It is this side of Grieg's compositional technic . . . that has so profoundly influenced modern Anglo-Saxon choral writing.' Certainly it would be hard to find, in all Grieg's music, such wealth of harmonic resource, or such variety of texture ranging from note-against-note homophony to ornate polyphony developed in unbroken phrases of unusually irregular lengths, as in the first psalm-setting, 'How fair is Thy face'. Particularly impressive is the tightening-up of the canonic imitation between soprano and tenor in the final stanza, leading to a powerful climax with sequences of diatonic discords, which subsides at the beginning of a tranquil coda, only to rise again to a fortissimo climax, with tense harmonies in which fourths and fifths predominate:

[1] In *Symposium*, p. 109.

The third psalm, 'Jesus Christ our Lord is risen', is effective in a different way, producing a medieval atmosphere by contrasting the unaccompanied, free-rhythm melismatic phrases of the bass soloist with the rich four-part polyphony of the choir. Grieg's harmony in this setting evidently owes something to Lindeman's (in No. 327 of *Ældre og nyere Norske Fjeldmelodier*)—yet another example of Grieg's immense debt to that great folk-music collector, organist and writer of congregational music.

8 Works for keyboard (other than those based on folk-music) and for strings with piano

Apart from the considerable part of his output consisting of works derived from folk-music, Grieg's keyboard music falls into two main groups.

First there are the numerous short pieces he produced throughout his career, partly because he followed the Romantic tradition in expressing poetic moods through carefully fashioned miniatures, partly because there was an unlimited demand for such things from the thousands of amateur pianists who formed the backbone of the musical public in the nineteenth and early twentieth centuries. Grieg's publishers, indulgent though they were to his fluctuating rate of composition, expected to be satisfied from time to time with the collections which they agreed to call *Lyric Pieces*, and which Grieg in a moment of outspoken exasperation once referred to as the 'lice and flies' on his artistic life. Beside the ten books specifically entitled *Lyric Pieces* there were other miscellaneous sets, including transcriptions of the composer's own songs and orchestral works, all of which the domestic pianist welcomed in those pre-gramophone times.

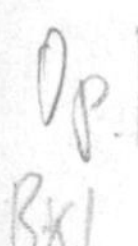

The earliest piano pieces are in some ways among the best. The *Four Pieces*, Op. 1, for example, show qualities of workmanship and originality which hardly deserve the composer's later dismissal of them as hack-work. Written in his student days, they are clearly influenced by admiration for Schumann; indeed, the three pieces of the set which the composer played at his final Leipzig examination originally bore the Schumannesque title of

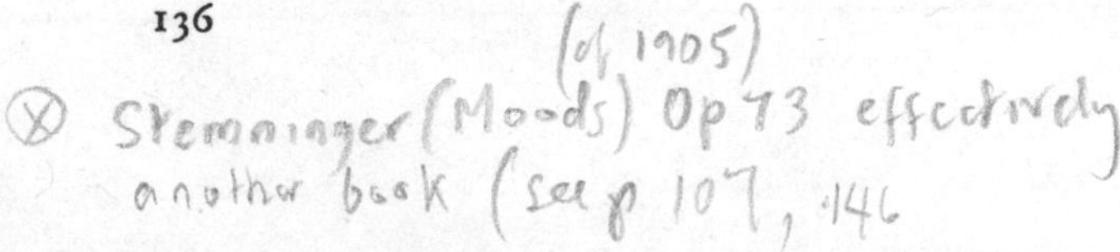

Drei Phantasiestücke. Far from being slavish imitations of their models, they bear the stamp of a positive talent backed by sound technique. In particular, two marks of Grieg's individuality are already apparent, especially in the second and fourth pieces: his fondness for chromatic chords and inner part-movement, and his feeling for the dance-rhythms of his native country; the *Allegro con moto* (No. 4), for example, suggests the *gangar* or processional dance.

Even these were by no means the composer's first attempts at writing for the piano. Schjelderup-Ebbe has examined and critically described a set of no fewer than twenty-three miniatures (*Smaastykker*),[1] some written at Leipzig in 1859, others possibly a little earlier; the first of them was played at the students' examination on 18th April 1959, and aroused the interest of Hauptmann, who had not at that time taught Grieg. Moreover, Olav Gurvin has brought to light three even more substantial pieces dating from April 1860,[2] which survive both in the Bergen Library and in the Stockholm Royal Academy. The third of these pieces, in the style of a scherzo, besides containing some bold harmonic progressions is animated by the dotted rhythms that were to become one of the composer's best-known finger-prints, as in the highly popular 'Wedding Procession' (Op. 19, No. 2).

We come next to a group of works written after Grieg left Leipzig, to spend most of the next two years (May 1863 to June 1865) in Denmark, where his talents flowered in the artistic climate of Copenhagen, and where he met the older Danish composers, Gade and Hartmann, and a group nearer his own age—Horneman, Winding, and Matthison-Hansen. Here

[1] *Edvard Grieg 1858–1867*, pp. 33 fol. The first book of *Lyric Pieces*, incidentally, was originally published under the title of *Lyriske Smaastykker* (see Appendix B, Catalogue of Works).
[2] *Norsk Musikkgranskning Årbok 1951–3*, pp. 90 fol. See also Schjelderup-Ebbe, op. cit., pp. 50–3.

also began the short-lived friendship with Nordraak that was to be a turning-point in his career, and here he met Nina Hagerup who was to become the inspiration of his song-writing. Not only in the songs but also in the instrumental works we now find a stronger lyrical element, as the graceful melodic lines of Romantic song, so characteristic of Danish music, combine with Grieg's acute harmonic sense.

The first of the Danish keyboard works, the *Poetic Tone-pictures* (Op. 3), is technically somewhat simpler than the Leipzig Op. 1, possibly because it was dedicated to an amateur musician, Benjamin Feddersen, who was Grieg's host during part of his stay in Denmark. Their modest elegance and gentle melancholy (the minor mode predominates) make them akin to the salon pieces of Gade, though there is more than a touch of Chopin in the nocturne-like No. 4 and of Mendelssohn in No. 6. It is in No. 5 (in F major) with its bare fourths and fifths—at one point superimposed—that the real Grieg emerges most clearly. This same harder Norse quality asserts itself even more unmistakably in the two piano works of about a year later, from the early summer of 1865. These are the *Humoresques* (Op. 6)[1] and the Piano Sonata (Op. 7). The former were dedicated to Rikard Nordraak and bear evidence of the impact of his personality, not merely in their heightened Norwegian colouring —the *springdans* rhythms, the imitations of hardanger-fiddle drones and chords, the exuberant vitality—but also in the suppression of those German Romantic traits Nordraak had deprecated as obscuring the true nature of Grieg's genius. Among the harmonic features that are present here in all their boldness, two are worthy of special mention: the frequent occurrence of chords of the ninth and the employment of pedal notes in a variety of contexts, including the rare supertonic

[1] The *Pictures of Folk-Life* (Folkelivsbilleder), Op. 19, were also originally published (in 1872) with the subtitle *Humoresker for Piano.*

pedal with its quasi-modal effect. Noteworthy also is the calculated roughness obtained by placing clusters of notes, often dissonant, in the lower octaves of the piano.

The Piano Sonata in E minor (Op. 7) shares much of the forthright vigour of the *Humoresques*. If this is again due in part to the stimulus of Nordraak's encouragement, the work also pays its tribute to the senior Danish composers, Gade, to whom it is dedicated, and J. P. E. Hartmann. While pointing out some striking resemblances between Grieg's third movement (*Alla Menuetto*) and a piano piece, *Vikingefruens Drøm*, by Hartmann, which was published in the year before Grieg's Sonata,[1] Schjelderup Ebbe strangely does not mention the similarity between the principal theme of Grieg's first movement, with its canonic treatment, and that of the first movement of Gade's Piano Sonata (also in E minor). These coincidences are instructive as showing that Grieg absorbed 'Norwegian' colour not only directly, from fellow-Norwegians like Bull, Kjerulf and Nordraak, but also indirectly, from the older Danish Romantic school which had long been under the influence of more generalized Scandinavian tendencies.

This was Grieg's first extant essay in sonata form, and on the whole it remains his most successful. It has a compactness and directness that are absent from the later string sonatas, even the loose construction of the finale [2] being to a great extent compensated for by harmonic astringency and rhythmic drive. The slow movement (*Andante molto*) foreshadows in a tentative way that of the Piano Concerto. The young Grieg's determination to master and excel in the larger forms is as yet unbroken, and one can understand his satisfaction with this sonata.

The remaining member of the group of instrumental works

[1] Schjelderup-Ebbe, op. cit., pp. 240–2.

[2] Twenty-five bars were excised from this movement in the later (Peters) edition.

composed at Rungsted during this fertile period is the Sonata in F major for Violin and Piano (Op. 8). The composer was to cherish a particular fondness for his three Violin Sonatas, and always welcomed opportunities of taking part in their performance; as late as 1900 he told Bjørnson that he considered them among his best works: 'They represent periods in my development—the first naïve, rich in ideas; the second national; and the third with a wider horizon.' We may therefore feel justified in considering them together, regardless of their widely separated dates.

It was the F major Sonata that first attracted the attention of Liszt, with immense advantage to Grieg's reputation and prospects. Gade also was delighted with it. Certainly it is hard to resist the appeal of the opening, with its two introductory chords right out of key, followed by a spontaneously sweeping paragraph of fifteen bars—one of the passages that might be cited in refutation of the criticism that Grieg could think only in short time-spans. As a whole this movement suffers, like others in the string sonatas, from its unenterprisingly literal recapitulation, a formal weakness that Grieg seemed unable to overcome. The second of the three movements has a folk-like theme with the Griegian finger-print of minor tonic-leading note-dominant (as in the opening of the Piano Concerto), and hardanger-fiddle effects, shared between piano and violin, making an appearance in the middle section. The finale too has a folk-music colouring imparted by the short repeated and sequential phrases recalling those of the *gangar*. Contrast is provided by the curious little subsidiary theme, moving chiefly by chromatic semitones, which is subjected in the development to a brief but severe contrapuntal treatment, almost as if in sly parody of the Leipzig student counterpoint exercises. There are many piquant harmonic details, like the series of broken triads moving upwards in thirds and progressively less closely related, a favourite device of Grieg's, and one that was to become a commonplace towards the end of the century, particularly in France, but in 1865 still sounded revolutionary enough:

Two years later Grieg produced the Sonata in G major for Violin and Piano (Op. 13). By now he was living and working in Norway, and the intensity of national feeling has deepened. The violin rhapsodizes eloquently in an elegiac prelude before giving way to the piano, which launches the main movement with the boisterous lilt of the *Humoresques*. The waltz-like second subject begins with northern iciness in the mediant minor, and reappears with this tonality again in the development. On its return the principal theme gains new interest through the extension of its phrase-length from four to six bars—another example of a flexibility not always credited to the composer. The second movement (*Allegretto tranquillo alla*

Romanza) has the kind of wistful minor-mode melodies, twining round the fifth of the scale, of which Grieg and Dvořák seem to share the secret. There are more allusions to traditional fiddle-technique in the ornamentation and double-stopping of the coda. The finale is another *springdans*, whose virtual identity with the main idea of the first movement is unfortunate in a work on this extended scale. Nevertheless, the violin writing throughout the Sonata has a brilliance that seems to reflect the lustre of Ole Bull, who was still at the height of his prowess as an international virtuoso, as well as the great talent of Johan Svendsen, another violinist-composer, to whom the work is dedicated.

Gade advised Grieg to make his next sonata 'less Norwegian', to which Grieg retorted that it would be more so. Twenty years went by, however, before he wrote his third Sonata for Violin and Piano, in C minor (Op. 45), and by this date (1887) his outlook had become, as he expressed it, more cosmopolitan and less national. César Franck's Sonata in A major had appeared in the previous year, and Brahms's in the same key (Op. 100) in that year also. Grieg's admiration for both composers may have stirred him to emulate them in this field.[1] The C minor Sonata has the air of addressing itself to an international public in large concert halls, and of adopting broader gestures and a less subtle kind of expression than the early 'Danish' and 'Norwegian' works. One cannot help feeling a sense of effort: this was Grieg's last attempt to write in the classical sonata forms, and it is hard to avoid the impression that the ideas are being stretched to cover the predetermined framework, the resulting thinness of construction being imperfectly disguised by busy but conventional figuration, syncopated accompaniments, and much sequential repetition. Yet the C minor remained

[1] Similarly, he may have begun the Piano Quintet, which never advanced beyond a few sketches, about the same time under the stimulus of Sinding's Quintet, performed in Christiania in 1885.

for long the most popular of the three Violin Sonatas, and even nowadays there are critics and performers who prefer it to the others.[1]

Chronologically between the second and third Violin Sonatas comes the Sonata in A minor for Cello and Piano (Op. 36), a gratefully written work forming a valued addition to the nineteenth-century repertory of the cello, whose technical and expressive possibilities it explores in considerable depth: the first movement even contains a miniature cadenza. The middle movement is closely related to the Homage March in the music to *Sigurd Jorsalfar*. The finale, after a short monologue for the cello (not unlike the prelude to *Solveig's Song*) plunges into a dance of the *halling* type, whose principal theme, transformed by change of mode and doubling of note-lengths, also does duty as second subject. Rhythmic and melodic monotony is therefore almost inevitable, and the whole movement tends to outstay its welcome.

The unevenness of the string sonatas, and especially the lack of constructional strength and variety in their outer movements, underline what is undeniably a serious fault in Grieg's creative powers: his failure either to adapt the classical forms as media for his novel and often arresting melodic, rhythmic and harmonic ideas—as did his contemporary, César Franck, whom he greatly admired—or, like Debussy, to evolve new types of form free from dependence on key-relationships and traditional procedures of thematic development.

Working on the lesser scale of his piano miniatures, however, he does from time to time approach the power of Debussy or Scriabin to make a complete, succinct and entirely original statement in the space of a page or two; as we shall see, he achieved this most often in his songs. Out of the sixty-odd

[1] This view is taken by Alan Frank, who, in *Symposium*, pp. 36 fol., discusses all three of the Violin Sonatas with sympathetic insight.

Lyric Pieces, spread over the ten books published between 1867 and 1901, a few stand out with this kind of distinction, such as 'To the Spring' (Op. 43, No. 6) and 'Bell-ringing' (Op. 54, No. 6). The former was one of the small group of piano pieces recorded by the composer in the earliest days of the gramophone; 'Bell-ringing' is unique in making a static construction out of the sonorities of superimposed perfect fifths, in reality an even more revolutionary conception than Debussy's 'La Cathédrale engloutie' which it anticipates by nearly two decades. One may also compare the 'Notturno' (Op. 54, No. 4) with Debussy's 'Clair de lune' belonging to the same year (1891). 'Quiet of the Woods' (Op. 71, No. 4), from the last book of the series, is another example which lingers in the memory through its impressionistic juxtaposition and spacing of chords:

Several of the *Lyric Pieces* command attention for the harmonic spice they give to what might otherwise be a banal type of salon piece; in this category are the various valse movements—like the 'Valse-impromptu' (Op. 47, No. 1) which makes characteristic play with confusion of modes, minor harmonies being set against a major tune, and the 'Valse mélancolique' (Op. 68, No. 6) with its piquant ninth and thirteenth chords—a piece that may well have given Ravel a hint for his *Valses nobles et sentimentales*; and in this connection may be mentioned also Grieg's own unjustly neglected *Valses-caprices* for piano duet (Op. 37).

The less-known later books of the series repay exploration. Book 6 (Op. 57), for example, has at least three pieces of uncommon harmonic interest: 'Vanished Days' (No. 1), 'Illusion' (No. 3), and 'Secrecy' (No. 4). In Book 7 (Op. 62), 'Phantom' (or 'Dream Vision', *Drømmesyn*) should not be overlooked. Book 8 (Op. 65) contains, beside the brilliant 'Wedding Day at Troldhaugen' (No. 6), the dark-coloured study, 'Melancholy' (No. 3) which might almost be taken for early Scriabin. In Book 10 (Op. 71), 'Once upon a time' (No. 1) brings together, as if in symbolic reconciliations, themes related to the folk-music of Sweden and Norway; 'Past and over' (*Forbi*, No. 6) is noteworthy for its highly chromatic intensity; and 'Quiet of the Woods' (No. 4) has already been quoted for its harmonic interest. It may be worth drawing attention to the fact that the whole series of *Lyric Pieces* is rounded off at the end of Book 10 by a 'Recollection' (No. 7) which re-harmonizes in valse style the 'Arietta' that opened Book 1 (Op. 12, No. 1).

While some of the slighter pieces have remained attractive even to professional pianists for their elegance and finish, like 'Butterfly' and 'Little Bird' in the popular Book 3 (Op. 43), others appear to have been conceived in orchestral terms, and several were actually arranged for orchestra by the composer or by other hands. The scoring of the plaintively chromatic 'Shepherd Boy' (Op. 54, No. 1) is Grieg's own, though Seidl was responsible for the original orchestration of the other pieces from the same book (Book 5) forming the *Lyric Suite*.[1] From Book 9 Grieg made two arrangements, the 'Lullaby' (Op. 68, No. 5) which he scored for strings, and the beautiful little tone-poem 'Evening in the Mountains' (Op. 68, No. 4), for which he chose the unusual combination of oboe, horn and strings.

Although Grieg firmly brought the *Lyric Pieces* to an end with Book 10 in 1901, his interest in writing for the piano was by no means exhausted. The three pieces published posthumously in 1908 may not show him at his best (the first of them, 'White Clouds', was completed by Röntgen), but the *Slåtter*, already described in the previous chapter, and *Moods* (Op. 73) are among the most important keyboard works. From *Moods* three pieces may be singled out: the first of the set, 'Resignation', is an impressive piece of *fin-de-siècle* introspection, the 'Study' (*Hommage à Chopin*) contrives to pay tribute to Chopin and at the same time to be inimitable Grieg, and the wonderfully picturesque 'Mountain Tune' (*Lualåt*) deserves a special place among the works inspired by the majesty and loneliness of Norwegian scenery.[2]

Leaving the Piano Concerto to be dealt with under the heading of the orchestral music, we complete this chapter by noticing two keyboard works that stand apart from the rest. The first of these is the *Funeral March for Rikard Nordraak*, which Grieg began in Rome on the day he heard of his friend's death. It is in every way a remarkable piece, with harmonic features that place it far in advance of its time. The outer sections have the rugged quality of the works Grieg produced under Nordraak's influence in the previous year—the *Humoresques* and the Piano Sonata. The middle section explores unfamiliar tonal regions,

[1] Seidl originally included an orchestral arrangement of 'Bellringing' (No. 5), but Grieg with sure instinct decided to omit this as being essentially pianistic.

[2] See Kathleen Dale's vivid description of this piece in *Symposium*, p. 57.

with a modal cadence that must surely be among the passages Ravel acknowledged to have influenced him; the *Pavane pour une infante défunte*, composed thirty-three years after Grieg's Nordraak March, irresistibly comes to mind:

The piano suite *From Holberg's Time* is an occasional work of a very different stamp. Written to order in 1884, under circumstances already described, it is an essay in pastiche attempted at a period when the imitation of older styles was much less common than it was to become a decade or so later, although Grieg may have met with Delibes's charming score for *Le Roi s'amuse*, written in 1882. The composer did not give the *Holberg Suite* a high place in his own esteem, calling it his 'perruque-piece'. The arrangement for string orchestra made in the following year,[1] however, met with considerable success —so much so, that ever since a quotation from the score found

[1] The circumstances of the string transcription are clearly set out in a letter to Röntgen dated Bergen, 1 February 1885 (Röntgen, pp. 23–4): 'A few days ago I got an invitation from Berlin to conduct my Piano Concerto there. But it won't do. The journey is too long and expensive. Instead I shall give a concert here, which is why I have arranged the poor Holberg Suite for string orchestra. It may sound quite well. I have set the finale (*Rigaudon*) for a solo violin and a solo viola, together with a whole lot of *pizzicati* in the rest of the orchestra. I'm hoping to collect 34 strings altogether. Then I'm to play the Cello Sonata with my brother, my wife is to sing some songs, and

its way into an English textbook as a model of idiomatic orchestral transcription, the string version has been tacitly accepted as superior to the keyboard original; indeed, it has even been maintained, on the strength of an ambiguous remark of the composer's, that the piano version, not the orchestral, was the arrangement. In fact at least two of the movements, the 'Prelude' and the 'Rigaudon', are essentially keyboard music, and although the scoring for strings is clever and effective up to a point, the original has a more authentic ring. The style is basically that of Bach's keyboard suites, with the addition of touches of piquancy suggestive of the French clavecinistes, as in such a passage as this:

Despite the composer's modesty about it, the *Holberg Suite* is a work of intrinsic merit, besides being a pioneer exercise in the revival of baroque idioms.[1]

---

then I shall pocket the money and bury it beneath Troldhaugen, the name of my villa: *Trold* means goblin, and *Haug* is hill. *Voilà tout.* It would be great if a real crowd of musical goblins took up their abode there!'

[1] Gade also was called on to celebrate the Holberg bicentenary, and produced a suite for large orchestra, *Holbergiana*. This is quite different in plan from Grieg's work, its four movements being related each to some episode in Holberg's plays. In the finale (*The Masked Ball*) an ad lib. chorus joins in the last bars with the threefold acclamation '*Vivat Holberg*'.

9 Various instrumental works, and music for the stage

One of the reproaches that Grieg often made against the Leipzig Conservatory was that it taught him little about the handling of instrumental resources other than the piano. Certainly his earlier attempts at writing for orchestra were only moderately successful, though this was due as much to his constitutional difficulty in planning musically on a large scale as to inexperience in scoring for orchestra. Both weaknesses are apparent in the Symphony in C minor and the Concert Overture *In Autumn*, and persist to some degree in the Piano Concerto, though in that work extensive revisions culminated in a definitive version with comparatively few imperfections of structure and orchestration.

The Symphony in C minor begun in 1863, probably at the suggestion of Gade, and finished at the beginning of May 1864, was soon to be discarded; only the two central movements, published for piano duet under the title of *Deux pièces symphoniques* (Op. 14), and accountably neglected by performers, and the autograph full score survive to justify the composer's decision. Schjelderup-Ebbe, who in general refuses to accept Grieg's strictures on his Leipzig training and on his earlier compositions, agrees that the Symphony is stylistically uneven, though he maintains that 'the orchestration, although not very imaginative and tending to be too heavy, with much doubling, is nevertheless quite sound and unmarked by any dilettantism'.[1] The same writer also considers that Grieg's treatment of the

[1] *Edvard Grieg 1858–1867*, p. 296.

orchestra here reflects his admiration for Schumann; in this connection, we have noted that in writing his article on that composer thirty years later Grieg was at pains to defend Schumann's orchestral works, and particularly the B flat major Symphony, against charges of incompetent scoring made by the Wagnerians.

Grieg's second essay in large-scale orchestral composition was the Concert Overture *In Autumn*, whose complicated history has already been described. The only form of the Overture we need now concern ourselves with is the second orchestral version, first performed, under the German title *Im Herbst*, at Birmingham in August 1888. The Overture makes extensive use of the song 'Autumn Storm' composed in 1865 to words by Christian Richardt, and also introduces a genuine Norwegian *springdans* from a book of hardanger-fiddle pieces published in Bergen early in 1865, a few months before the original version of the work was written. This theme appears in the coda of the Overture. Monrad Johansen, perhaps following the Birmingham programme note presumably based on Grieg's information, calls this 'the harvesters' cheerful song', though there is no clear evidence that the instrumental tune has any such connection;[1] and it occurs also in modified form near the end of the exposition. 'Autumn Storm' is, rather exceptionally for Grieg, a non-strophic song of elaborate construction, with much variety of tempo, key and melodic material. The Overture begins with a slow introduction which makes no reference to the song, but

[1] One suspects some linguistic confusion, the word *slått* having two distinct meanings: a musical air (cf. p. 124, n. 2) and mowing hay (*slåttefolk* are mowers or haymakers). The tune in question was originally published in *VIII Norske Slaatter for Hardangerfele* (Bergen, 1865). As Grieg noted in his diary for 12 March 1865 that his brother John had just sent him *Slaattevisen* ('the harvest song'?) from Bergen for his Overture, the composer may have tacitly accepted the 'harvest' interpretation.

creates a bleak atmosphere by means of melodic and harmonic progressions that gravitate round the fifth degree of the scale, producing a Mixolydian modal effect. In the *Allegro* section only the first part of the song is quoted, but as far as it goes—which is to the point where the key changes from D minor to the relative major, and the tempo from *molto allegro* to *poco andante*—the quotation is almost note-for-note. The second subject introduces a new theme, but is rounded off with the folk-tune reference previously mentioned. In the course of development ideas are still being added to the borrowed material and worked together with it. It is this section of the Overture that appears to many as academically over-contrived, though once again Schjelderup-Ebbe takes up a somewhat different attitude:

From the viewpoint of sheer development technique this whole section is convincingly handled. The material is constantly presented in new lights; it is broken up into fragments or extended, and appears in a variety of keys and moods. What *is* lacking, however, is the cohesion that is necessary to the creation of living music.[1]

With all its obvious faults, this is not a work to be entirely written off. It made some impression on its first performance in the revised version under the composer's baton, and later conductors have found it worth reviving from time to time. A recording (not currently available) made by Beecham and the Royal Philharmonic Orchestra brought out unsuspected touches of colour and imagination; no doubt Beecham's interest in the work was to some extent related to its prophetic hints of the orchestral nature-painting of Sibelius and Delius.

After another two-year interval, in 1868, Grieg produced his third and by far his most convincing essay in large-scale orchestral composition. Although critics, among them Shaw and

[1] Op. cit., p. 296.

Debussy, have never been slow to draw attention to flaws of taste and technique in the Concerto in A minor for Piano and Orchestra (Op. 16), and although it has not only been over-performed but also shamefully exploited and bowdlerized, it maintains a remarkably firm hold on life and loses with the years little of its vitality and freshness. Its success is due to a fortunate combination of factors: the composer at one of his rare high peaks of inventiveness, his willingness to follow Schumann's concept of the Romantic concerto without being completely subservient to it, a bold admixture of Lisztian bravura in the writing for solo part, and a happy blending of his own inborn harmonic originality with the national colouring he had, during the past few years, been assimilating to his style. Examples of this last characteristic are the tonic-leading note-dominant motive in the soloist's opening bars, the dotted rhythms of the theme that follows and its varied repetition, the augmented fourths of the next melodic idea, with its short sequential phrases, the folk-fiddler type of figuration in the *animato* section, the song-like theme of the slow movement enriched harmonically and colouristically in the manner of the later folk-song arrangements, and the *halling* and *springdans* rhythms of the finale.

The Concerto as now performed represents at least one major revision and several phases of re-touching; in fact, Grieg was never entirely satisfied with either the solo or the orchestral aspect of the work, and was altering details of both right up to the time of his death. The first published full score issued by Fritzsch of Leipzig shows an intermediate stage, giving the second subject theme of the first movement, for example, to a solo trumpet, not to the cellos; this was Liszt's suggestion, but the composer had the good sense to cancel it, reverting to what may well have been his first thoughts at this point.[1]

[1] The differences between the Fritzsch score and the later ones published by Peters are examined by Gerald Abraham in *Symposium*, pp.

An almost inseparable companion of the Concerto on Grieg's concert tours was the first *Peer Gynt* Suite (Op. 46), made up of four of the longer pieces from the twenty-odd numbers written either for the first stage production of Ibsen's play in 1876 or for its subsequent revivals.[1] If ever music has been played to death, it is these four pieces. It derives much of its charm from the blending of national colour, evoking the background of the drama, with the portrayal of exotic scenes and situations, like 'Morning Mood' and 'Anitra's Dance', in terms of the refined tradition of Copenhagen entertainment music. 'The Death of Åse' has more harmonic distinction, with some striking excursions into neo-modality, and is also a little classic of writing for string orchestra. 'In the Hall of the Mountain King' (to use its most familiar English title) is a diabolic *halling*, even in its purely instrumental version (the stage version has choral parts added) a *tour de force* of monothematic cumulative writing such as Ravel was to carry to a higher power of virtuosity in his *Boléro* half a century later. The second *Peer Gynt* Suite, assembled in 1891 (Op. 55), has never enjoyed—or suffered from—the same amount of popularity as the first, though it includes in the storm picture of 'Peer Gynt's Homecoming' one of the composer's best pieces of scoring for large orchestra. Also worthy of note are the effective writing for strings alone in the central section of the 'Arabian Dance', and the first number of the Suite, which is the Prelude to the second

---

28–31. The edition of the Concerto published by Schirmer in 1919, with the orchestral part for a second piano, gives a number of minor alterations in the solo part sanctioned by the composer in discussion with Percy Grainger at Troldhaugen in the summer of 1907.

[1] The numbers included in the posthumous full score are listed and described in *Symposium*, pp. 104–5. Further notes on the work are given in *Music & Letters*, xxvi (1945), pp. 66–77.

Act of the play, where contrasting musical ideas symbolize the lawless impetuosity of Peer and the baleful world of the trolls.

The incidental music required for Bjørnson's *Sigurd Jorsalfar* was on a smaller scale, comprising only five pieces, three of them instrumental; the latter were made into an orchestral Suite (Op. 56), in which the *Homage March* from Act II is considerably extended, mainly by the addition of a trio section. The quartet of cellos used in the opening of this March is an interesting idea, especially in view of the resemblance of the melody to that of the slow movement of the Cello Sonata. The first movement of the Suite was originally a piece for solo violin and piano, a gavotte with a companion piece which became the Minuet in the first Violin Sonata. When transferred to the *Sigurd* score the gavotte became a march, '*ved Mandjævningen*', to accompany the scene in which the rival merits of the two kings are, according to Viking custom, ceremoniously enumerated and compared. The *Intermezzo*, the middle movement of the Suite, formed the prelude to the scene where Borghild, who is one of the causes of dissension between the kings, awakens from her troubled dreams.

Bjørnson took the story of Sigurd from the *Heimskringla Saga*, and he drew upon the same source of history and legend for the dramatic poem *Bergliot* which Grieg set as a melodrama. Despite its unfamiliar literary material and its hybrid form, this work, now seldom heard, had considerable success in its day, especially in Paris at the height of a fashion for Nordic literature, mythology and art. Bjørnson gave his poem a dramatic unity, basing it upon an episode centred on a tragic heroine-figure, to which the Norwegian actress Laura Gundersen added the strength of her stage personality when the melodrama was performed for the first time with orchestrated accompaniment in 1885. The episode begins at the point in the saga where Bergliot's husband, a peasant-proprietor (*bonde*), has been treacherously slain by Harald Hårdråde. Bergliot reproaches her tenants and kinsmen for allowing the king to escape and tries to rally them for revenge. This part of the work is declaimed in free speech-rhythm, first in detached phrases interspersed with *tremolando* strings, drum rolls and horn and trumpet calls. With the beginning of Bergliot's lament for the dead man the speaker gradually falls into musically measured recitative; Bergliot calls for divine vengeance from 'the new God', and Einar's funeral procession begins. The scoring of this slow march is unusual—wind over timpani in fourths and other percussion, and double basses in octaves like the tolling of bells. Bergliot's final words are a classic quotation: 'Drive slowly, for we shall reach home soon enough.'[1]

There are features of the harmonic idiom of *Bergliot* that may conceivably have influenced French musical impressionism; the modal effect of unrelated chords over a scalar base in the opening of Debussy's 'Danseuses de Delphes', for example, is anticipated in such a progression as the following from *Bergliot*:

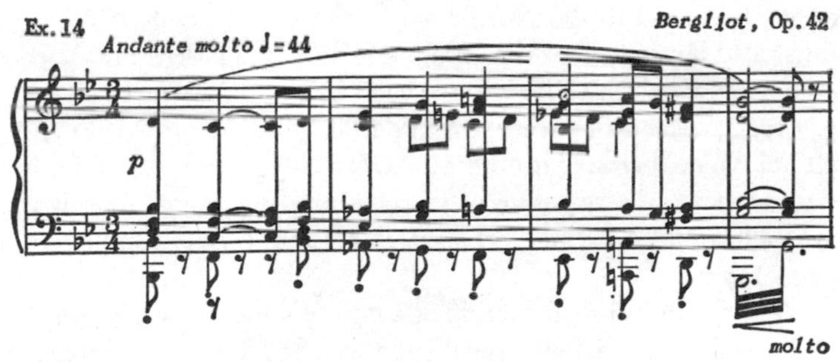

The unfinished opera *Olav Trygvason* also derives its subject-

[1] *Kjør langsomt;*
ti vi kommer tidsnok hjem.

matter from saga literature. An episode from the life of this national hero had already been used as the basis of the cantata *Landkjenning*; Bjørnson's verses describe Olav's return to Norway, after an upbringing in England, to claim his realm and establish the Christian faith there, and Grieg's setting is a straightforward, even obvious one, intended for massed singing by amateur male voices with organ accompaniment (to which orchestral parts were added for a later revival). The opera was meant to carry the story further, reaching its climax in the triumph of Christianity over the dark rites of Norse paganism. It is possible that one reason why Bjørnson lost interest in the project was his growing impatience with the dogmas of institutional Christianity. The three scenes he completed, however, are centred in the ritual of a Norse temple and offer the composer much scope for picturesque writing in the invocations of the high priest and a prophetess, a march with ceremonial horns round the sacred fires, and choral dances that seem distantly related to those in the almost contemporary *Prince Igor*, though it would be difficult to show that Grieg and Borodin knew of each other's work; a more likely model for *Olav Trygvason* might be found in the Nordic stage music of Hartmann. Grieg must also have remembered the scene with the Norns in *Götterdämmerung*, on which he was to write so eloquently in 1876, and resolved to keep the orchestra in subordination to the solo and choral voice parts. Throughout *Olav Trygvason*, whether in free or measured recitative or in the choral sections, Grieg is as scrupulous as ever in verbal declamation (see Example 15, page 157).

Yet despite its initial success as a choral suite, *Olav Trygvason* could make little lasting appeal even to a Scandinavian audience. Bjørnson had loaded his text so heavily with recondite antiquarian allusions that even Grieg himself could not unravel them, and had to beg the author to supply a glossary. Also, without its later scenes (Olav was to appear in the temple

Ex. 15

(Eternal faith of the gods, thou lovest all life;
Eternal faith of the gods, breathing in everything!)

doorway at the close of the ritual scenes, and the whole opera was to end with a mass baptism of white-robed converts), the work inevitably lacked credibility and coherence.

From 1871, when collaboration between Grieg and Bjørnson began in earnest, dates a short choral work with orchestra, *Foran Sydens Kloster* (Before a Southern Convent, Op. 20). The text is an episode from *Arnljot Gelline*, and tells its story in rhymed dialogue between the characters, in the manner of the traditional ballad *Edward*. An unknown girl knocks on the convent door for sanctuary, is questioned by the abbess or guest-mistress, and reveals that her father has been killed by her lover. The two voices (soprano and contralto) are accompanied by a large orchestra (without trombones) imaginatively used, and towards the end, when the nuns are heard singing in the convent chapel, the organ is added. Despite its atmosphere of romanticized medievalism, the cantata has dramatic tension and might well be considered for occasional performance by women's choirs.

Another work of ballad character, and one on which Grieg himself placed a high value, is the short cantata for solo baritone accompanied by two horns and strings, *Den Bergtekne* (*The Mountain Thrall*, Op. 32). The Old Norwegian verses, taken from Landstad's collection of folk ballads, embody a version of the legend familiar to English readers through Keats's *La Belle Dame sans Merci* and also recall the scenes with the troll-king's daughter in *Peer Gynt*. A young man wandering in the woods near an enchanted 'rune-stone' is bewitched by a giant's daughter and forgets his way home again. The giants pursue him, and he finds himself in isolation, the only human being in a hostile nature-world where even the animals and fishes have the companionship of their own kind. The false relations of the opening chords of Grieg's setting, and the brooding horn theme that follows, create a sense of desolation and fear:

At the climax of the ballad an effect of almost hysterical terror is produced by the use of the falsetto voice and the chromatic harmonies of divided strings and horns:

(Falsetto)
i - konn up i tré
3
3

cresc. molto
ff largamente
al-le så he - ve dei ma - ka-mann, men in - gin så he - ve
cresc.
molto
2 horns
ff
ff
ff
cresc.
C.B.

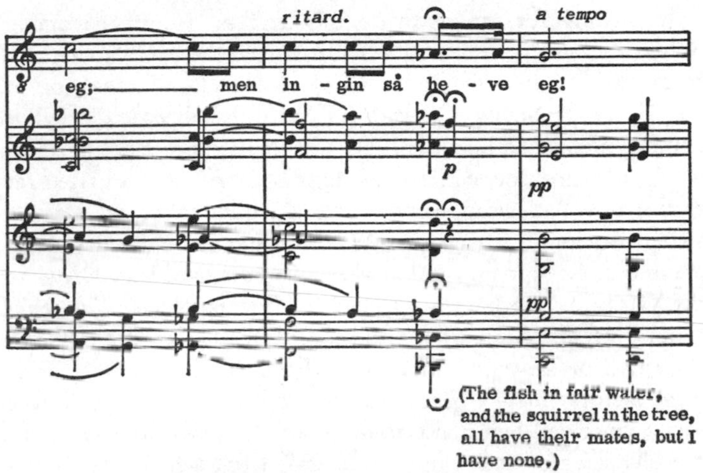

Although *The Mountain Thrall* is among the composer's least-known works, it concentrates into a short space of time some of his deepest feeling for the spirit and symbolism of Norwegian folklore.

The score also illustrates the fact that he generally wrote better for strings with a few solo wind than for full orchestra, and best of all for strings alone. The sound of massed strings fascinated him, and inspired him as a composer to score adventurously for them and as a conductor to extract from them the greatest possible range of expression. He deserves a place beside Tchaikovsky and Dvořák in the development of the string orchestra, a medium which had been little exploited since the first half of the eighteenth century. Grieg's arrangements of two of the Vinje songs under the title of *Elegiac Melodies* (Op. 34) remains one of the best-sounding works in the repertory of the romantic string orchestra.

In writing for string quartet his success is more debatable. While the string orchestra version of the *Holberg Suite* could be quoted in a respectable text-book as a model of transcription, the G minor String Quartet (Op. 27) has been pilloried in another manual as being entirely unsuited to the medium. This work was not the composer's first attempt at a quartet (an earlier one has disappeared), and surrounded as he was by string players of distinction and consulting as he did the Heckmann quartet on many technical details, it is hard to believe that the G minor work is a product of inexperience. The chief ground of objection to it—the long stretches of homophonic and quasi-orchestral texture—is perhaps to be accounted for by three factors: first, a preoccupation with chord progressions as such, conceived habitually in terms of the keyboard; secondly, the character of the song, 'Fiddlers', from which the motto-theme is taken; and thirdly, perhaps a real intention of breaking with the classical quartet styles and attempting something novel in the medium. Grieg himself strongly resisted any suggestion that it was unidiomatic: 'It is true [he told his Leipzig publishers[1]], that it is not written in conformity with the requirements of the Leipzig school, but it is wrong to assert that it is unsuited to strings, much less that it is fundamentally keyboard music.'

It is only fair to notice that the composer admits a considerable amount of variety of texture on his own terms. The second movement (*Romanze*) is at once the most elaborately organized and the most satisfying from the linear aspect. The principal motive, a happy melodic inspiration, is heard three times, with a contrasting theme, in quicker tempo and based on the motto idea, separating the three presentations. The following passage shows the figuration of the subsidiary theme combining with the principal one when the latter makes its first reappearance:

[1] Zschinsky-Troxler, 28 October 1878.

Not the least interesting tribute to the merits of Grieg's Quartet is the influence it seems to have had on Debussy's String Quartet, also in G minor, which was written fifteen years later, in 1893. Debussy also uses a motto theme, one that is identical in the pitch of its first four notes with Grieg's 'Fiddlers' motive; and like Grieg, Debussy introduces this theme into each of his four movements, though with more variation and greater subtlety. There is more contrapuntal writing in the Debussy Quartet than in the Grieg; yet the former also has some assertive homophonic passages, and the repeated octave quavers in the final bars of the first movements of both works are remarkably similar.[1]

In 1891 Grieg began a second String Quartet, in F major. He left the first two movements in an almost complete state, and these were edited by Julius Röntgen and published by Peters; Röntgen also completed the slow movement (*Adagio*, in B flat major) and the Finale (*Allegro giocoso*, F major) from the composer's sketches, now in the Bergen Library. As far as one can judge, this work would have been more traditional in style and structure. It also gives an impression of being less spontaneous. Neither the ideas nor their treatment are particularly novel or striking. The principal subject of the first movement, for example, faintly recalls that of the early Violin Sonata in the same key (Op. 8) but lacks its youthful *élan*, and its working-out is no more than conscientious. The *Allegretto scherzando*, D minor, harks back to the early 'Norwegian' style of the *Humoresques*, or, in the naïvety of its trio section, to an even earlier period (see music Example 1); its animation and humour might, however, justify an occasional performance as a separate movement.

[1] These are but a few of the more obvious parallels; for other points of similarity see the note on Grieg's Quartet by Gerald Abraham in *Symposium*, p. 8. Alan Frank analyses both this work and the unfinished Quartet in *Symposium*, pp. 41–4.

1 C		2 R			3 S		4 T	
A		O			L		R	
5 L	6 O	B		7	I		E	
8 F	A	I	9 R		G		A	
	10 K	N	I	G	H	11 T	S	
	T		O		12 T	O	O	13
14	R		T			15 O	N	E
	E		E			T		
16	E		R		17 C	H	A	T

10 The solo songs

There are several reasons why Grieg's songs with piano, to the number of nearly 150, should contain much of his best work.

The composer himself unhesitatingly gave most of the credit to Nina's exceptionally sympathetic gifts of interpretation. The inspiration of her artistry continued from the time of their engagement in 1864, through the years spent in Christiania, (1866 to 1874) which he described as the full flowering of her voice, until nearly the end of the century when she gave up singing in public. He was to write no more songs after 1900, when the Benzon settings (Ops. 69 and 70) appeared.

His second piece of good fortune was that the span of his life coincided almost exactly with the golden age of Norwegian lyric poetry. Although he was only two years old when Wergeland died, he was to come into contact, in some cases very closely, with Welhaven, Andreas Munch, Jørgen Moe, Bjørnson, Ibsen, Vinje, Garborg and Vilhelm Krag, and to set verses by all of them. In addition, through the years he spent in Denmark and the many friends he had there he was in touch with Danish Romantic literature, which had a generation's start over the corresponding movement in Norway. Among the Danish poets Grieg set were Christian Winther, Christian Richardt, Hans Christian Andersen and lesser men like Drachmann and Benzon. Grieg was outstandingly sensitive to language, both spoken and written, and never regarded verse as merely a vehicle or substructure for his own art. He read widely, was always concerned with correct declamation, and often fretted over the problems of translating his songs from Scandinavian languages into those with a wider currency.

It is necessary to refer here to a third factor contributing towards Grieg's interest and success in the field of the solo song. There existed already in the Scandinavian lands a particular kind of lyric song, the *romance*, differing in history and character from the German Romantic *Lied*. It was more like what nineteenth-century England knew as the 'ballad'; though it never descended to the banalities of the worst of that species, it shared with it the undramatic vocal line, the stylized emotion, the unobtrusive piano accompaniment and usually the strophic form. The quality of both verse and music in the *romance* was often high. Among the musicians who, before Grieg, helped to establish the tradition were Weyse and Heise in Denmark, Lindblad in Sweden and Nordraak and Kjerulf in Norway. Grieg viewed the line of Scandinavian song-writing as continuing beyond his own work in such composers as Christian Sinding in Norway, Peter Lange-Müller in Denmark, and Emil Sjögren in Sweden.

Grieg was conscious that the character of his songs was governed to a great extent by the language he set, according to whether this was German, Danish, Dano-Norwegian or the *Landsmål* of Vinje and Garborg. He believed that the best Norwegian poetry (in both forms of the language) was deeply impregnated with the spirit of the ancient Eddas and sagas, where

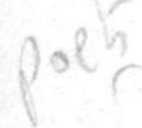

> one soon perceives the wonderful power and conciseness of expression, the ability to say much in few words. The more deeply the heart is moved, the more reticent, the more enigmatic is the expression. The language always remains dry, serious, and dignified. The stormy ocean of the passions is sensed rather than seen. It is accounted crude [*brutal*] to show one's most intimate feelings, and hence their expression is generally brief and restrained [*knapp wie keusch*]. This saga-literature is the basis on which Bjørnson and Ibsen have built. . . . What the

poets have achieved in this respect is what I have aimed for in the music, perhaps most of all in the settings of the deeply-felt lyrics of the peasant-poets Vinje and Garborg. The exuberant wealth of outward trapping [*Apparat*] characteristic of the German has thus never been part of the Norseman's nature.[1]

Despite his unwavering admiration for Wagner, and notwithstanding the influence of Wagnerian dramatic declamation in his later songs, Grieg refused to follow some contemporary German composers in depriving the voice of its priority. It was evidently with Hugo Wolf and Richard Strauss chiefly in mind that he made his own position clear: 'I do not wish to see the melodic element concentrated mainly in the piano part, and I have no sympathy with attempts to transfer the Wagnerian opera-style to the *Lied*. The unfoldment [*Dramatik*] of a *Lied* must, I feel, always differ entirely from that of a Music-Drama.'[2]

In considering Grieg's songs it is convenient to follow his own classification by languages, since this corresponds to a great extent with the successive periods at which they were composed.[3] As a student in Leipzig, and with his reputation to make in a musical world that was steeped in German culture, both literary and musical, it was natural for the young Grieg to include among his earliest publications a set of *Four Songs for Alto* (Op. 2), to poems by Chamisso and Heine,[4] and, in the year of his engagement, six more German songs, to texts by Chamisso, Heine, and Uhland (Op. 4), dedicated to 'Fräulein Nina Hagerup'. Most of these German songs are non-strophic

[1] Communication to Finck, in *Artikler og Taler*, p. 53.

[2] ibid., p. 63.

[3] It is the plan adopted in Astra Desmond's chapter on the songs in *Grieg: a Symposium*, pp. 71 fol. This is the most complete study of the subject available.

[4] Dedicated to Wibecke Meyer, who sang Nos. 1 and 4 of the set at Grieg's first concert in Bergen in May 1862.

Lieder in the tradition of Schubert and Schumann. Of the first set, the best is No. 3, Heine's 'Ich stand in dunkeln Träumen', offering as it does much scope for Grieg's already well-developed sense of harmonic colour. The six songs of Op. 4, though still indebted to Schumann, show growing freedom in the treatment of the voice and in harmonic resource: the dissonances of No. 3, 'Abschied', are particularly bold, and No. 6, 'Wo sind sie hin?' contains some remarkable writing; Heine's verses are tinged with nordic Romanticism, and this seems to have given Grieg a special interest in them. He is not yet ready, however, to respond completely to a poem of such tragic concentration, and finds it necessary to balance the two strophes with a ritornello for the piano, foreshadowing the style of the Piano Sonata.[1]

Grieg's other settings of German texts include the *Six Songs* (Op. 48) and the posthumously published 'Der Jäger' (Schultz) and 'Osterlied' (Böttger), together with the fine Heine song, 'Hör' ich das Liedchen klingen' (Op. 39, No. 6), which, however, was set to a Norwegian translation by Nordahl Rolfsen. All these were composed at a much later period than the first two sets of German songs, and were designed for a very different kind of voice. It is instructive to consider them in the context of the composer's views on the suitability of music-drama style to the solo *Lied*. The Op. 48 songs were dedicated to the Swedish-born Wagnerian soprano Ellen Gulbranson, and by a reversal of the usual process are sometimes sung in Norwegian instead of German. Grieg must have been satisfied that Gulbranson had the sensibility to distinguish between operatic and lyric song-styles, for he welcomed the wider currency she gave a number of his Norwegian songs through her international recitals. By any standards, the Op. 48 is a fine set of *Lieder*: the

[1] The Op. 4 Songs are subjected to detailed analysis in Schjelderup-Ebbe, *Edvard Grieg 1858–1867*, pp. 180–9.

voice, though never losing its well-defined melodic outline, is given leaps of sixths, sevenths, and octaves in Heine's 'Gruss', in Uhland's 'Lauf der Welt', in Goethe's 'Zur Rosenzeit' and in Bodenstedt's 'Ein Traum'. This last is a non-strophic *Lied*, almost completely in the central tradition, though the composer seems to assert his Norse individuality in the little descending figure given to the piano in the opening stanzas. The setting of Geibel's 'Dereinst, Gedanke mein' illustrates, though in connection with a famous German lyric, the Norse restraint and brevity of expression Grieg remarked on; there is a close similarity between its harmonic idiom, in which the simplest triadic progressions are intermingled with chromatic dissonances, and the style of the Vinje songs (Op. 33), where the composer is at his most Norwegian. The remaining song of Op. 48, Walther von der Vogelweide's 'Die verschwiegene Nachtigall', recalls the folksong settings of Brahms.

The Danish songs fall into two main groups: those written during, or soon after, Grieg's years in Copenhagen and Rungsted after graduating from the Leipzig Conservatory and before establishing himself in Norway; and the Drachmann and Benzon songs that he wrote much later. The Christian Winther set of *Four Romances* published as Op. 10[1] is so far from representing the young composer at his best that one may assume that Nina Hagerup was the principal agent in producing the marked improvement in quality shown in *Melodies of the Heart*, to four lyrics by H. C. Andersen (Op. 5). We can take these in conjunction with other Andersen settings written between 1864 and 1869, and included in Op. 15 and Op. 18 (the latter, entitled *Romances*, is subdivided into two books). Here we find several of the charming Danish lyrics which Nina interpreted so beautifully, and which are still perhaps the least neglected of the

[1] It is suggested in *Grieg: a Symposium* that these may date from before the Leipzig period, but Schjelderup-Ebbe is in favour of a date of 1864 or thereabouts.

composer's songs: unfortunately, the situation can only be expressed in this negative way.

Op. 5 contains the most popular of all Grieg's songs, 'I love thee' (*Jeg elsker Dig!*), the delight of every lusty student baritone, who usually learns the German translation with its second stanza added by Frank van der Stucken; this redundancy ruins the carefully built-up tension between Andersen's regular four-line stanza and the asymmetrical structure of the music, and, as Astra Desmond points out,[1] can only produce an anticlimax, especially if the composer's marking *poco accelerando* is observed for a second time. 'Two Brown Eyes' (Op. 5, No. 1) is another compact *romance*, interweaving an almost entirely diatonic vocal melody with an accompaniment that intensifies momentarily at the emotional climax, with a series of dominant-interrelated harmonies creating, as so often with the composer, a sense of ambiguity between major and minor before swinging back to the tonic major (see Example 18, page 171).

The other two songs of Op. 5, 'You cannot grasp the waves' eternal course' and 'My thought is a great mountain', are longer and more turbulent, and show the influence of the Schubertian *Lied*; the former is in varied two-strophic form, in the latter the music is continuous. Both have well-wrought pianistic accompaniments with some adventurous changes of key and mode.

The collections published as Op. 15 and the two books of Op. 18 contain further Andersen settings. The spirit of the Danish *romance* reigns supremely here, with folksong-like strophic setting of simple character, like 'Wandering in the Woods' (Op. 18, No. 1), 'She is so white', 'A poet's last song', and others of more unusual structure, like 'The Cottage' (Op. 18, Vol. II, No. 3) with its delicately ornamented vocal line, and 'The Rosebud' (Op. 18, Vol. II, No. 4), with its magical glide, for four bars in each of the two stanzas, into the key of

[1] *Symposium*, p. 77.

As in the original version: see Schjelderup–Ebbe, op. cit., pages 205–6 for a number of divergences between the Danish edition of 1865 and the text and music of this song in the Collected Edition of 1890.

the flattened submediant. 'Poesy' (Op. 18, No. 5) shows, especially in the arpeggio accompaniment over an interesting bass, and an eloquent ritornello after each stanza, how the influence of Schumann still lingers, though Schumann would hardly have marred the effectiveness of a carefully constructed stanza by repeating it twice in identical form. Another Danish poet, Christian Richardt, provided the text for the most elaborate song of the whole series, 'Autumn Storm' (Op. 18, No. 4), which was soon afterwards to become the basis of the Overture *In Autumn*. No deep emotion is to be found in either words or music; the poem draws, in an amiable Danish way, lessons of husbandry and thrift from the changing seasons, and Grieg responds to its various moods, linking them by means of a few basic motives.

Among the posthumous songs is a little-known setting of H. C. Andersen's poem 'The Soldier', which Schumann had already set, along with three other Andersen poems, all translated into German by Chamisso, in his *Fünf Lieder* (Op. 40, 1840). Schumann makes some telling musical points, but Grieg's setting is far more imaginative. The subject of the poem was suggested to Andersen by a horrifying memory from childhood of the execution of a soldier stationed in Odense; it is one that Mussorgsky, as Schjelderup-Ebbe points out, might have treated in much the same way as Grieg.[1] The soldier is the only friend of one of the men in the firing-squad. All nine of them take aim and fire, but eight miss, for their hands are trembling with compassion. The friend alone shoots him through the heart. The slow march to the execution place is depicted in a throbbing, dissonantly chromatic piano part, while the singer expresses his mounting anguish:

[1] *Edvard Grieg 1858–1867*, p. 258. I understand from Øystein Gaukstad that David Monrad Johansen in a letter compared Grieg's unpublished setting of Kipling's 'Gentlemen-Rankers' to Mussorgsky's 'Field-Marshal Death', adding that this seemed to be 'an isolated phenomenon in Grieg's output'.

As the climax of the narrative approaches, the singer breaks down into recitative, with a final dramatic outcry:

A wider knowledge of this great tragic song might do much to dispel the popular misconception of both Andersen and Grieg as picturesquely childlike figures, untouched by the harsh realities of an adult world.

Although Andersen and other Danish poets are most often drawn upon at this period, we find that even before the autumn of 1866, when Grieg began his professional career in Christiania, he had become aware of Norwegian poetry and was setting it to music. Several of the *Romances and Ballads* (Op. 9) to texts by Andreas Munch were composed as early as 1864. Munch was one of the founding fathers of Norwegian Romantic literature. In 1849, at an exhibition of national painting in Christiania, a famous picture by Tidemand, *Bridal procession on the Hardanger fjord*, had been made the subject of verses by Munch, and the poem had been set as a choral piece by Kjerulf. For many years, until the rise of Ibsen and Bjørnson, Munch was the leading figure in national poetry and drama. In 1864 he retired to Denmark, where Grieg may have met him. In the Op. 9 settings the Norwegian tone is muted alike in verse and music, 'The Harp', 'Cradle-song' and 'Sunset' being typical examples of the melancholy strophic Dano-Norwegian *romance*. The fourth song of the set, 'The Departure', is more elaborate, however. A ship rides at anchor, ready to sail at dawn; its gently rocking motion is depicted in the 9/8 rhythm of the piano part, while the voice describes the scene in a flexible line that rises and falls buoyantly. The key changes from C major to A flat major as the poet and his young wife stand on deck, dreaming of the voyage together, and of their future happiness by 'Arno's and Tiber's shores'. Here the key changes again abruptly (A flat major to E major), with excited tremolando writing for the piano. The voyage begins in full daylight (C major again) but ends bleakly, with a modal chill in the harmony; the young bride was not to know that her life would soon be over. Both Monrad Johansen and Schjelderup-Ebbe link the subject of this song with Grieg's voyage to Italy and the death of Nordraak, but this seems less probable than that Munch's poem refers to his own journey to Italy in 1847, with the tragic loss of his wife three years later.[1]

Another of the older generation of Norwegian poets represented in the 'Danish' collection of Op. 18, though by a song

[1] Munch also wrote the texts for two occasional works by Grieg. These were the cantata for chorus and military band for the unveiling of the Christie monument in Bergen on 17 May 1868, and the cantata for the unveiling of the Kjerulf statue in Christiania in 1874.

written in 1869, is Jørgen Moe. He was joint editor with P. Chr. Asbjørnsen of the folk tales (*Norske Folke-Eventyr*) that were published at the time of Grieg's birth and were to give his life, like those of all Norwegians from that time onward, a permanent background of folk-imagery (one has only to think of the villa named Troll-hill—*Troldhaugen*—and of the snow-bound Voksenkollen sanatorium above Christiania which became, in the imagination of Grieg when he was a patient there, the fantastic Soria Moria Castle). Moe also wrote the verses of 'The Herd-girl's Sunday' to Ole Bull's famous violin melody. Grieg drew little upon Moe's poetry; there is one (but fairly popular) song, 'The Young Birch Tree' (Op. 18, Vol. II, No. 2) and there are two male-voice quartets, 'The Bear Hunt' and 'Evening Mood', written in 1867.

Grieg set as a song only one poem by the great novelist Jonas Lie;[1] this is 'High on the grassy slope' (Op. 39, No. 3), and belongs to a much later date (1885). For some reason it never got into the German edition, but it should not be overlooked, for the poem has wit and freshness and Grieg's music responds well to it, with a happy use of the various registers of the piano.

The first-fruits of the long partnership between Grieg and Bjørnson appear in *Four Songs from 'The Fisher-Lass'* (Op. 21). Bjørnson's lyric verse was more often than not written expressly for singing; though no musician himself, he regarded music as the natural accompaniment of poetry, identifying himself with the musical nationalism of Ole Bull, Halfdan Kjerulf, Rikard Nordraak and Grieg. One of Kjerulf's Bjørnson settings, 'The Princess', may even be preferred to Grieg's, successful though the latter is in suggesting an atmosphere of medieval romance through the alternation of monodic passages in the piano part,

[1] A short work for male voices, written for a choral festival held in Christiania in 1896, has a text by Jonas Lie.

delicately ornamented, with sonorous chromatic harmony. In 'The First Meeting' Bjørnson's lyric compresses in eight short lines an almost Wordsworthian vision of the interpenetration of human and natural worlds, with a wealth of sound imagery:

> The sweetness of the first meeting
> is like singing in the forest,
> like singing over the water
> in the sun's last glow.
> It is like a horn-call in the mountains,
> those resounding moments
> wherein we are made at one with nature
> in wonderment.[1]

In his response to this beautiful little poem (the first of the *Fisher-Lass* songs, Op. 21) Grieg has entered fully into his heritage as a Norwegian composer, with an ecstatic sweep of melody that seems not so much to be supported by as to grow out of his unerring harmonic sense. After 'The First Meeting' the most original song of the Op. 21 set is 'I give my song to the Spring' (No. 3), where there are anticipations, in the gliding chromatic harmonies beneath fresh, diatonic melody, of the great Vinje song 'The Spring' that was still ten years away. The impetuous side of Bjørnson's personality is well brought out in 'Thanks for thy counsel' (No. 4), a vigorous setting which enhances the impression conveyed in the poem of a Viking ship riding over stormy and uncharted seas.

To the same vintage Bjørnson year (1870) belongs the song

[1] Det første møtes sødme
det er som sang i skogen,
det er som sang på vågen
i solens siste rødme, –
det er som horn i uren,
de tonende sekunder
hvori vi med naturen
forenes i et under.

'From Monte Pincio' (Op. 39, No. 1). Written in the year of the liberation of Rome from French military dominance and of the unification of Italy, the poem rings with Bjørnson's passion for freedom and self-determination wherever he found them, and with his conviction that the regenerated Italian nation would advance in peace and amity. The largeness of scale and variety of movement in Grieg's setting make this one of the most imposing of all his songs, and account for its early admission to the international song repertory. Grieg's setting begins with harmonies anticipating the famous opening of the *Largo* of Dvořák's 'New World' Symphony (written in 1893, twenty-three years after Grieg's song):[1]

He sets only the first and last stanzas of Bjørnson's poem, treating each of them sectionally, first with one of his rapturous, wide-ranging melodies, followed by a quicker episode in the style of Italian popular song, which towards the end of the stanza disintegrates into the sounds of rejoicing as they vanish into the night.

Other Bjørnson songs composed in the next year or so include 'The Princess', already mentioned, and 'Hidden Love' (Op. 39, No. 2), an outstandingly beautiful song, whose theme of

[1] It is interesting to note that Grieg orchestrated the accompaniment of 'From Monte Pincio' in 1894.

tragic misunderstanding needs the restraint of the Norwegian text to make its full effect; the opening phrases are akin to those of 'Solveig's Song' written for *Peer Gynt* two years later.

In the six Ibsen songs (Op. 25) terseness and economy are even more in evidence, and again Grieg shows his sympathy with the qualities he regarded as the hall-marks of Norwegian poetry at its finest. The first song of the set, 'Minstrels' (*Spillemænd*), supplied the motto-theme for the String Quartet in G minor. Ibsen's words allude to the *nøkk* of Norse popular lore —the spirit of the waterfall from whom a musician can learn the most precious secrets of his art, though at the risk of losing his peace of mind for ever. It may be that Grieg linked this conception, half-consciously, with the spell that the unending search for excellence lays upon a group of dedicated musicians. What is certain is that the intensity of Ibsen's poem is reflected in one of Grieg's most completely unified structures; the central declamatory section of the song is marked by scrupulous attention to verbal rhythm, underlined in minute fluctuations of tempo and dynamics, and there is a striking contrast between the archaic simplicity of the opening (the motto of the Quartet), and the enrichment of the same motive on its return, with full, dissonant chords in the lower register of the piano.

'A Swan' (Op. 25, No. 2) also ranks among the greatest of the composer's songs. Again, Ibsen's poem is brief and charged with symbolism, some of it doubtless personal, though the swan is a not uncommon motive in Nordic folklore, and Grieg's respect for the deep but reticent emotion implicit in the words is indicated by the direction *langsomt og tilbageholdt* ('slow and held in check', 'restrained'); the voice-part flows in a broad, rhythmically plastic line above a chordal accompaniment gently suffused with chromatic alterations and unessential notes. The brevity of the poem, and its formal perfection of metre and rhyme, make translation almost an impossibility, not least because neither English nor German can find a counterpart to the disyllable *svane* which is the final word of the song. In his anxiety that Ibsen's poem should be understood, Grieg insisted that the climax at the words '*ja da, da löd der!*' (German: 'Ja da—da sangst du!') should be *ff*, with a further crescendo at the end of the phrase; but although his manuscript makes the intention clear enough, the German edition published by Peters marks a *diminuendo* at this point.[1] (See plates 4–5.)

Another example of concentration in both poem and setting is the fifth song of the Ibsen set,[2] whose desolate title and final word, *borte*, resists the translator almost as much as 'En Svane': the obvious equivalents 'away', 'gone', 'left', and 'departed' are all commonplace and, except for the last, will not fit the final trochaic cadence with its rising intonation. Like 'Borte', the 'Album Verse' ('I called thee my messenger of joy', Op. 25, No. 3), occupies but a single page, its despairingly broken phrases punctuated by drooping fourths, diminished and augmented. Two of the Ibsen songs are of sunnier character: 'A Bird-song' (No. 6), with its delicious interplay of voice and piano, and the charming 'With a Water-lily' (No. 4), which, even if it had no other merits, should dispel the notion that Grieg could think only in two- and four-bar phrases; the accompaniment, though doubling the voice at most points, has a life of its own and reminds us yet again how much the composer owed to Schumann.

Besides the Ibsen songs Grieg published in the same year (1876) a collection of five settings of verses by John Paulsen, a minor poet whom he had known from early days in Bergen. These *Five Poems* (Op. 26) were the first of three sets of songs Grieg wrote to Paulsen's verses, the others being the cycle

[1] Other problems of translation, unsolved in the German version, are discussed by Astra Desmond, *Symposium*, p. 83.

[2] The poem is thought to have been inspired by Thea Bruun, a young Norwegian Ibsen met in Genzano in 1864. She died of consumption at an early age (Meyer, *Henrik Ibsen*, Vol. II, pp. 236–7).

Norway (Op. 58) and the *Elegiac Poems* (Op. 59); in fact the Paulsen songs outnumber Grieg's settings of any other poet. Though admired, at least in his youthful days, even by as stern a judge as Ibsen, Paulsen never fulfilled his promise as poet and dramatist, but it was one of his consolations that both Grieg and Svendsen had drawn freely upon his work; apart from the poems thus rescued from oblivion, Paulsen is now remembered chiefly for his volumes of memoirs, which provide interesting anecdotes about his more distinguished contemporaries, especially Ibsen and to a lesser degree Grieg also. The Op. 26 songs contain some excellent things. Supreme among them is 'With a Primrose', a not unworthy companion to Ibsen's 'With a Water-lily'.[1] Another song of this set, 'The Ambitious One' (Op. 26, No. 3), though less known because it was never included in the German edition, has a piano part of unusual brilliance and complexity.

We come now to the songs of the Lofthus period, which the composer always regarded as among the most fertile of his life, when he felt completely identified with the land, the people, and the literature of Norway. The isolated setting of the old ballad *The Mountain Thrall* (Op. 32) has been referred to in the previous chapter. Grieg's most important discovery at this time, however, was the poetry of Aasmund Olavsson Vinje, who had been born in a peasant family in Telemark, struggled into schoolmastering, law studies, and journalism, and became a supporter of the *landsmål* movement, writing his best verse in that rugged and sonorous language based on regional dialects and first systematized by Ivar Aasen. Vinje's outspokenness about government policy on the question of the union with

[1] Both were among Nina Grieg's favourite songs. Forty years later, in May 1915, she wrote (in English) to Anna Brodsky in Manchester describing the late spring at Troldhaugen: 'It is still snowing every day and freezing in the night. The trees are black and dry, without a leaf, and *one* single little cold primula in the garden.'

Sweden cost him his lowly official post, and he died in poverty, but not before he had reinvigorated Norwegian literature, both in poetry and prose. Like Grieg, he was an ardent lover of the mountains, and declared that after death his spirit would linger on those wild snow-clad heights.

In the twelve Vinje songs of Op. 33 (divided into two books) Grieg uses for the most part an unmodified strophic type of setting, as being best suited to the folksong-like nature of the verse. 'The Youth', an elegy on the poet who through his own suffering and death has created inspired song, is to be sung 'with free declamation', the voice-part flowing almost in speech-rhythm above dissonant harmonies in a low register of the keyboard. 'The Spring', also strophic, is beyond question Grieg's most beautiful melody, universally known through its string version as the second of the *Elegiac Melodies* (Op. 34), where it is entitled more explicitly 'The Last Spring'. The poem, with its wonderful description of a northern land released from its icy bondage—a transformation the poet may be witnessing for the last time—is for technical reasons difficult to translate; English does not possess a large enough store of trochaic disyllables to reproduce the effect of Vinje's recurrent feminine rhymes, which Grieg has set to rising and falling thirds. 'The Wounded Heart' was transcribed as the first of the *Elegiac Melodies*; this poem also deals with Spring, in terms anticipating Eliot's 'April is the cruellest month', and Grieg emphasizes its stern courage with a setting that begins each stanza with grinding dissonances and restless tonality, resolved in the end through a liberating enharmonic change. 'The Whortleberry', a little nature-parable of dedication and sacrifice, begins innocently, but ends with a reharmonization of the original melody with some of the composer's most poignant chromatic progressions above a dominant pedal. In 'Beside a Stream' the poet again draws a parable from the sight of a group of trees inclining towards the brook, which all the time is gnawing at their roots;

this exceptionally is a non-strophic song, with much use of Grieg's favourite expressive device, ambiguity of mode, and an inspired coda for which the poem gives no authority whatever: the words 'Du Skog' (lit. 'Thou wood') are reiterated in a lingering cadence:

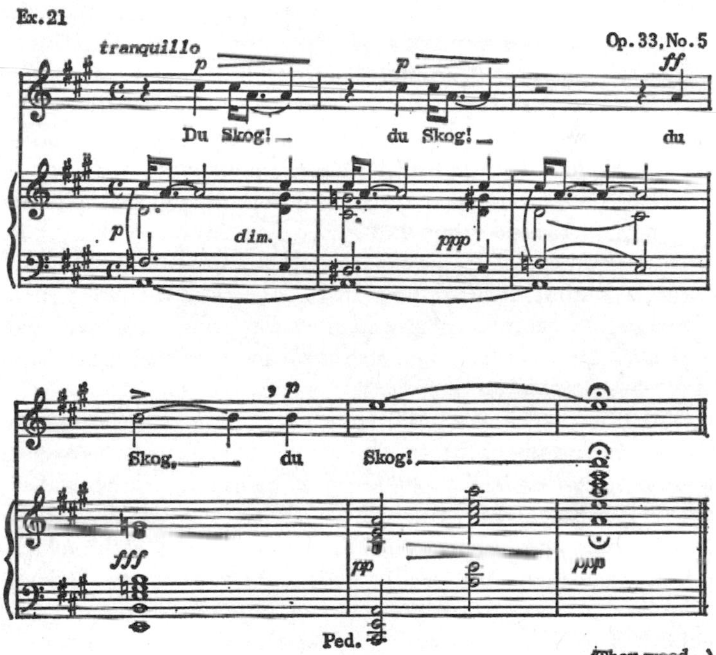

'A Vision' introduces a change of mood, with an engaging waltz lilt and an ecstatic episode as its central section. 'Old Mother', a simple folk-like strophic setting, was composed at an earlier date than the rest of the cycle. 'The First . . .' reverts to the stark, fatalistic tone of the beginning of the cycle, and is set in an austere, quasi-modal style. 'At Rundarne' breathes nostalgia for the scenes of the poet's childhood; musically the style is that of a *romance*, redeemed from sentimentality by the anguished chromatic counter-melodies appearing in the course of each stanza. 'A Broken Friendship' is a sour little poem about an older lover cheated by a young interloper, set in two musically identical strophes, with bitingly dissonant eleventh chords. 'Faith' is an ironical parody of hypocritical religiosity, which Grieg sets, apparently in all innocence, as a devotional hymn. The final song of the collection, 'The Goal', also was composed under a misapprehension about the meaning of the text. Grieg took it to be written in praise of social comradeship, and gave it a hearty march-like tune with a middle section in the style of a march-trio; whereas Vinje wrote the verses in robust alliterative fashion as an appeal to the readers of his journal *Dølen*, urging them to continue their support for the reform of the Norwegian language. The composer later found a way round this awkward topicality by arranging the song as an instrumental movement for strings, under the title *Norsk* (Op. 53, No. 1).

The discrepancies between Vinje's intentions and Grieg's in the last two songs of the set, and the tendency for the verses to decline in interest in the second book, deprive the collection of the unity needed for a true song-cycle such as the *Haugtussa* songs were to prove. Nevertheless the Vinje songs (with which may be included the posthumous 'Over Hamar's Ruins', composed at the same period as Op. 33 but for some reason not published in it) contain enough material to make up coherent recital-groups, with 'Spring' as the natural climax of any of them.

After the emotional depth of the best of the Vinje songs, the cycle entitled *Travel Memories from Mountain and Fjord* (Op. 44) offers little more than poetical and musical album-sketches. Even the expectations of scenic description aroused by the title remain unfulfilled; instead, Drachmann produces a series of portraits of girls and women who caught his roving eye during the Jotunheim tour with Grieg in the summer of 1886. There are, however, a prologue and an epilogue, forming as it were a scenic background to the portrait-display, and these Grieg set with the free rhythmic declamation he had already used in the first Vinje song. The epilogue introduces a Tyrolean yodelling song that Drachmann was fond of giving vent to when in the mountains.

The same partnership was more successful in the set of six songs of Op. 49. Here the atmosphere is recognizably Danish, the verse being less concentrated in form and expression than that of the Norwegian poets, and Grieg's music correspondingly more exuberant and decorative. The first song of the set, 'Saw you the lad who brushed past?' is overpowering in its hearty rhetoric, with a piano accompaniment that seems to have been conceived in orchestral rather than keyboard terms; it has a close affinity in style with the third song, 'Greetings, you ladies'. There is greater subtlety in 'Rock, O wave', whose opening words give the composer his cue for some delightful keyboard figuration; the diffuse construction of the song, in modified strophic form with some wide-ranging modulations, matches the vaguely erotic poem with its neo-classical imagery. Much more finely wrought, and indeed the gem of the collection, is 'Spring Rain', with its delicate impressionist accompaniment of broken ninth chords. The sharply contrasted ideas in 'Christmas Snow'—the snow as a beautifying and calming influence, but also arousing mournful thoughts on the transience of life and happiness—allow Grieg to range from the simplest harmonies to some of his most pungent dissonances in the *agitato* syncopated episodes. 'Now evening is light and long' is the least ambitious of the set—a three-stanza strophic *romance* with some effective pianistic interludes alternating with unaccompanied vocal phrases.

For his next three song-collections Grieg returned to Norwegian texts. In the Paulsen cycle *Norway* (Op. 58) one feels that the composer must have been responding to the obligations of friendship rather than to any deep-seated creative impulse. Yet even Paulsen's rather pallid lyrics have the power, perhaps through the sincerity of their patriotic sentiments, to evoke an intimate musical expressiveness that is missing from the more pretentious Drachmann settings just considered. The last song in this Paulsen set, 'The Emigrant', though a naïvely artless rhyme, moves the composer to create a melody that comes very near to folksong, and to round it off with one of his most haunting modal cadences.

Paulsen's *Elegiac Poems*, which Grieg set in the same year (1894) as Op. 59, are of more uniformly high quality, and seem to stimulate the composer's harmonic imagination, though in general the accompaniments are technically restricted; exceptions are the falling leaves suggested by the piano figuration of 'When I die', the throbbing syncopations of 'To One' (the second of the two songs with this title), and the Brahmsian arpeggios of 'Now you are resting in the earth'. In 'On Norway's bare mountains' both poet and musician seem to have caught something of the epigrammatic qualities of the poem by Heine on which Paulsen's is based.

The Vilhelm Krag settings (Op. 60), though little known, include some of Grieg's finest Norwegian songs. 'Little Kirsten' is an imaginative re-creation of a familiar folk-ballad situation, with charming pictorial touches—the girl at her weaving, the cuckoo calling in the woods. Folk-lore also pervades the third song, 'While I wait', which is full of allusions to children's songs and games; the wild geese flying, the yellow duckling, the dancing on St John's Eve, the nursery rhyme 'Bro, bro, brille' all offer the composer occasion for fanciful and humorous word-painting, combined with what is for Grieg considerable variety of phrase-length. Altogether, this is one of the most attractive of his lighter songs, whose craftsmanship is a delight to dwell on. The fourth song, 'A bird cried', reaches even greater heights. The poem (*Der skreg en fugl*) has been described by a Norwegian writer[1] as showing 'perhaps the most concentrated feeling of any in the language'. Grieg's introduction and postlude are founded on a gull's cry heard on the Hardanger fjord. The desolate scene, with the dark bird giving its wounded call in 'the autumn-grey day', beating its tired wings, is wonderfully depicted in the tension between the voice-line and the semitonally moving bass of the accompaniment. In the last ten bars (out of the total of twenty-six that comprise the whole song), the harmonization is entirely by parallel seventh chords —an effect of pure impressionism (see Example 22, page 188).

The same year Grieg began the little album of *Children's Songs* (Op. 61), to texts written or selected by Nordahl Rolfsen, a Bergen writer and publisher of children's books whose influence on Norwegian education was to be long and far-reaching. These settings from Rolfsen's school books are without any doubt the best children's songs written by any nineteenth-century composer, being free from the mawkishness of the more celebrated ones by Schumann and Brahms. The Norwegian spirit blows over them like fresh ozone, from the appropriate opening, 'The Sea', in which, as Grieg said, the sharpened fourth of the scale must 'sound like sea-salt'; through Bjørnson's 'Animal Song' (*Lok*, taken from the story 'A Happy Lad'), the virile 'Fisherman's Song' to words by the Nordland parson-poet, Petter Dass, the rhyme by Rolfsen himself about the hardworking family horse *Blakken* set to one of Grieg's simplest and happiest tunes in a trotting rhythmic pattern, a song in praise of the Norwegian mountains, and, to round off the set, a patriotic hymn of the least arrogant kind. It is worth noting that the

[1] Wilhelm Keilhau, *Det norske folks liv og historie*, Vol. 3 (Oslo, 1935), p. 257. The setting of the same words by Christian Sinding only serves to heighten by comparison Grieg's originality and economy.

(glided on dark wings away to sea.)

published English versions of these songs, by Natalie Macfarren, are exceptionally good.

The last of Grieg's Norwegian songs are among his greatest achievements. They form the cycle *Haugtussa* (Op. 67), the texts being taken from the long series of poems in *landsmål* by Arne Garborg, published in May 1895. Something has already been said in an earlier chapter about the origin and nature of Garborg's work. It is an extremely complex and profound conception, with several layers of meaning. One may appreciate its technical virtuosity, become absorbed in its rich folk-lore and nature-painting, attempt to ravel out its psychological and religious implications, or even take the trouble to identify the contemporary events and personalities it satirizes in certain of its episodes. Although the narrative thread is tenuous, it is not difficult to recognize that disappointed love is among the trials that beset the 'Little Maid' (*Veslemøy*), and it is this aspect of the work that Grieg isolates and dwells upon; his selection from the poems is, in fact, taken entirely from the earlier part of the work, thus leaving aside the demonic and satirical elements which recall the Dovre-King scenes in *Peer Gynt*. Only in the first song, 'The Singing', does a voice from the other world of the 'Blue Hill' call, with the insidious sweetness of Goethe's Erlking, promising the girl untold happiness if she consents to ply her silver spinning-wheel among the hill-folk. Grieg sets each stanza in two halves, the first to a flexible, wide-ranging minor mode melody, the second to a dancing lilt with harp-like accompaniment. A portrait of *Veslemøy* follows, the tenderness of Garborg's description matched by the simplicity of Grieg's setting, with its tinge of melancholy in the Phrygian colouring of melody and harmony. In 'Bilberry Slopes' the girl's dreaming, as she watches over the herd on the hillside and hopes timidly for a visit from 'the nice lad from Skare-Bròt', is expressed through a song of fresh spontaneity, contrasting in its innocence with the sinister luring song that begins the cycle, though both are in the same key. 'Meeting' is filled with the chromatic progressions that Grieg, like Mozart, always brings to an intensified emotional situation. The fragment of melody heard in the first bar of the piano introduction, an allusion to a familiar hardanger-fiddle cadence, has by now established itself as a kind of *Leitmotiv*: we have already heard it in 'The Singing' and 'Bilberry Slopes'.

The second half of the cycle breaks away from the key-centre of F which has unified the first group of songs. In 'Love' the girl dwells on her happiness in a rapturous melody which, as so often with Grieg, seems to imitate the intonation of the spoken language, with its frequent rising phrases that sound to the southern English ear like questions:

(The wild youth has beguiled my thoughts, I am caught like a bird in a trap; the wild youth, he looks so fine-- he knows that the bird will never escape.)

This undergoes a series of free variations, at first in the lively rhythm of the *springdans*, later with a sudden reversion to the former pensive mood, though with new and deeply expressive transformations. For the last section of the song the melody returns to its original form and harmonization. This type of structure is related to the traditional song-form known as *stev*. 'Kidlings' Dance' restores the atmosphere of care-free childhood[1] as the girl calls to her animals, playing with the sounds of their names; the song is in fact a more extended treatment of the same idea in the children's 'Animal Song' (Op. 61, No. 3). 'Evil Day' expresses in two ballad-like stanzas Veslemøy's despair at losing 'the lad from Skare-Bròt', and the cycle ends with lines taken from the next poem in Garborg's sequence, 'By the Brook' (*Ved Gjætle-Bekken*), whose onomatopoeic word-play must remind any English listener of Tennyson's familiar lyric from *The Princess*. As in Schubert's *Die schöne Müllerin*, the sound and sight of moving water are magically suggested in Grieg's accompaniment, for which the piano piece 'The Brook' (Op. 62, No. 4) might be regarded as a preliminary study. Grieg recalls Schubert also in choosing for the final consolatory song of the brook a keynote a third above that of the opening of the cycle, though he alludes to the original key (F) in the central section of his A major song. While his general plan here is strophic, Grieg's setting is remarkable for its subtle variations of melodic interval, tonality, metre and tempo and, despite its apparent simplicity, it is one of the most elaborately organized of his compositions.[2]

Although Grieg set no more Norwegian poetry after *Haugtussa* his song-writing was not quite at an end. In 1900 he published two sets of songs (Op. 69 and Op. 70) to texts by

[1] In Garborg's work, however, these verses occur between 'Meeting' and 'Love'.

[2] Manuscript sketches in the Bergen Library (and a set of photostat transcripts in the British Museum (H. 3536. d) show that Grieg set other portions of *Haugtussa*, including part of the Prologue, but decided against publication (see Appendix B).

Otto Benzon, a Danish chemist and playwright. They have a good deal in common with the Drachmann songs, especially in their tendency towards diffuseness, in contrast to the concentration and economy of the finest of the Norwegian songs; and again the style is, as the composer realized, cosmopolitan rather than Scandinavian, and adapted to the scale of the large concert hall recital rather than to the more homely and intimate atmosphere in which Grieg's songs had usually been listened to when Nina was still his chief interpreter. At their best, the Benzon songs are immensely professional, and they contain some beautiful ideas; but when inspiration flags the lapse is made all the more obvious by the composer's recourse to such clichés as chord reiterations, tremolandos, syncopations, arpeggios and sequences of augmented triads. Some of these make their unfortunate appearance in 'A boat is rocking on the wave', though the attractive undulating and rippling figures of the opening go far to redeem this first song of the Op. 69 set. 'To my son', a poem in the form of a letter to a child, has little enough to offer a composer, and even so is stretched out in the setting to an unconscionable length. The subject of 'At Mother's grave' again is unlikely to commend itself to modern singers or their audiences, though its mournfulness evokes some of Grieg's richest harmonies; as he himself suggested, it might make an effective solo piece for cello, perhaps, or better still for viola. Despite its coyness, 'Snail, Snail, come out of your home' is treated with musical imagination, and has a particularly effective piano part. 'Dream' is an interesting composition, in *Lied*-form but showing strong French influence, with a careful balance between voice and piano part and much harmonic subtlety.

In the Op. 70 set the composer appears to be trying to reconcile his former concept of lyric song with some of the features of Germanic music-drama, and the results are not always convincing. 'Eros' (Op. 70, No. 1), for example, is filled with uncharacteristic Wagnerian yearnings, and the piano-writing imitates orchestral textures. 'I live a life of longing' is potentially finer, with more idiomatic keyboard figuration and bold enharmonic key changes, but three long strophes set to identical music bring into operation the law of diminishing returns. The best of the collection, 'Lucent Night', has the merit of conciseness in words and music; the familiar theme of the lover's discontent with the shortness of the night is put into a northern setting, where the midnight sun allows little space between dusk and dawn. Of the remaining songs in the set, 'Beware' reverts to the folksong type of *romance*, while 'The Poet's Song', which Grieg wrote for the baritone Thorvald Lammers, is on a grandiose scale, with a quasi-operatic vocal part and an accompaniment that would require orchestrating to bring it to life.

This chapter has been written in the conviction that Grieg's songs constitute his most distinctive, and perhaps most lasting, contribution to Romantic music. The reason why they are not better known is obvious enough. The fact that the majority of them have texts in minor European languages inevitably restricts their accessibility for listeners and still more for performers. It is true that they were given a wider currency in the composer's lifetime by being translated into German, then the *lingua franca* of the musical world. Although he accepted this as a compromise, especially since his publishers were a German organization and carried weight in the matter, Grieg was by no means happy with the expedient, as he admitted in his notes to Finck:

When I compose a song, my concern is not to make music but, first and foremost, to do justice to the poet's intentions. I have tried to let the poem reveal itself, and indeed to raise it to a higher power. If I have achieved this aim, then the music also has been successful: not otherwise, however beautiful it may be. But if a Scandinavian poet, whose language the foreigner neither sings nor understands, is garbled in translation, not only he but also the composer suffers. Unfortunately I have often had bad luck in my attempts to get good translations. . . . My Leipzig publishers, C. F. Peters, have indeed made strenuous efforts to obtain adequate translations, but the result, even in favourable circumstances, is usually that the translations are *made to fit the music* and seem unnatural.[1]

In any case, German is open to many objections as a substitute for Norwegian and Danish. Not only is its sentence-structure different (more so than English), but it contains voiced sibilants that are alien to Scandinavian speech. Its poetic diction, too, frequently carries the wrong kind of romantic associations. Ibsen's 'A Swan' has already been quoted as an example of a text that suffers badly from translation, the German alternatives for the opening phrase ('Mein Schwan, mein stiller' or 'Du stiller Schwan') sounding clumsy in comparison with the clarity of the original ('Min hvide Svane'). The magnificent climax of Bjørnson's 'The First Meeting' fares ill in another way, the German translation ruining the effect of the threefold repetition of 'Under' ('Wonder') by underlaying different words. The continued use of the German versions by English singers is a practice which can no longer be justified, any more than would be the performance nowadays of Tchaikovsky's songs in German or Mussorgsky's in French, although this was common enough in days when librarians still classified Russian among 'minor languages'. Today even the Swedish and Finnish songs of Sibelius and Kilpinen are, if sung at all, usually given with their original words. Yet a number of causes have conspired to keep the unsatisfactory German translations of Grieg's songs in circulation. There is the prestige of the Leipzig editions, though not all of these are now in print. There is the persistent fallacy that Grieg is a composer of *Lieder*, and that German is therefore the most appropriate medium for them. There is the

[1] *Artikler og Taler*, p. 56. Grieg made an exception to the mediocre run of translators in the case of the Leipzig poet Herzen who, though he did not know Norwegian, was sensitive to both poetical and musical values.

attitude of singers who feel that a foreign composer ought to be sung in *some* kind of foreign language, and choose German of which they have some knowledge in preference to the Scandinavian diction it would cost additional time and money to learn. There is the dearth of satisfactory English translations, since, bad as many of the German ones are, the English published alongside them are often worse: as a sample, the opening of 'The First Meeting' (see p. 177) in the official English translation in one of the Peters albums begins 'The thrill of love's first eye-glance . . .'

Fortunately we have the recorded recitals of Kirsten Flagstad and Birgit Nilsson, with English translations on leaflets. These at least serve as an introduction to Grieg's work in a field where he excelled, though still more material is needed for the full re-appraisal that is long overdue.

11 Grieg's personality and influence

The conventional portrait of Grieg as man and musician, derived from an uncritical reproduction of the statements and opinions of his earlier biographers, represents him as a frail, dreamy recluse set against a background of tourist-brochure scenery, with such talents as he possessed fully extended in the production of salon pieces and orchestral works, mostly of a programmatic kind, whose appeal is continually waning.

In reality, as his own countrymen have long been aware, he was a character to be reckoned with, and a composer whose most significant work tends to be neglected or misunderstood. Gran Bøgh describes him as

> a typical Bergenser. . . . Quicksilver in debate, his repartee was like that of a rapier and . . . his point of view was . . . always expressed with a disarming candour. [He was] irresistible when in a good mood, with his power to stimulate thought, [but] not an easy person to get on with at close quarters.[1]

His letters and journals help to fill out this more complex and lifelike picture, with their mixture of poetry, idealism, philosophy and practical commonsense, their flights of vivid description, their bursts of warm friendliness, their alternations of hopefulness and pessimism, stoical resolution and whimsical self-pity, their artistic integrity and (especially in writing to his Danish friends) a vein of earthiness that might cause some surprise if rendered faithfully into English.

[1] *Edvard Grieg* (Bergen, 1953), p. 71.

No assessment of Grieg's work can afford to leave out of account the isolated position he occupied as a nationalist composer. We have only to compare his situation with that of his Russian contemporaries, who were able to support and complement one another's efforts, to acknowledge a common source of national style and sense of mission (Glinka) and to turn for technical guidance to a common mentor (Balakirev). Grieg on the other hand belonged to what was only the second generation of Norwegian (as distinct from Dano-Norwegian) composers, the first being represented by figures of limited talent or opportunity: Ole Bull, Kjerulf, and Udbye. It is true that Grieg was only one of a large number of composers born in Norway between the late 1830s and the middle 1850s, including Winter-Hjelm (1837), Svendsen (1840), Nordraak (1842), Selmer (1844), Haarklou (1847), Capellen (1845), Agathe Backer Gröndahl (1847), Ole Olsen (1850), Iver Holter (1850) and Christian Sinding (1856). Of these, however, the most dynamic if not the most talented died young (Nordraak), or worked chiefly abroad (like Svendsen and Selmer), or chose specialized fields (like Capellen, who wrote mainly organ and church music, and Holter, who was a distinguished choral conductor), or after a promising start became reactionary in their tastes (Winter-Hjelm) or showed comparatively little interest in developing on nationalist lines (like Christian Sinding, who in any case was separated from Grieg by deep-rooted temperamental differences). In Denmark the abler composers—Gade and Hartmann—belonged to an older generation, while Grieg's contemporaries like Matthison-Hansen, Winding, and Horneman were far from being his equals in creative endowment.

Although the sense of isolation which Grieg felt most bitterly during his years in Christiania doubtless strengthened his originality and independent outlook, it combined with his frail health to produce bouts of discouragement and depression. It was also one of the causes of the restlessness that drove him to make exhausting journeys abroad, to refresh himself at the main centres of European musical life—Leipzig, Vienna and Paris—where he could meet with creative artists of the calibre of Brahms and Tchaikovsky, or to visit cities like London and Amsterdam, where he could gain the satisfaction and reassurance of hearing his major works adequately performed.

By the end of the century he had in his turn become a kind of father-figure to younger composers, more especially those outside the main German-Austrian tradition: in the Scandinavian countries, Sibelius (whose early *Karelia* Overture, Op. 10—to take only one example—is heavily indebted to Grieg's theatre music); Carl Nielsen; Sjögren, Alfvén and other Swedish nationalists; and in the English-speaking world, Delius, Grainger and MacDowell. This brings us to a consideration of the nature and extent of Grieg's legacy, based on a survey of his work as a whole and not on those parts of it which, even in his lifetime, came to be over-publicized and over-performed.

The previous chapter has attempted to demonstrate that the songs form the most valuable section of his output. The fact that most of them lie outside, or on the periphery, of the German *Lied* tradition should not in itself diminish their importance; the songs of Mussorgsky and Fauré are now evaluated on their own terms and in their own right, and not in relation to the *Lieder* of Brahms and Wolf. Similarly, we should not hestiate to claim for the Ibsen songs (Op. 25), the Vinje *Melodier* (Op. 33) and the *Haugtussa* cycle (Op. 67) a distinction of the same order as *La Bonne Chanson* and *Songs and Dances of Death*.

It would be patently absurd to make similar claims for Grieg's orchestral works, despite the unassailable position of the Piano Concerto; his useful contributions to the nineteenth-century repertory of the string orchestra, however, have already been pointed out. String-players also seem to be turning with renewed interest to the Sonatas, whose defects of form are counterbalanced by much excellent writing for the instruments and by an abundance of melodic and harmonic interest. With the purely keyboard works the situation is more difficult to clarify. With the exception of the Sonata and the *Ballade* there is nothing on a large scale, while the best of the shorter pieces are hidden away in miscellaneous collections among a great deal of unpretentious material, and the few professional pianists who have given them any attention have usually followed the composer's own example by keeping to a handful of popular favourites, not all of them representative of Grieg at his best. Only in recent years have the superior merits of the folk-music arrangements, and especially those forming homogeneous collections (Op. 66 and Op. 72), been recognized. It is here, in their choral counterparts Op. 30 and Op. 74, in the songs, and in a few other instrumental pieces, that we find the most interesting examples of that aspect of Grieg's art which gives him a special place among late-Romantic and nationalist composers, and which is reflected in the styles of many composers of the generation following his, not only in Scandinavia, but in other countries including our own: the names of Delius, Warlock, Moeran, Bax and Ireland are among those that at once come to mind. The aspect of his musical personality referred to is his deep interest in harmony.

Grieg's harmonic sense governs and informs all other factors in his musical language. His melodic outlines, for example, more often than not grow out of harmonic ideas, as when his exploration of diatonic seventh and ninth chords gives rise to 'pentatonic' formulae in such passages as the openings of the songs 'Fra Monte Pincio' and 'Blåbærli', or the orchestral 'Morning Mood' in *Peer Gynt*. The similarity of some of these melodic outlines to those of folksong was apparent to Grieg himself, and led him to a fuller realization of the 'hidden harmonies' of Norwegian traditional music; but it is necessary to repeat that his musical language was not so much derived from the latter as possessing a rare affinity and sympathy with it.

The development of Grieg's harmonic vocabulary[1] begins with his assimilation of the procedures of the Leipzig late-classical and early-Romantic traditions, including the linking of distantly related keys by means of enharmonic modulation; a charming example in an early song, his setting of H. C. Andersen's *The Rosebud*, has already been cited. But side by side with mainstream tendencies in expressive Romantic harmony we find that Grieg, even in his student days, was beginning to display some more idiosyncratic features. These include a liking for chromatic progressions—rarely in upper melodic lines, more often in the movement of his basses, most frequently of all in the inner parts; quasi-modal colour, as in the trio of the Nordraak Funeral March; an abundance of single and double pedal notes, by no means restricted to tonic and dominant; and a variety of unorthodox treatment of dissonant chords, beginning with second inversions freely approached and quitted, continuing with the emancipation of higher diatonic and chromatic discords, and culminating in the kind of parallel movement illustrated in the Krag song 'Der skreg en fugl' (see music Example 22) that was to become a commonplace of *fin-de-siècle* impressionist harmony. This last point is clearly made in Alfred Einstein's reference to the advanced nature of much of Grieg's harmonic language: 'Many of his ideas, in their boldness and tenderness, began to step over into the territory of the "impression", and a history of post-Wagnerian impressionism would have to concern itself with him as one of its ancestors, or at least as one of its godfathers.' [2]

While it is an over-simplification to attempt to explain the individuality of Grieg's national-Romantic idiom as the product

[1] The most complete studies of this subject are contained in Dag Schjelderup-Ebbe's *A Study of Grieg's Harmony* and in his *Edvard Grieg 1858–1867* which is subtitled 'with special reference to the evolution of his harmonic style'. See Appendix D, Bibliography.

[2] *Music in the Romantic Era* (New York, 1947), p. 321.

of his involvement with folk-music, it is true to say that his harmonic development reached its climax in the later folk-tune arrangements of Op. 66, Op. 72 and Op. 74. The whole relationship is best summarized in his own words:

The realm of harmonies was always my dream-world, and the relationship between my harmonic idiom and Norwegian folk-music was a mystery to myself. I have discovered that the dark profundities of our folksongs contain in all their richness unsuspected harmonic possibilities. In my folksong arrangements (Op. 66) and similar works I have attempted to give expression to my perception of the hidden harmonies of our folk-music. To this end, I have been particularly attracted towards the use of chromatic progressions in the harmonic texture.[1]

It was Grieg's misfortune never to succeed, except in his songs, his folk-music arrangements, and some of his shorter piano pieces, in devising structures that were really suited to his impressionist idiom. Throughout his life he continued to bemoan his inability to handle 'the larger forms', not realizing that these were invalid for his restricted but strongly individual processes of musical inventiveness and expression. His chamber music in particular suffers from a fundamental inconsistency of content and form; only in the G minor String Quartet did he make a resolute attempt to break away from the antecedents he had been brought up to respect, and even this was only successful to a limited extent, though Debussy, who was gifted with far greater ability to create new types of form or transmute older ones, did Grieg's Quartet the honour of using it as a working model for his own Quartet.

Incompatibility of ideas and form lies at the root of the unevenness of Grieg's output, both in quality and regularity of production, rather than the chronic ill-health and the regional isolation that were subsidiary handicaps. At moments, all too

[1] Notes to Finck, printed in *Artikler og Taler*, pp. 51–2.

rare, when his originality of harmonic language and his responsiveness to poetry or natural beauty achieve a true equilibrium, he speaks with a voice unique in the rich and varied chorus of the Romantic age. As that shrewd and sympathetic French critic, Camille Bellaigue, observed in an extended concert notice in 1890,[1] the one thing Grieg seldom lacks is an idea. Its presentation, its organic working-out may be deficient—'son talent semble fait d'imagination plus que de réflexion'—but still the idea compels attention for its own sake. Unique and irreplaceable, it often shows a remarkable power of retaining and renewing its sharp clarity and untarnished freshness in the memory and imagination.

[1] *Revue musicale*, Paris (1890), pp. 672–81. Bellaigue's just estimate of the strength and weakness of Grieg's talent may be paralleled from other acute French critics of the period. Thus Louis Laloy (*La Musique retrouvée*, pp. 85–6) recalls d'Indy's references to Grieg in his Schola Cantorum lectures: '. . . ce musicien tout en trouvailles et incapable de logique; mais plus sensible au charme d'un accord qu'aux déductions du développement.'

Appendix A Calendar

YEAR	AGE	LIFE	CONTEMPORARY MUSICIANS
1843		Edvard Grieg born, 15 June, at Bergen, Norway.	Berlioz 40; Berwald 47; Bizet 5; Borodin 10; Brahms 10; Bruckner 19; Bull 33; Franck 21; Gade 26; Gounod 34; Hartmann 38; Horneman 3; Kjerulf 28; Lalo 20; Lindblad 31; Lindeman 31; Liszt 32; Mendelssohn 34; Mussorgsky 4; Nordraak 1; Schumann 33; Smetana 19; Söderman 2; Sullivan 1; Svendsen 3; Tchaikovsky 3; Tellefsen 20; Verdi 30; Wagner 30.
1844	1		Rimsky-Korsakov born, 18 March.
1845	2		Fauré born, 12 May.
1846	3		Wegelius born, 10 Nov.
1847	4		Mendelssohn (38) dies, 4 Nov.
1848	5		
1849	6		Chopin (39) dies, 17 Oct.
1850	7		
1851	8		
1852	9		
1853	10	Grieg family moves to Landås, near Bergen.	Sjögren born, 16 June.

YEAR	AGE	LIFE	CONTEMPORARY MUSICIANS
1854	11		
1855	12		
1856	13		Kajanus born, 2 Dec.; Sinding born, 11 Jan. Schumann (46) dies, 29 July.
1857	14		Elgar born, 2 June. Glinka (54) dies, 15 Feb.
1858	15	Ole Bull visits the Griegs at Landås, and advises that Edvard be sent to study in Leipzig. Edvard's earliest extant piano pieces composed. He enters the Leipzig Conservatory in October.	
1859	16	*Neun Kinderstücke* for piano, included in the *23 Smaastykker*, most of which were probably written at Leipzig.	Spohr (75) dies, 22 Oct.
1860	17	*3 Klaverstykker*. Studies at Leipzig interrupted by severe illness.	Mahler born, 7 July; Wolf born, 13 March.
1861	18	*Vier Stücke für das Pianoforte*, Op. 1. *Vier Lieder für eine Altstimme*, Op. 2.	MacDowell born, 18 Dec.
1862	19	Grieg finishes course at Leipzig Conservatory (Easter). Concert in Bergen, 21 May.	Debussy born, 22 Aug.; Delius born, 29 Jan.
1863	20	During the next three years, Grieg lives chiefly in Denmark, meeting Gade, J. P. E. Hartmann,	

YEAR	AGE	LIFE	CONTEMPORARY MUSICIANS
		Nordraak, and the writer H. C. Andersen. *Poetiske Tonebilleder*, Op. 3.	
1864	21	Symphony in C minor. *Sex Digte*, Op. 4. Betrothal to Nina Hagerup. Beginning of close friendship with Nordraak.	Halvorsen born, 15 March; Richard Strauss born, 11 June.
1865	22	Summer at Rungsted, Denmark. *Fire Romancer*, Op. 10. *Hjertets Melodier*, Op. 5. *Humoresker*, Op. 6. Piano Sonata in E minor, Op. 7. Sonata in F for Violin and Piano, Op. 8. First visit to Italy (autumn).	Carl Nielsen born, 9 June; Sibelius born, 8 Dec.
1866	23	Death of Nordraak in Berlin, 20 March. Grieg receives the news in Rome, 6 April, and writes the Funeral March in Nordraak's memory. Overture *I Höst* completed. Grieg returns to Denmark, and seeks employment in Christiania, where he gives a concert (15 Oct.).	Busoni born, 1 April; Satie born, 17 May.
1867	24	Grieg's marriage to Nina Hagerup. Directs Christiania Harmonic Society. Sonata No. 2 in G for Violin and Piano, Op. 13. First book of *Lyric Pieces*, Op. 12.	Peterson-Berger born, 27 Feb.

YEAR	AGE	LIFE	CONTEMPORARY MUSICIANS
1868	25	Birth of daughter, Alexandra. Piano Concerto, Op. 16, written in Denmark.	Berwald (72) dies, 23 Sept.; Kjerulf (53) dies, 11 Aug.; Rossini (76) dies, 13 Nov.
1869	26	Letter of encouragement from Liszt, inviting Grieg to visit him. Holiday at Landås. Death of Alexandra. Grieg's discovery of Lindeman's collection of folk-music. Second visit to Rome.	Berlioz (66) dies, 8 March.
1870	27	Meetings with Liszt in Rome. Beginning of collaboration with Bjørnson. *Norwegian Dances and Songs*, Op. 17.	
1871	28	Cantata, *Foran Sydens Kloster*, Op. 20, and melodrama, *Bergliot*, Op. 42, both to texts by Bjørnson.	Stenhammar born, 7 Feb.
1872	29	Songs from Bjørnson's *Fiskerjenten* completed, Op. 21. Plans for opera on subject of *Olav Trygvason*. *Folkelivsbilleder*, Op. 19. *Sigurd Jorsalfar* produced, and cantata *Landkjenning* performed.	Alfvén born, 1 May; Scriabin born, 6 Jan.; Vaughan Williams born, 12 Oct.
1873	30	*Olav Trygvason* begun, but the project breaks down. Grieg made a Knight of St Olav.	Reger born, 19 March; Rachmaninov born, 1 April.
1874	31	Invitation from Ibsen to compose music for stage	Schoenberg born, 13 Sept.; Tellefsen (51) dies, 7 Oct.

YEAR	AGE	LIFE	CONTEMPORARY MUSICIANS
		production of *Peer Gynt*. Grieg obtains a government stipend, and is able to spend more time out of Christiania.	
1875	32	Death of Grieg's parents. *Ballade*, Op. 24.	Bizet (37) dies, 3 June; Ravel born, 7 March.
1876	33	*Peer Gynt* produced. Ibsen songs, Op. 25, and songs to texts by Paulsen, Op. 26. Grieg attends performances of *The Ring* at Bayreuth.	Söderman (44) dies, 10 Feb.
1877	34	Summer and winter spent in Hardanger district. Some of the Vinje songs, Op. 33, composed, and also the *Album for Male Voices*, Op. 30, and *Den Bergtekne*, Op. 32.	
1878	35	String Quartet, Op. 27, completed, but during this year and the following one little else composed.	Lindblad (77) dies, 28 Aug.; Palmgren born, 16 Feb.
1879	36	Concerts in Copenhagen, Bergen, Leipzig and Bonn.	
1880	37	Vinje Songs, Op. 33, completed. Grieg undertakes to direct Bergen *Harmonien*.	Ole Bull (70) dies, 17 Aug.
1881	38	Contract with Leipzig publishing firm of Peters. *Norwegian Dances* for piano duet, Op. 35.	Bartók born, 25 March; Mussorgsky (42) dies, 28 March.

YEAR	AGE	LIFE	CONTEMPORARY MUSICIANS
1882	39	Grieg ends his engagement with *Harmonien.*	Kodály born, 16 Dec.; Stravinsky born, 17 June.
1883	40	*Lyric Pieces,* Book II, Op. 38. *Valses-caprices,* Op. 37. Sonata in A minor for Cello and Piano, Op. 36. Concert tour in Germany and Holland; beginning of friendship with Julius Röntgen.	Wagner (70) dies, 13 Feb.; Webern born, 3 Dec.
1884	41	Holiday in Italy. Building of Troldhaugen begun. Cantata and Suite, Op. 40, for Holberg bicentenary.	Smetana (60) dies, 12 May.
1885	42	Move to Troldhaugen. Meeting with Brahms in Leipzig.	
1886	43	Mountain tour with Drachmann; song-cycle, *Fra Fjeld og Fjord,* Op. 44. *Lyric Pieces,* Book III, Op. 43.	Liszt (75) dies, 31 July.
1887	44	Sonata No. 3 in C minor for Violin and Piano, Op. 45. Meeting with Delius in Leipzig.	Borodin (54) dies, 28 Feb.; L. M. Lindeman (75) dies, May 23; Valen born, 25 Aug.
1888	45	First concert tours in England. Overture (Op. 11) rescored for Birmingham Festival. *Lyric Pieces,* Book IV, Op. 47. Meeting with Tchaikovsky in Leipzig.	
1889	46	Concerts in London,	

YEAR	AGE	LIFE	CONTEMPORARY MUSICIANS
		Paris, and Brussels. Songs to German texts, Op. 48, and Drachmann songs, Op. 49. Reconciliation with Bjørnson.	
1890	47	Concerts in Paris, Germany, and Sweden. A further gap in composition.	Franck (78) dies, 8 Nov; Gade (73) dies, 21 Dec.
1891	48	*Variations* for two pianos, Op. 51. *Lyric Pieces,* Book V, Op. 54. 25th anniversary of Grieg's first concert in Christiania.	Delibes (55) dies, 16 Jan.
1892	49	The Griegs celebrate their silver wedding.	Lalo (69) dies, 22 April; Rosenberg born, 21 June.
1893	50	*Lyric Pieces,* Book VI, Op. 57.	Gounod (75) dies, 18 Oct.; Tchaikovsky (53) dies, 6 Nov.
1894	51	Renewed song-composition: *Norge,* Op. 58 and *Elegiske Digte,* Op. 59, to texts by Paulsen; the five Krag songs, Op. 60; and the Children's Songs, Op. 61.	
1895	52	*Haugtussa* song-cycle, Op. 67. *Lyric Pieces,* Book VII, Op. 62.	Hindemith born, 16 Nov.
1896	53	*Norwegian Folk-Tunes,* Op. 66. *Lyric Pieces,* Book VIII, Op. 65.	Bruckner (72) dies, 11 Oct.
1897	54	Concerts in Vienna, Holland, and Great	Brahms (64) dies, 3 April.

YEAR	AGE	LIFE	CONTEMPORARY MUSICIANS
		Britain (London, Manchester, Birmingham, Edinburgh, Cheltenham, and Brighton).	
1898	55	Norwegian Music Festival at Bergen. *Symphonic Dances*, Op. 64. *Lyric Pieces*, Book IX, Op. 68.	
1899	56	Opening of National Theatre, Christiania. Grieg refuses invitation to Paris as mark of disapproval of conduct of the Dreyfus case.	
1900	57	Two sets of songs to texts by Otto Benzon, Op. 69 and Op. 70.	J. P. E. Hartmann (95) dies, 10 March; Sullivan (58) dies, 22 Nov.
1901	58	*Lyric Pieces*, Book X, Op. 71. Transcription of hardanger-fiddle tunes by Halvorsen, and Grieg's piano arrangement (Op. 72) begun.	Verdi (88) dies, 27 Jan.
1902	59	Concert tours, including one to Warsaw.	
1903	60	Sixtieth birthday celebrations. Successful visit to Paris, despite hostile demonstrations.	Wolf (43) dies, 22 Feb.
1904	61	Meetings with German Kaiser at Bergen.	Dvořák (63) dies, 1 May.
1905	62	*Stemninger*, Op. 73. Political crisis in Norway and Sweden ends with separation of the crowns.	

YEAR	AGE	LIFE	CONTEMPORARY MUSICIANS
1906	63	*Four Psalms*, Op. 74. Last visit to England.	Horneman (65) dies, 8 June; Wegelius (60) dies, 22 March; Shostakovich born, 25 Sept.
1907	64	Grieg dies in Bergen Hospital, 4 September.	

Appendix B Catalogue of Works

The dates given are, except when otherwise stated, those of composition.

ORCHESTRAL WORKS

OP.		DATE
—	Symphony in C minor (see under Keyboard Works, Op. 14)	1863–4
11	Concert Overture *Im Herbst* (In Autumn)[1] (see under Keyboard Works, *I Höst*, 1867)	1866, reorchestrated 1887
16	Concerto in A minor for piano and orchestra	1868, revised 1906–7
34	*Two Elegiac Melodies* for string orchestra, arranged from the Vinje Songs, Op. 33, I, Nos. 3 and 2: No. 1 *Herzwunden* (The Wounded Heart) No. 2 *Letzter Frühling* (The Last Spring)	1881
40	Suite *Fra Holbergs Tid* (From Holberg's Time) for string orchestra (see also under Keyboard Works)	1885
46	*Peer Gynt* Suite No. 1 (see under Dramatic Works) 1 *Morgenstemning* (Morning Mood) 2 *Åses Død* (The Death of Åse) 3 *Anitras Dans* (Anitra's Dance) 4 *I Dovregubbens Hall* (In the Hall of the Mountain King)	revised and reorchestrated 1888
51	*Old Norwegian Melody with Variations* (see under Keyboard Works) (*Altnorwegische Romanze mit Variationen*)	orchestrated 1900

[1] The Overture in its reorchestrated form was performed and published under the German title.

OP. DATE

53 *Zwei Melodien für Streichorchester nach eigenen Liedern* (*Two Melodies* for string orchestra, arranged from the Vinje song Op. 33, II, No. 6, and the Bjørnson song Op. 21, No. 1) 1891

No. 1 *Norsk* (Norwegian)

No. 2 *Det første Møte* (The First Meeting)

55 *Peer Gynt* Suite No. 2 (see under Dramatic Works) revised and reorchestrated 1891

1 *Bruderovet—Ingrids Klage* (The Abduction of the Bride—Ingrid's Lament)

2 *Arabisk Dans* (Arabian Dance)

3 *Peer Gynts Hjemfart* (Peer Gynt's Homecoming)

4 *Solveigs Sang* (Solveig's Song)

56 Three Orchestral Pieces from *Sigurd Jorsalfar* (see under Dramatic Works) revised and reorchestrated 1892

1 *Prelude: In the King's Hall*

2 *Intermezzo: Borghild's Dream*

3 *Homage March*

(For original Norwegian titles see Op. 22 (Dramatic Works); see also under Chamber Music for origin of *Prelude*.)

63 *Zwei nordische Weisen* (Two Scandinavian melodies for string orchestra) 1894–5

No. 1 *Im Volkston* (*In folk style*, based on a melody by Fr. Due)

No. 2 *Kuhreigen und Bauerntanz* (*Cow-call and Peasant Dance*, from Op. 17, Nos. 22 and 18)

64 *Symphonic Dances* (see also works for piano duet) 1898

No. 1 *Allegro moderato e marcato*

No. 2 *Allegretto grazioso*

No. 3 *Allegro giocoso*

No. 4 *Andante: Allegro molto e risoluto*

68 No. 4 *Aften på Højfjeldet* (Evening in the Mountains), arranged for strings, oboe, and horn

No. 5 *Bådnlåt* (Cradle Song), arranged for string orchestra 1898

OP.		DATE
—	*'Resignation'* (*Studie von Edmund Neupert*) arranged for small orchestra by Grieg, who had already (in 1895) arranged Neupert's melody, with specially-written text, *'Syng mig hjem'*, by Bjørnson, for voice with string orchestra and horn.	

DRAMATIC WORKS

22 Incidental music to Bjørnson's *Sigurd Jorsalfar* 1872

1 *Borghilds Drøm* (Borghild's Dream: Intermezzo, Act I)
2 *Ved Mandjævningen* (The Matching Game: Introduction to Act II)
3 *Kvad: Norrønafolket* (Northland Folk: male soloist and chorus)
4 *Hyldningsmarsjen* (Homage March, Act III)
5 *Kongekvadet* (The King's Song, Act III: male soloist and chorus)

23 Incidental music to Ibsen's *Peer Gynt* 1874–5; reorchestrated 1886 and later, with additional numbers. The full score published posthumously contains the following:

1 Prelude to Act I: *I Bryllupsgården* (At the Wedding)
2 *Brudefølget drager forbi* (Wedding March from Op. 19, No. 2, orch. Halvorsen)
3 *Halling* and *Springdans* (for solo violin, off-stage)
4 Prelude to Act II: *Bruderovet-Ingrids Klage* (see *Peer Gynt* Suite II)
5 *Peer Gynt and the Sæter-girls*
6 Close of the scene with the Green-clad Woman
7 *I Dovregubbens Hall* (as in Suite I, but with the addition of chorus parts)
8 *Dance of the Mountain-King's Daughter*
9 *Peer Gynt hunted by the Trolls* (melodrama, leading to Scene with the Bøyg)

OP.		DATE
	10 Prelude to Act III	
	11 *Solveig's Song* (orchestral version, as in Suite II)	
	12 *Åses Død* (The Death of Åse: as in Suite I)	
	13 Prelude to Act IV: *Morgenstemning*, as in Suite I	
	14 *The Thief and the Receiver* (scena for two solo basses and orchestra)	
	15 *Arabian Dance:* as in Suite II, but with an optional chorus of women's voices	
	16 *Anitra's Dance*, as in Suite I	
	17 *Peer Gynt's Serenade*	
	18 *Solveig's Song:* first sung version, with flutes, clarinets, and muted strings	
	19 Prelude to Act V: *Peer Gynts Hjemfart*, as in Suite II	
	20 *Solveig's Song:* second version, unaccompanied	
	21 *Scene at night, on the heath:* melodrama with chorus	
	22 *Chorale*	
	23 *Solveig's Lullaby:* voice with strings and harp.	
42	*Bergliot*, text by Bjørnson set for declamation with piano	1871
	orchestrated	1885
50	*Olav Trygvason*, unfinished opera to text by Bjørnson	1873
	orchestrated and published as *Scenes from Olav Trygvason*	1888

CHAMBER MUSIC

—	String Quartet in D minor (not extant)	? 1861
8	Sonata No. 1 in F, for Violin and Piano	1865
—	Gavotte for Violin and Piano (adapted as *Ved Mandjævningen*, Op. 22, No. 2)	1867
13	Sonata No. 2 in G, for Violin and Piano	1867
27	String Quartet in G minor	1877–8
—	Andante in C minor, for Piano, Violin, and Cello (MS.)	1878
36	Sonata in A minor, for Cello and Piano	1882–3
45	Sonata No. 3, in C minor, for Violin and Piano	1887
—	String Quartet in F (first two movements)	1891

Gavotte from 'Gavots' of Pays de Gap in S. France — feet raised.

OP. DATE

KEYBOARD WORKS

'Op. 1' *Variations on a German Melody* (not extant) — *c.* 1855
— *Smaastykker for Pianoforte* (23 pieces) (MS.) — *c.* 1858–9
— *3 Klaveerstykker* (3 Piano pieces) (MS.) — 1860
1 *Vier Stücke für das Pianoforte* (4 piano pieces) — 1861
No. 1 *Allegro con leggerezza*
No. 2 *Non allegro e molto espressivo*
No. 3 *Mazurka*
No. 4 *Allegro con moto*
3 *Poetiske Tonebilleder* (Poetic Tone-pictures) — 1863
No. 1 *Allegro ma non troppo*
No. 2 *Allegro cantabile*
No. 3 *Con moto*
No. 4 *Andante con sentimento*
No. 5 *Allegro moderato*
No. 6 *Allegro scherzando*
— *Deux pièces symphoniques* — 1864
Arrangement for piano duet of the slow movement and scherzo of the unpublished Symphony in C minor
6 *Humoresker* — 1865
No. 1 *Tempo di valse*
No. 2 *Tempo di Menuetto ed energico*
No. 3 *Allegretto con grazia*
No. 4 *Allegro alla burla*
7 Sonata for Piano, in E minor — 1865
11 *I Höst. En fantasi for Pianoforte til 4 Händer* — 1867
Piano duet version of the Concert Overture *In Autumn*. A version for two pianos, 8 hands, also exists in MS.
— *Sørgemarsj over Richard Nordraak* (Funeral March for Nordraak) — 1866
(Also arr. for military band and for brass band by Grieg)
12 *Lyriske Smaastykker* (Lyric Pieces), Book I — 1867
No. 1 *Arietta*
No. 2 *Vals* (Waltz)

OP. DATE

No. 3 *Vægtersang* (Watchman's Song)
No. 4 *Elverdans, Alfedans* (Fairy Dance)
No. 5 *Folkevise* (Folk-song)
No. 6 *Norsk* (Norwegian)
No. 7 *Stambogsblad, Albumblad* (Album Leaf)
No. 8 *Fædrelandssang* (National Song)
No. 7 had already been published in 1864. No. 8 was arranged for mixed voices to a text by Bjørnson in 1868

17 25 *Norske Folkeviser og Dandser* (25 Norwegian Folk-songs and Dances) 1870
No. 1 *Springdans* (Springlåt)
No. 2 *Ungersvenden han bad sin pige* (The swain asked his girl)
No. 3 *Springdans*
No. 4 *Niels Tallefjorn den kaute karen* (N.T. the proud fellow)
No. 5 *Jölstring* (Dance from Jölster)
No. 6 *Brulåt* (Wedding Tune)
No. 7 *Halling*
No. 8 *Aa grisen hadde eit tryne* (O, the pig had a snout)
No. 9 *Naar mit öie* . . . (When my eyes . . .)
No. 10 *Aa Ole engang i sinde* . . . (When Ole once in anger . . .)
No. 11 *På Dovrefjeld i Norge* (In the Dovre Mountains in Norway)
No. 12 *Solfager og Ormekongen* (S. and the Snake-King)
No. 13 *Reiseslatt* (or *Reiselåt*) (Wedding March)
No. 14 *Jeg sjunger med sorrigfuldt hjerte* (I sing with a sorrowful heart)
No. 15 *Den sidste laurdags kvelden* (Last Saturday evening)
No. 16 *Je veit ei lita jente* (I know a little maiden)
No. 17 *Aa kleggen han sa no te flugga si* (Said the gadfly to the fly)
No. 18 *Stabbe-Låten* (Stumping Dance)

OP.		DATE
	No. 19 *Hölje Dale*	
	No. 20 *Halling*	
	No. 21 *Sæbygga* (The man from Setesdal)	
	No. 22 *So lokka me over den myra* (Cow-calling song)	
	No. 23 *Saag du nokke kjæringa mi* (Did you see my love)	
—	*Albumblad* in B flat (published separately)	?1878
	No. 24 *Bruläten* (Wedding Tune)	
	No. 25 *Rabnabryllaup i Kraakalund* (The ravens' wedding)	
19	*Folkelivsbilleder* (Scenes from Folk Life)	1872
	No. 1 *Fjeldslåt* (Mountain Tune)	
	No. 2 *Brudefølget drar (drager) forbi* (The wedding procession passes by)	
	No. 3 *Fra Karnavalet* (From the Carnival)	
24	*Ballade i form av variasjoner over en norsk folketone* (Ballade in the form of variations on a Norwegian folk-tune)	1875
—	*Sex norske Fjeldmelodier* (Six Norwegian Mountain Tunes)	*c.* 1875
	No. 1 *Springdans*	
	No. 2 *Bådnlåt* (Lullaby)	
	No. 3 *Springdans*	
	No. 4 *Sjugur å Trollbrura* (Sigurd and the Troll-bride)	
	No. 5 *Halling*	
	No. 6 *Guten å gjenta på fjöshellen* (The boy and girl in the cow-byre)	
28	*Albumblade* (Album Leaves)	(first published 1878)
	No. 1 in A flat	1864
	No. 2 in F	1874
	No. 3 in A	1876
	No. 4 in C sharp minor	1878
29	*Improvisata over to norske folkeviser* (Improvisations on two Norwegian folk-songs)	1878
	No. 1 *Guten å gjenta på fjöshellen*	
	No. 2 *Dæ var eigong en Kungje* (There was once a King)	

OP.		DATE
35	*Firhændige Danse* (Norwegische Tänze, Norwegian Dances for piano duet)	1881
	No. 1 *Allegro marcato*	
	No. 2 *Allegretto tranquillo e grazioso*	
	No. 3 *Allegro moderato alla marcia*	
	No. 4 *Allegro molto*	
37	*Valses caprices* for piano duet	1883
	No. 1 in C sharp minor	
	No. 2 in E minor	
38	*Lyrisker Stykker* (Lyric Pieces, Neue Lyrische Stückchen)	1883
	No. 1 *Vuggevise* (Cradle Song)	
	No. 2 *Folkevise* (Folk-song)	
	No. 3 *Melodie*	
	No. 4 *Halling*	
	No. 5 *Springdans*	
	No. 6 *Elegie*	
	No. 7 *Vals* (Waltz)	
	No. 8 *Kanon*	
40	*Fra Holbergs Tid: Suite i gammel stil for Pianoforte* (From Holberg's Time: Suite in olden style . . .)	1884, published 1885
	No. 1 *Prelude*	
	No. 2 *Sarabande*	
	No. 3 *Gavotte*	
	No. 4 *Air*	
	No. 5 *Rigaudon*	
41	*Klaverstykker efter egne Sange* (Transcriptions of Grieg's own songs)	1885
	No. 1 *Vuggesang* (Cradle Song, Op. 9, No. 2)	
	No. 2 *Liden Håkon* (Little Håkon, Op. 15, No. 1)	
	No. 3 *Jeg elsker dig* (I love thee, Op. 5, No. 3)	
	No. 4 *Hun er saa hvid* (She is so white, Op. 18, No. 2)	
	No. 5 *Prinsessen* (The Princess)	
	No. 6 *Jeg giver mit digt til våren* (I give my song to the Spring, Op. 21, No. 3)	

OP.		DATE
43	*Lyriske Stykker* (Lyrische Stücke, Lyric Pieces), Book III	1886
	No. 1 *Sommerfugl* (Schmetterling, Butterfly)	
	No. 2 *Ensom Vandrer* (Einsamer Wanderer, Lonely Wanderer)	
	No. 3 *I Hjemmet* (In der Heimat, In my Native Land)	
	No. 4 *Liden Fugl* (Vöglein, Little Bird)	
	No. 5 *Erotik* (Love-song)	
	No. 6 *Til Foråret* (An den Frühling, To the Spring)	
47	*Lyriske Stykker*, Book IV	1887–8
	No. 1 *Valse-Impromptu*	
	No. 2 *Albumblad*	
	No. 3 *Melodie*	
	No. 4 *Halling*	
	No. 5 *Melankoli*	
	No. 6 *Springdans*	
	No. 7 *Elegie*	
51	*Gammel norsk melodi med variasjoner* (Old Norwegian Melody with Variations, for two pianos)	1891
	See also under Orchestral Works.	
52	*Klaverstykker efter egne Sange* (Song Transcriptions)	1891
	No. 1 *Modersorg* (Mother's Grief, Op. 15, No. 4)	
	No. 2 *Det første møte* (The First Meeting, Op. 21, No. 1)	
	No. 3 *Du fatter ei Bølgernes evige Gang* (You cannot grasp the waves' eternal course, Op. 5, No. 2)	
	No. 4 *Solveigs Sang* (from *Peer Gynt*)	
	No. 5 *Kjærlighed* (Love, Op. 15, No. 2)	
	No. 6 *Du gamle Mor* (Old Mother, Op. 33 II, No. 1)	
54	*Lyriske Stykker*, Book V	1891
	No. 1 *Gjætergut* (Hirtenknabe, Shepherd Boy)	
	No. 2 *Gangar* (Norwegischer Bauernmarsch, Processional Dance)	
	No. 3 *Troldtog* (Zug der Zwerge, Trolls' March)	
	No. 4 *Notturno*	
	No. 5 *Scherzo*	
	No. 6 *Klokkeklang* (Glockengeläute, Bell-ringing)	

OP.		DATE
57	*Lyriske Stykker*, Book VI	1893
	No. 1 *Svundne Dage* (Entschwundene Tage, Vanished Days)	
	No. 2 *Gade*	
	No. 3 *Illusion*	
	No. 4 *Hemmelighed* (Geheimnis, Secrecy)	
	No. 5 *Hun danser* (Sie tanzt, She dances)	
	No. 6 *Hjemve* (Heimweh, Home-sickness)	
62	*Lyriske Stykker* (Lyric Pieces), Book VII	1895
	No. 1 *Sylphe*	
	No. 2 *Takk* (Dank, Gratitude)	
	No. 3 *Fransk Serenade* (French Serenade)	
	No. 4 *Bækken* (Bächlein, The Brook)	
	No. 5 *Drømmesyn* (Traumgesicht, Phantom)	
	No. 6 *Hjemad* (Heimwärts, Homeward)	
64	Symphonic Dances for piano duet (Symphonische Tänze über norwegische Motive)	1898
	No. 1 *Allegro moderato e marcato*	
	No. 2 *Allegretto grazioso*	
	No. 3 *Allegro giocoso*	
	No. 4 *Andante: Allegro molto e risoluto*	
	(See also Orchestral Works)	
65	*Lyriske Stykker* (Lyric Pieces), Book VIII	1896
	No. 1 *Fra Ungdomsdagene* (Aus jungen Tagen, From Days of Youth)	
	No. 2 *Bondens Sang* (Lied des Bauern, Peasants' Song)	
	No. 3 *Tungsind* (Schwermut, Melancholy)	
	No. 4 *Salon*	
	No. 5 *I Balladetone* (In Ballad Style)	
	No. 6 *Bryllupsdag på Troldhaugen* (Hochzeitstag auf Troldhaugen, Wedding Day at Troldhaugen)	
66	*19 hidtil utrykte norske Folkeviser* (19 previously unprinted Norwegian folksongs)	1896
	No. 1 *Kulok* (Cow-call)	
	No. 2 *Det er den største Dårlighed* (It is the greatest foolishness)	

OP. DATE

No. 3 *En Konge hersked i Østerland* (A King ruled in the East)
No. 4 *Siri Dale Visen* (The Siri Dale Song)
No. 5 *Det var i min Ungdom* (It was in my youth)
No. 6 *Lok og Bådnlåt* (Call and lullaby)
No. 7 *Bådnlåt* (Lullaby)
No. 8 *Lok* (Call)
No. 9 *Liten va Guten* (It was a little lad)
No. 10 *Morgo ska du få gifte deg* (Tomorrow you shall marry)
No. 11 *Der stander to Piger* (There stood two girls)
No. 12 *Ranveig*
No. 13 *En liten grå Man* (A little grey man)
No. 14 *I Ola-dalom, i Ola-Kjønn* (In Ola Valley, in Ola Lake)
No. 15 *Bådnlåt* (Lullaby)
No. 16 *Ho vesle Astrid vor* (Little Astrid)
No. 17 *Bådnlåt* (Lullaby)
No. 18 *Jeg går i tusind Tanker* (I wander deep in thought)
No. 19 *Gjendines Bådnlåt* (Gjendine's Lullaby)

68 *Lyriske Stykker* (Lyric Pieces), Book IX 1898
No. 1 *Matrosernes Opsang* (Matrosenlied, Sailors' Chorus)
No. 2 *Bedstemors Menuet* (Grandmother's Minuet)
No. 3 *For dine Fødder* (Zu deinen Füssen, At your Feet)
No. 4 *Aften på Højfeldet* (Abend im Hochgebirge, Evening in the Mountains)
No. 5 *Bådnlåt* (An der Wiege, Lullaby)
No. 6 *Valse mélancolique*
(See also Orchestral Works)

71 *Lyriske Stykker* (Lyric Pieces), Book X 1901
No. 1 *Der var engang* (Es war einmal, Once upon a time)

OP.		DATE
	No. 2 *Sommeraften*[1] (Sommerabend, Summer Evening)	
	No. 3 *Småtrold* (Kobold, Puck)	
	No. 4 *Skovstilhed* (Waldesstille, Quiet of the Woods)	
	No. 5 *Halling*	
	No. 6 *Forbi* (Vorüber, Past and Over)	
	No. 7 *Efterklang* (Nachklänge, Recollection)	
72	*Slåtter* (Norwegian Peasant Dance-Tunes)	1902
	No. 1 *Giböens Bruremarsch* (Bridal March)	
	No. 2 *John Væstafæ's Springdans*	
	No. 3 *Bruremarsch fra Telemarken*	
	No. 4 *Haugelåt* (Tune from the Fairy Hill)	
	No. 5 *Prillaren fra Os Præstegjeld* (Tune for the Goat-horn)	
	No. 6 *Gangar (efter 'Møllargutten')*	
	No. 7 *Røtnamsknut* (Halling)	
	No. 8 *Bruremarsch (efter 'Møllargutten')*	
	No. 9 *Nils Rekve's Halling*	
	No. 10 *Knut Luråsen's Halling I*	
	No. 11 *Knut Luråsen's Halling II*	
	No. 12 *Springdans (efter 'Møllargutten')*	
	No. 13 *Håvar Gibøens Draum* (H.G.s Dream) (*Springdans*)	
	No. 14 *Tussebrurefæra på Vossevangen* (The Goblins' Bridal Procession)	
	No. 15 *Skuldalsbruri* (Skuldal's Bride) (*Gangar*)	
	No. 16 *Kivlemøyerne* (The Girls of Kivledal) (*Springdans*)	
	No. 17 *Kivlemøyerne* (The Girls of Kivledal) (*Gangar*)	
73	*Stemninger* (Stimmungen, Moods)	1905
	No. 1 *Resignation*	
	No. 2 *Scherzo-Impromptu*	
	No. 3 *Natligt Ridt* (Nächtlicher Ritt, Night Ride)	
	No. 4 *Folketone* (Folk tune from Valders)	

[1] *Sommerkvæld* in MS.

OP.		DATE
	No. 5 *Studie* (Hommage à Chopin)	
	No. 6 *Studenternes Serenade*	
	No. 7 *Lualåt* (Gebirgsweise, Mountain Tune)	
—	*Tre Klaverstykker* (Three Piano Pieces, published posthumously, 1908)	
	No. 1 *Dansen går* (Im wilden Tanz, Wild Dance)	
	No. 2 *Tusseslåt* (Gnomenzug, Gnomes' Procession) composed 1898	
	No. 3 *Hvide Skyer* (Sturmwolken, White Clouds) begun 1891, completed by Röntgen 1908	
—	Parts for second piano to solo keyboard works by Mozart:	1877
	Sonata in F (K 533)	
	Fantasia (K 475) and Sonata (K 457) in C minor	
	Sonata in C major (K 545)	
	Sonata in G (K 283)	

SOLO SONGS

—	*Den syngende Menighed* (The Singing Congregation) (N.F.S. Grundtvig) (MS.)	1860
2	*Vier Lieder für eine Altstimme und Pianoforte*	1861
	No. 1 *Die Müllerin* (Chamisso)	
	No. 2 *Eingehüllt in grauen Wolken* (Heine)	
	No. 3 *Ich stand in dunkeln Träumen* (Heine)	
	No. 4 *Was soll ich sagen?* (Chamisso)	
—	*Ich denke dein* (Goethe) (not extant)	? 1862
4	*Sex Digte* (Six Songs)	1863–4
	No. 1 *Die Waise* (Chamisso)	
	No. 2 *Morgenthau* (Chamisso)	
	No. 3 *Abschied* (Heine)	
	No. 4 *Jägerlied* (Uhland)	
	No. 5 *Das alte Lied* (Heine)	
	No. 6 *Wo sind sie hin?* (Heine)	

OP.		DATE
—	*Til Kirken hun vandrede* (To church she went) (C. Groth, trans. B. Feddersen) (MS.)	1864
5	*Hjertets Melodier* (Melodies of the Heart) (H. C. Andersen)	1864–5
	No. 1 *To brune Øine* (Two Brown Eyes)	
	No. 2 *Du fatter ei Bølgernes evige Gang* (You cannot grasp the waves' eternal course)	
	No. 3 *Jeg elsker dig!* (I love thee)	
	No. 4 *Min Tanke er et mægtigt Fjeld* (My thought is a great mountain)	
—	*Min lille Fugl* (My Little Bird) (H. C. Andersen)	1865
9	*Romancer og Ballader* (Romances and Ballads) (Andreas Munch)	
	No. 1 *Harpen* (The Harp)	1866
	No. 2 *Vuggesang* (Cradle Song)	1866
	No. 3 *Solnedgang* (Sunset)	1863
	No. 4 *Udfarten* (The Departure)	1866
—	*Vesle Gut* (Little Lad) (K. Janson) (MS.)	1866
10	*Fire Romancer* (Four Romances) (Chr. Winther)	? 1864
	No. 1 *Taksigelse* (Gratitude)	
	No. 2 *Skovsang* (Woodland Song)	
	No. 3 *Blomsternes tale* (The Flowers' Message)	
	No. 4 *Sang paa Fjeldet* (Song on the Mountain)	
15	*Romancer*	
	No. 1 *Margretes Vuggesang af 'Kongsæmnerne'* (Margaret's *Lullaby from 'The Pretenders'*) (Ibsen)	1868
	No. 2 *Kjærlighed* (Love) (H. C. Andersen)	1864
	No. 3 *Langelandsk Folkemelodi* (Folksong from Langeland) (H. C. Andersen)	? 1864
	No. 4 *Modersorg* (A Mother's Sorrow) (C. Richardt)	1870
	Odalisken synger (Song of the Odalisque) (Carl Bruun)	1870
18	*Romancer og Sange* (Romances and Songs), Book I	
	No. 1 *Vandring i Skoven* (Wandering in the Woods) (Andersen)	1869
	No. 2 *Hun er saa hvid* (She is so white) (Andersen)	1869

OP.		DATE
	No. 3 *En Digters sidste Sang* (A Poet's Last Song) (Andersen)	1869
	No. 4 *Efteraarsstormen* (The Autumn Storm) (Chr. Richardt)	1865
	Book II	
	No. 1 *Poesien* (Poesy) (Andersen)	1869
	No. 2 *Ungbirken* (The Young Birch Tree) (Jørgen Moe)	1869
	No. 3 *Hytten* (The Cottage) (Andersen)	1869
	No. 4 *Rosenknoppen* (The Rosebud) (Andersen)	1869
	No. 5 *Serenade til Welhaven* (Bjørnson) (with accompaniment for male voices)	1868
—	*Prinsessen* (The Princess) (Bjørnson)	1871
21	*Fire Digte af Bjørnson's 'Fiskerjenten'* (Four Songs from Bjørnson's 'The Fisher Lass') first published	1875
	No. 1 *Det første møte* (The First Meeting)	1873
	No. 2 *God morgen* (Good Morning)	1870
	No. 3 *Jeg giver mit digt til våren* (I give my song to the Spring)	1872
	No. 4 *Tak for dit råd* (Thanks for thy counsel)	1872
25	*Sex Digte* (Six Songs) (Ibsen)	1876
	No. 1 *Spillemænd* (Fiddlers)	
	No. 2 *En Svane* (A Swan)	
	No. 3 *Stambogsrim* (Album Verse)	
	No. 4 *Med en vandlilje* (With a Water-lily)	
	No. 5 *Borte* (Departed)	
	No. 6 *En fuglevise* (A Bird-song)	
26	*Fem Digte* (Five Songs) (John Paulsen)	1876
	No. 1 *Et Håb* (A Hope)	
	No. 2 *Jeg reiste en deilig sommerkvæld* (I walked one lovely summer evening)	
	No. 3 *Den ærgjerrige* (The Ambitious One)	
	No. 4 *Med en primula veris* (With a Primrose)	
	No. 5 *På skogstien* (On the Woodland Path)	
32	*Den Bergtekne* (The Mountain Thrall) (Old Norwegian Ballad) (for solo baritone, strings, and two horns)	1878

OP.		DATE
33	*12 Melodier til Digte af A. O. Vinje* (12 Songs to Poems by A. O. Vinje) Book I (first published 1881)[1]	
	No. 1 *Guten* (The Youth)	1880
	No. 2 *Våren* (Spring)	1880
	No. 3 *Den Sårede*[2] (The Wounded Heart)	1880
	No. 4 *Tyttebæret*[2] (The Whortleberry)	1880
	No. 5 *Langs ei Aa* (Beside a Stream)	1877
	No. 6 *Eit Syn* (A Vision)	1880
	Book II	
	No. 1 *Gamle Mor* (Old Mother)	1873
	No. 2 *Det Første* (The First)	1880
	No. 3 *Ved Rundarne* (At Rundarne)	1880
	No. 4 *Et Vennestykke* (A Broken Friendship)	1880
	No. 5 *Trudom* (Faith)	1880
	No. 6 *Fyremål* (The Goal)	1880
39	*Romancer (ældre og nyere)* (Romances, old and new)	published 1884
	No. 1 *Fra Monte Pincio* (From Monte Pincio) (Bjørnson)	1870
	No. 2 *Dulgt kjærlighed* (Hidden Love) (Bjørnson[3])	1872–3
	No. 3 *I liden høit deroppe* (High on the grassy slope) (Jonas Lie)	1884
	No. 4 *Millom rosor* (Among Roses) (Kristoffer Janson)	1869
	No. 5 *Ved en ung hustrus båre* (At the bier of a young wife) (O. P. Monrad)	1873
	No. 6 *Hører jeg sangen klinge* (When I hear that song) (Heine, trans. Nordahl Rolfsen)	1884
44	*Rejseminder fra Fjeld og Fjord* (Travel Memories from Mountain and Fjord) (Holger Drachmann)	1886

[1] Two unpublished songs to Vinje texts are *Gjenta* (The Girl), dated in the MS. 30 April 1880, and *Atteglöyma* (The Old Maid) dated 3 May 1880.

[2] Alternative spellings *Den særde, Tyteberet.*

[3] A setting of Bjørnson's *Den hvide, røde Rose,* composed in 1873, remains in MS.

OP.		DATE
	No. 1 *Prolog*	
	No. 2 *Johanne*	
	No. 3 *Ragnhild*	
	No. 4 *Ingebjørg*	
	No. 5 *Ragna*	
	No. 6 *Epilog*	
48	*Seks Sange* (Six Songs, to German original texts with Norwegian translations by Nordahl Rolfsen)	1888
	No. 1 *Gruss* (Hilsen) (Heine)	
	No. 2 *Dereinst, Gedanke mein* (Jeg ved, min Tanke) (Geibel)	
	No. 3 *Lauf der Welt* (Verdens Gang) (Uhland)	
	No. 4 *Die verschwiegene Nachtigall* (Nattergalen) (Walther von der Vogelweide)	
	No. 5 *Zur Rosenzeit* (I Rosentiden) (Goethe)	
	No. 6 *Ein Traum* (En Drøm) (Bodenstedt)	
—	*Osterlied* (Easter Song) (A. Böttger)	1889
49	*Seks Digte* (Six Poems) (Holger Drachmann[1])	1887
	No. 1 *Saa du Knøsen?* (Saw you the lad?)	
	No. 2 *Vug, O Vove* (Rock, O wave)	
	No. 3 *Vær hilset, I Damer* (Greetings, you ladies)	
	No. 4 *Nu er Aftnen lys og lang* (Now evening is light and long)	
	No. 5 *Julesne* (Christmas Snow)	
	No. 6 *Forårsregn* (Spring Rain)	
58	*Norge* (Norway) (John Paulsen)	1893–4
	No. 1 *Hjemkomst* (Homecoming)	
	No. 2 *Til Norge* (To Norway)	
	No. 3 *Henrik Wergeland*	
	No. 4 *Turisten* (The Tourist)	
	No. 5 *Udvandreren* (The Emigrant)	
59	*Elegiske Digte* (Elegiac Poems) (John Paulsen)	1894
	No. 1 *Når jeg vil dø* (When I wish to die)	

[1] A setting of Drachmann's *Du retter tidt dit Øiepaar* (Thou often turnest thine eyes), composed in 1889, remains in MS.

OP.		DATE
	No. 2 *På Norges nøgne fjelde* (On Norway's bare mountains) (after Heine)	
	No. 3 *Til En* I (To One)	
	No. 4 *Til En* II	
	No. 5 *Farvel* (Farewell)	
	No. 6 *Nu hviler du i jorden* (Now you are resting in the earth)	
60	*Digte av Vilhelm Krag* (Poems by Vilhelm Krag)	1894
	No. 1 *Liden Kirsten* (Little Kirsten)	
	No. 2 *Moderen synger: Gretchen liggor i Kiste* (The mother sings: Gretchen lies in her coffin)	
	No. 3 *Mens jeg venter* (While I wait)	
	No. 4 *Der skreg en fugl* (A bird cried)	
	No. 5 *Og jeg vil ha mig en hjertenskjær* (And I will take a sweetheart)	
61	*Barnlige Sange* (Children's Songs)	1894–5
	No. 1 *Havet* (The Sea) (Nordahl Rolfsen)	
	No. 2 *Sang til Juletræet* (Christmas Song) (Johan Krohn)	
	No. 3 *Lok* (Animal Song) (Bjørnson)	
	No. 4 *Fiskervise* (Fisherman's Song) (Petter Dass)	
	No. 5 *Kveldsang for Blakken* (Dobbin's Good-night Song)	
	No. 6 *De norske fjelde* (The Norwegian Mountains)	
	No. 7 *Fædrelands-Salme* (Fatherland Hymn) (Runeberg, trans. Rolfsen)	
67	*Haugtussa Sang-Cyclus* (Arne Garborg) (first published 1898)	1895–8
	No. 1 *Det syng* (The Singing)	
	No. 2 *Veslemøy* (Little Maid)	
	No. 3 *Blaabærli* (Bilberry Slopes)	
	No. 4 *Møte* (Meeting)	
	No. 5 *Elsk* (Love)	
	No. 6 *Killingdans* (Kidlings' Dance)	
	No. 7 *Vond Dag* (Evil Day)	
	No. 8 *Ved Gjætle-Bekken* (By the Brook)	

OP.		DATE
	(Settings of 5 other *Haugtussa* poems exist as MS. sketches in the Bergen Library: *Til deg hu hei; Sporven* (arranged for female voice choir); *Veslemøy undrast*; *Ho mor*; and *Det er haust*.)	
69	*Fem Digte* (Five Poems) (Otto Benzon)	1900
	No. 1 *Der gynger en Baad paa Bølge* (A boat is rocking on the wave)	
	No. 2 *Til min Dreng* (To my son)	
	No. 3 *Ved Moders Grav* (At Mother's grave)	
	No. 4 *Snegl, Snegl!* (Snail, Snail!)	
	No. 5 *Drømme* (Dream)	
70	*Fem Digte* (Five Poems) (Otto Benzon)	1900
	No. 1 *Eros*	
	No. 2 *Jeg lever et Liv i Længsel* (I live a life of longing)	
	No. 3 *Lys Nat* (Lucent Night)	
	No. 4 *Se dig for, naar du vælger din Vej* (Beware when you choose your way)	
	No. 5 *Digtervise* (Poet's Song)	
	(Another song to words by Benzon, *Til en Djævel* (To a Devil), remains in MS., dated 19 February 1900.)	
—	*Ave Maris Stella*	1898
	(see also under Choral Works)	
—	*Efterladte Sange* (Posthumous Songs, Hansen Edition, Book I)	
	No. 1 *Den blonde Pige* (The Fair-haired Girl) (Bjørnson)	1867
	No. 2 *Dig elsker jeg!* (I love thee!) ('Caralis')	1865
	No. 3 *Taaren* (The Tear) (Andersen)	1865
	No. 4 *Soldaten* (The Soldier) (Andersen)	1865
	(Hansen Edition, Book II)	
	No. 1 *På Hamars Ruiner* (Over Hamar's Ruins) (Vinje)	1880
	No. 2 *Jeg elsket . . .* (I loved . . .) (Bjørnson)	1891
	No. 3 *Simpel Sang* (Simple Song) (Drachmann)	1889
	No. 4 *Suk* (Sigh) (Bjørnson)	1873

OP.		DATE
	No. 5 *Julens Vuggesang* (Christmas Lullaby) (Adolf Langsted)	1900
	No. 6 *Der Jäger* (The Huntsman) (Wilhelm Schulz)	1905 or earlier
—	*Gentlemen-Menige* (Gentlemen-Rankers) Kipling, trans. Rosenkrantz Johnsen (MS. only, 17 December 1900)	
—	*Til L. M. Lindemans Sølvbryllup* (For L. M. Lindeman's silver wedding) (MS. only, September 1873)	

CHORAL WORKS

OP.		DATE
—	Til Studentersangforeningen i København (*4 Sange for Mandsstemmer*) (4 Songs for Male Voices, written for the Copenhagen Students' Choral Society) (MS.)	1863–4
	No. 1 *Norsk Krigssang* (Norwegian War Song) (Wergeland)	
	No. 2 *Fredriksborg* (C. Richardt)	
	No. 3 *Studereliv* (Student Life) (Richardt)	
	No. 4 *Den sildige Rose* (The Late Rose) (A. Munch)	
—	*Rückblick* (Chorus with piano) (not extant)	? 1863
—	*Danmark* (Andersen) (Mixed voice chorus with piano)	1864
—	*Bjørnskytten* (The Bear Hunt) (Jørgen Moe) for male voice quartet	1867
—	*Aftenstemning* (Evening Mood) (Jørgen Moe) for male voice quartet	1867
—	*Den norske Sjømand* (The Norwegian Sailor) (Bjørnson) for male voices	1868
—	*Serenade to Welhaven* (Bjørnson) See Solo Songs, Op. 18, II, No. 5	1868
—	*Til Karl Hals ved 25 Aarsjubilæet* (Cantata for the 25th Anniversary of Hals Brothers' Piano Factory) for tenor solo, mixed voice choir, and pianos (Bjørnson)	1873
—	*Kantate ved Afsløringen af Christiemonumentet* (Cantata for the Unveiling of the Christie Monument) (A. Munch) (Choir and Military Band)	1868

OP.		DATE
20	*Foran Sydens Kloster* (Before a Southern Convent) (Bjørnson) for soprano and contralto soloists, women's chorus and orchestra	1871
30	*Album for Mandssang (Kor og Soli) frit efter norske Folkeviser* (Album for Male Voices (choir and soloists) freely arranged from Norwegian folksongs) No. 1 *Jeg lagde mig så sildig* (I lay down so late) No. 2 *Bådn-Låt* (Children's Song) No. 3 *Torø liti* (Little Torø) No. 4 *Halling* No. 5 *Dæ æ den største Dårleheit* (It is the greatest foolishness) No. 6 *Går e ut ein Kveld* (When I go out in the evening) No. 7 *Han Ole* No. 8 *Halling* No. 9 *Deiligste blandt Kvinder* (Fairest Among Women) No. 10 *Den store, hvide Flok* (The Great White Host) No. 11 *Fantegutten* (The Gipsy Lad) No. 12 *Røtnams Knut*	1877–8
31	*Landkjenning* (Land-sighting) (Bjørnson) for baritone solo, male voice chorus, orchestra, and organ	1872, revised 1881
—	*Stille nu!* (Funeral song for J. S. Welhaven) (Jørgen Moe) (The same music, to a text by the composer's brother, John Grieg, was sung at the funeral of Alexander Grieg on 19 September 1875.)	1873
—	*Til Generalkonsul Chr. Tønsberg på hans 60-årige Fødselsdag* (Johan Bøgh)	1873
—	*Kantata ved Kjerulfstøttens Afsløring* (Cantata for the Unveiling of the Kjerulf Statue) (Andreas Munch) (Male voices) (MS.)	1874

OP.		DATE
—	*Opsang for Frihedsfolket i Norden* (Chorus for the Supporters of Freedom in Scandinavia) (Bjørnson)	1874
—	*Vort Løsen* (Our Watchword) (Olav Lofthus) (Male voices) (dedicated to the Bergen Manual Workers' Choral Society)	1883
—	*Min deiligste Tanke* (My finest thought) (Olav Lofthus) (Male voices)	1881
—	*Trondhjem's Velkomsthilsen til Sangerne* (Trondhjem's Greeting to the Singers) (Sigv. Skavlan) (Male voices)	1883
—	*Kantate ved Holbergmonumentets Afsløring* (Cantata for the Unveiling of the Holberg Memorial) (male voices) (Nordahl Rolfsen)	1884
—	*Kristianiensernes Sangerhilsen* (Greeting from Christiania's Singers) (Jonas Lie) (Male voices)	1896
—	*Valgsang* (Election Song) (Bjørnson) (Male voices)	1894
—	*Flagvise* (Song of the Flag) (Johan Brun) (Male voices)	1893
—	*Vestanvejr* (Westerly Wind) (Jonas Dahl) (MS.) (Male voices)	1896
—	*Ave Maris Stella* Arrangement for mixed voice choir of the solo song	1898
74	*4 Salmer fritt efter gamle norske Kirkemelodier* (4 Psalms, freely arranged from old Norwegian Church Tunes) for mixed voice choir with baritone solo No. 1 *Hvad est du dog skjøn* (How fair is thy face) (Laurentius Laurentii) No. 2 *Guds Søn har gjordt mig fri* (God's Son hath made me free) (Brorson) No. 3 *Jesus Christus er opfaren* (Jesus Christ hath ascended) (Hans Thommisøn) No. 4 *I Himmelen* (In Heaven) (Brorson)	1906

Appendix C Personalia

Abraham, Max (1831–1900), head of publishing firm of Peters in Leipzig. Became a regular correspondent and a personal friend of Grieg's.

Andersen, Hans Christian (1805–75), Danish author, known chiefly through his fairy tales, but who also wrote novels and lyric poems, several of which were set by Grieg.

Benzon, Otto (1856–1927), Danish chemist, dramatist, poet and sportsman. Author of the texts of Grieg's songs, Op. 69 and Op. 70.

Beyer, Frants (1851–1918), native of Bergen. Studied law and held administrative posts. An amateur musician who at one time studied piano with Grieg in Christiania. Later became one of the composer's closest friends and his nearest neighbour, having a villa at Næsset, opposite Troldhaugen. Grieg's letters to Beyer (see Bibliography) are valuable source material.

Bjørnson, Bjørnstjerne (1832–1910), Norwegian poet, playwright, orator and leading patriot. One of the most influential figures of his time in Norwegian literature, social life and politics. Greatly admired at home and abroad for his liberal outlook and fearless outspokenness. Frequently collaborated with Grieg in songs and stage works. His son Bjørn became a noted actor and theatre director, and his daughter Bergliot married Ibsen's son.

Brodsky, Adolf (1851–1929), Russian-born violinist and conductor. Successively professor at Leipzig Conservatory, leader of the Damrosch Orchestra in New York (1890–94), leader of the Hallé Orchestra (1895) and Principal of the Royal Manchester College of Music.

Bull, Ole Bornemann (1810–80), Norwegian violinist, born at Bergen. Played in Paris and other European centres. Founded first Norwegian national theatre in 1850. Made several tours in America, where he attempted to found a colony for Norwegian emigrants (Oleana), and took American citizenship in 1853. His more ambitious compositions for violin and orchestra are now forgotten and remain in manuscript, but his melody *Sæterjentens Søndag* (The Herd-girl's Sunday) ranks only second to Nordraak's national hymn in popularity.

Delius, Frederick (1862–1934), was strongly attracted by Scandinavian literature and scenery and by the music of Grieg, whom he first met in 1887. Grieg encouraged him to devote himself entirely to music, and invited him to join in mountain excursions in Norway.

Drachmann, Holger (1846–1908), Danish poet and novelist, amateur artist and lover of music. Accompanied Grieg on a tour in the Hardanger district, and wrote the texts of the songs Op. 44 (*Fra Fjeld og Fjord*) and Op. 49.

Due, Fredrik (1853–1906), Norwegian diplomat, from 1890 to 1899 *Ministre plénipotentiaire* for Sweden and Norway in Paris. Amateur musician who published songs and piano pieces; Grieg's Op. 63, No. 1 is based on one of his melodies.

Gade, Niels Vilhelm (1817–90), Danish composer and organist. Studied in Copenhagen and Leipzig, where he was closely associated with Mendelssohn. Returned to Copenhagen in 1848, and worked as church musician, conductor, and director of the Conservatory.

Garborg, Arne (1851–1925), Norwegian poet, novelist and journalist. Became leader of the *landsmål* movement, and wrote his *Haugtussa* in that form of Norwegian.

Grainger, Percy Aldridge (1882–1961), Australian-American pianist, composer and collector of English and Scandinavian folk music. Grieg, near the end of his life, considered Grainger the ideal interpreter of his piano music, and Grainger was strongly influenced by Grieg in his own arrangements of folk-tunes.

Gröndahl, Agathe Backer (1847–1907), Norwegian pianist and composer. Studied with Lindeman and Kjerulf. Played Grieg's Concerto in various European centres, including London. Her son Fridtjof Backer-Grøndahl also was a noted Grieg interpreter.

Gundersen, Laura (1832–98), native of Bergen, became a leading actress. Grieg's melodrama *Bergliot*, in which she declaimed Bjørnson's poem, was dedicated to her.

Halvorsen, Johan (1864–1935), Norwegian violinist, conductor and composer. Among his appointments were the conductorship of *Harmonien* (Bergen) and that of the orchestra of the National Theatre, Christiania.

Hartmann, Johann Peter Emilius (1805–1900), Danish composer, grandson of Johann Ernst H., to whom the Danish national song *King Christian* ... is attributed. J. P. E. Hartmann composed operas, ballets, a symphony and numerous other instrumental and vocal works, some of which may have influenced Grieg's earlier style.

Horneman, C. F. Emil (1841–1906), Danish composer, fellow-student with Grieg at Leipzig and known chiefly for his opera *Aladdin*.

Ibsen, Henrik (1828–1906), Norwegian poet and dramatist. Grieg set several of his earlier poems, and provided incidental music for the first stage production of his drama *Peer Gynt* in 1876.

Josephson, Ludvig Oskar (1832–99), Swedish dramatic author and Director of the Christiania Theatre 1873–7.

Kjerulf, Halfdan (1815–68), Norwegian composer and teacher; studied in Christiania with Carl Arnold, in Copenhagen with Gade and in Leipzig with Richter. Composed original songs and piano pieces and folk-music arrangements.

Krag, Vilhelm (1876–1933), poet and novelist associated with the southern coastland region of Norway. Influenced by Danish poets Holger Drachmann and J. P. Jacobsen. Grieg set five of his poems in Op. 60.

Lammers, Thorvald (1841–1921), Norwegian singer, conductor and composer. Especially admired for his interpretations of Norwegian folksongs and of Grieg's Vinje songs. Dedicatee of the Drachmann songs (Op. 49).

Lie(-Nissen), Erika (1845–1903), Norwegian pianist, friend of Nordraak and one of the earliest performers of Grieg's Concerto.

Lindeman, Ludvig Mathias (1812–87), Norwegian composer (chiefly of church music), virtuoso organist and collector of folk-music. Son of organist of Trondhjem Cathedral, and himself became organist of Our Saviour's Church, Christiania. The first part of his monumental folk-music collection, *Ældre og nyere Fjeldmelodier*, appeared in 1853.

Matthison-Hansen, Gottfred (1832–1909), Danish organist and composer. In 1865 formed with Grieg, Horneman and Nordraak the music society *Euterpe* for the performance of Scandinavian works.

Munch, Andreas (1811–84), Norwegian poet. From 1866 lived chiefly in Copenhagen, where he may have met Grieg.

Neruda, Wilma (or *Wilhelmina*) (1839–1911), Moravian-born violinist. Married the Swedish composer and conductor Ludvig Norman and after his death became, in 1888, the second wife of Sir Charles Hallé.

Neupert, Edmund (1842–88), Norwegian pianist, to whom Grieg dedicated his Piano Concerto. In 1868 became professor of piano at Copenhagen Conservatory.

Nordraak, Rikard (1842–66), Norwegian composer, cousin of Bjørnson, to whose national hymn *Ja, vi elsker dette Landet* he composed the music. His meeting with Grieg in Copenhagen has always been regarded as a turning-point in Grieg's career.

Paulsen, John (1851–1924), native of Bergen, poet and dramatist and the author of several books of memoirs. Grieg composed three sets of songs to his verses (Op. 26, Op. 58 and Op. 59).

Ravnkilde, Niels (1823–90), Danish pianist who settled in Rome as a private teacher of piano and became president of the Scandinavian Society there.

Reinecke, Carl (1824–1910), German pianist, conductor and composer. Professor of composition at the Leipzig Conservatory and conductor of the Gewandhaus concerts.

Rolfsen, Nordahl (1848–1928), native of Bergen, author and publisher of educational books which for many years had wide circulation in Norway.

Röntgen, Julius (1855–1932), son of a Dutch violinist who became professor at Leipzig and leader of the Gewandhaus orchestra. Julius was born in Leipzig, but settled in Amsterdam as composer and conductor, becoming director of the Conservatory there in 1914. He was one of Grieg's most intimate friends, and wrote a biography of him.

Schjelderup, Gerhard (1859–1933), Norwegian composer trained in Paris under Massenet; works include several operas to Norwegian texts and two important books: *Norges Musikhistorie* (with O. M. Sandvik, 1921) and *Ed. Grieg* (with W. Niemann, 1908).

Selmer, Johan Peter (1844–1910), Norwegian composer and conductor of the Christiania Music Society from 1883 to 1886. Spent many years in Paris and other southern European centres.

Sgambati, Giovanni (1841–1914), Italian composer and pianist, pupil of Liszt. Grieg thought highly of his chamber music.

Sinding, Christian (1856–1941), Norwegian violinist, pianist and composer. At one time a pupil of Lindeman, and later studied in Leipzig and Munich. Unlike Grieg, achieved considerable success in the larger classical forms, but showed fewer nationalist tendencies.

Tellefsen, Thomas Dyke Acland (1823–74), Norwegian pianist and composer, born in Trondhjem but spent most of his life in Paris, where he was at one time a pupil of Chopin.

Vinje, Aasmund Olavsson (1818–70), Norwegian poet and prose author, born of peasant stock in Telemark. Mainly self-educated, engaged in teaching, journalism, politics and literature, and became the first important writer in *landsmål*.

Welhaven, Johan (1807–73), Norwegian poet and literary historian.

Wergeland, Henrik (1808–45), the greatest Norwegian poet of the earlier Romantic period.

Winding, August (1835–99), Danish composer and pianist. Travelled with Grieg to Italy in 1869.

Winter Hjelm, Otto (1837–1931), Norwegian organist and composer, music critic of the Christiania newspaper *Aftenposten*. Grieg's collaborator in an attempt to found a school of music in the Norwegian capital.

Appendix D Bibliography

Abraham, Gerald (ed.), *Grieg, a Symposium.* (London, 1948.)

Bauer, W., 'Die Harmonik in den Werken von Edvard Grieg'. (Dissertation, Vienna, 1931.)

Behrend, W., *Niels W. Gade.* (Leipzig, 1918.)

Berg, Sigurd, 'Nogle brev fra Edvard Grieg til Niels Ravnkilde'. (*Ord och Bild,* No. 4, Stockholm, 1947.)

Bergen Public Library, *Katalog over Griegutstillingen 22. Mai–7. Juni 1962.*

Björndal, Arne, *Norsk folkemusikk.* (Bergen 1952.)

Beyer, Marie, *Breve fra Edvard Grieg til Frants Beyer 1872–1907.* (Christiania, 1923.)

Bull, Francis, *Tradisjoner og minner.* (Oslo, 1945.)

Bull, Maria: *Minder fra Bergens første nationale scene.* (Bergen, 1905.)

Bøe, Finn, *Trekk av Edvard Griegs personlighet.* (Oslo, 1949.)

Cappelen, G., *Die Freiheit und Unfreiheit der Töne und Intervalle als Kriterium der Stimmführung nebst einem Anhang: Grieg-Analysen als Bestätigungsnachweis und Wegweiser der neuen Musiktheorie.* (Leipzig, 1904.)

Cederblad, J., *Edvard Grieg.* (Stockholm, 1948.)

Cherbuliez, A. E., *Edvard Grieg: Leben und Werk.* (Zürich, 1947.)

Closson, Ernest, *Edvard Grieg et la musique scandinave.* (Paris, 1892.)

Cuypers, Jules, *Grieg.* (Haarlem, 1948.)

Dale, Kathleen, 'Edvard Grieg's Pianoforte Music'. (*Music and Letters,* Vol. XXIV, 1943.)

Day, L. A., *Grieg.* (New York, 1945.)

Derry, T. K., *A Short History of Norway.* (2nd edition, London, 1968.)

Desmond, Astra, 'Grieg's Songs'. (*Music and Letters,* Vol. XXII, 1941.)

Downs, B. W., *Modern Norwegian Literature 1860–1918*. (Cambridge, 1966.)

Eggen, E., 'Grieg og Nordraak'. (*Syn og Segn*, Oslo, 1912.)

Feddersen, B. J., 'Fra Griegs Ungdom'. (*Illustreret Tidende*, Copenhagen, 1899.)

Fellerer, K. G., *Edvard Grieg*. (Potsdam, 1942.)

Finck, Henry T., *Edvard Grieg*. (New York and London, 1906.)
Grieg and his Music. (New York, 1929.)
Song and Song Writers. (New York, 1900.)

Fischer, Kurt von, *Griegs Harmonik und die nordländische Folklore*. (Berne and Leipzig, 1938.)

Fischer, Trygve, 'Den instrumentale viseform hos Grieg'. (*Norsk Musikkgranskning Årbok 1942*, Oslo, 1943.)

Foss, Hubert, 'Edvard Hagerup Grieg'. (*The Heritage of Music*, Vol. III, Oxford, 1951.)

Freiheiter, I. J., 'Harmonica Edwarda Griega'. (Dissertation, Lwow, 1931 : extract ed. Eggen, E., in *Tonekunst*, Oslo, 1932.)

Gaukstad, Øystein, 'Edvard Grieg 1843–1943 : en bibliografi'. (*Norsk Musikkgranskning Årbok 1942*, Oslo, 1943.)
(ed.) *Edvard Grieg: Artikler og Taler*. (Oslo, 1957.)

Gilman, Lawrence, 'The Place of Grieg'. (*Nature in Music*, New York, 1914.)

Greni, L., 'Grieg og folkemusikken'. (*Syn og Segn*, Oslo, 1954.)
Rikard Nordraak. (Oslo, 1942.)

Grainger, P. A., 'Grieg's last opus'. (*Hinrichsen's Musical Year Book, Vol. VII*, London, 1952.)
'Personal Recollections of Grieg'. (*Musical Times, Vol. XLVIII, No. 777*, London, Nov. 1907.)

Greig, J. Russell, 'Grieg and his Scottish Ancestry'. (*Hinrichsen's Musical Year Book, Vol. VII*, London, 1952.)

Grieg, Harald, *En Forleggers Erindringer*. (2nd ed., Oslo, 1971.)

Grinde, Nils, 'Halfdan Kjerulfs klavermusikk'. (*Norsk Musikkgranskning Årbok 1959–61*, Oslo, 1961.)

Grønwold, H. A., *Norske Musiker*. (Christiania, 1883.)

Gurvin, Olav, 'Three Compositions from Edvard Grieg's Youth'. (*Norsk Musikkgranskning Årbok 1951–3*, Oslo, 1953.)
'Rikard Nordraaks musikk . . .' (*Syn og Segn*, Oslo, 1942.)

Hammerich, Angul, *J. P. E. Hartmann*. (Copenhagen, 1916.)
Hauch, Gunnar, *Breve fra Grieg: et Udvalg*. (Copenhagen, 1922.)
Horton, John, *Grieg*. (London, 1950.)
'Grieg'. (*Grove's Dictionary of Music and Musicians*, 5th edition, London, 1954.)
'Grieg's Slåtter for Pianoforte'. (*Music and Letters*, Vol. XXVI, 1945.)
'Ibsen, Grieg, and *Peer Gynt*'. (*Music and Letters*, Vol. XXVI, 1945.)
'Scandinavian Music: a Short History'. (London, 1963.)
'Johan Severin Svendsen'. (*The Listener*, 5 October 1944.)
Hove, R., *J. P. E. Hartmann*. (Copenhagen, 1934.)
Hurum, H. J., *I Edvard Griegs verden*. (Oslo, 1959.)
Jacobs, R. L., 'Grieg and the Sonata'. (*The Listener*, 19 July 1945.)
Jefferson, Alan, *Delius*. (London, 1972.)
Jordan, S., *Edvard Grieg. En oversikt over hans liv og verker*. (Bergen, 1954.) (*Supplement*, Bergen, 1959.)
Kahl, W., 'Grieg'. (*Die Musik in Geschichte und Gegenwart*, Cassel and Basel, 1956.)
Kortsen, Bjarne, *Four Unknown Cantatas by Grieg* (Bergen, 1972.)
'Grieg's String Quartet and Robert Heckmann'. (*Music and Letters*, Jan. 1968.)
Grieg the Writer. 2 vols. (Bergen, 1973.)
Kretzschmar, H., *Griegs Lyrische Stücke: eine Würdigung*. (Preface to collected edition, Leipzig, 1902.)
Lee, E. Markham, *Grieg*. (London, 1908.)
Laloy, L. *La Musique retrouvée*. (Paris, 1928.)
Levasheva, O. E. *Edvard Grig*. (Moscow, 1962.)
Lindeman, L. M., *Ældre og nyere norske Fjeldmelodier samlede og bearbeidede for Pianoforte*. (Christiania, 1853–1907: facsimile reprint, ed. O. M. Sandvik.)
Linge, O., *Ole Bull*. (Oslo, 1953.)
Mason, D. G., *From Grieg to Brahms*. (New York, 1902 and 1904.)
Monrad Johansen, D., *Edvard Grieg*. (Oslo, 1934, 1943, and 1956. English trans. by Madge Robertson, New York, 1938 and 1945.)

Niemann, W., 'Kjerulf und Grieg'. (*Die nordische Klaviermusik*, Leipzig, 1918.)
Die Musik Skandinaviens. (Leipzig, 1906.)
Platzhoff-Lejeune, E., 'Aus Briefen Edvard Griegs an einen Schweizer'. (*Die Musik*, Jhrg. VII, No. 2, 1907–8.)
Rokseth, Yvonne, *Grieg*. (Paris, 1933.)
Röntgen, Julius, *Grieg*. (The Hague, 1930.)
'Edvard Griegs musikalischer Nachlass'. (*Die Musik*, Jhrg. VII, No. 5, 1907–8.)
Sandvik, O. M., 'Griegs Melodikk'. (*Norske Musikkgranskning Årbok 1942*, Oslo, 1943.)
'L. M. Lindeman og Edvard Grieg in deres forhold til norsk folkemusikk'. (*Syn og Segn*, Oslo, 1922.)
L. M. Lindeman og Folkemelodien, (Oslo, 1950.)
(see also under *Lindeman, L. M.*)
'Folk Music (Norwegian)' (*Grove's Dictionary of Music and Musicians*, 5th edition, London, 1954.)
Sawyer, F., 'The Tendencies of Modern Harmony as Exemplified in the Works of Dvořák and Grieg.' (Proceedings of the Musical Association, Vol. XXII, London, 1895–6.)
Schjelderup, G., *Edvard Grieg og hans Værker*. (Copenhagen, 1903.)
and Niemann, W., *Ed. Grieg. Biographie und Würdigung seiner Werke*. (Leipzig, 1908.)
Schjelderup-Ebbe, Dag, *A Study of Grieg's Harmony. With special Reference to his Contributions to Musical Impressionism*. (Oslo, 1953.)
Edvard Grieg 1858–1867. (Oslo and London, 1964.)
'En ukjent artikkel om Nordraak av Grieg'. (*Aftenposten*, Oslo, 5 July, 1961.)
'Grieg och folktonen'. (*Musikrevy*, Stockholm, 1957.)
'Neue Ansichten über die früheste Periode Edvard Griegs'. (*Dansk Aarbog for Musikforskning*, 1961.)
Smith, M., *The Life of Ole Bull*. (Princeton, 1943.)
Stein, R. H., *Grieg*. (Berlin and Leipzig, 1921.)
Stoecklin, P. de, *Grieg*. (Paris, 1926.)
Tchaikovsky, P. 'Diary of my Tour in 1888'. (In *Tchaikovsky; his life and works*, trans. Rosa Newmarch, London, 1908.)

Törnblom, F. H., *Grieg*. (Stockholm, 1943.)
Torsteinson, S., *Troldhaugen* (Bergen, 1966.)
Tveitt, G., 'Edvard Grieg og norsk Folkemusikk'. (*Dansk Musiktidsskrift*, June 1943.)
Wallner, Bo, *Vår tids musik i Norden*. (Stockholm, 1968.)
Winter-Hjelm, O., 'Om Norsk Musik og nogle Kompositioner af Edvard Grieg'. (*Morgenbladet*, Christiania, 14 and 16 Sept., 1866.)
Zschinsky-Troxler, Elsa von, *Edvard Grieg: Briefe an die Verleger der Edition Peters 1866–1907*. (Leipzig, 1932.)

ADDENDA

Bird, John, *Percy Grainger*. (London, 1976.)
Carley, Lionel, *Delius: the Paris Years*. (London, 1975.)
Fuller-Maitland, J. A., Obituary of Edvard Grieg, in *Journal of the Folk Song Society*, No. 11. (London, 1907.)
Gaukstad, Øystein, 'Grieg som lystspillkomponist', in *Cursus Librorum*, No. 9. (Oslo, 1971.)
Toner fra Valdres. (Leira, Valdres, 1977.)
Gérard-Arlberg, Gilles, 'Nr. 6 rue Vercingétorix', in *Konstrevy*. (Stockholm, 35/2, 1958, pp. 64–8.)
Schjelderup, Gerik, *Gerhard Schjelderup*. (Oslo, 1976.)

Appendix E The Grieg Collection, Bergen, Norway

The Grieg Collection (*Griegsamlingen*) bequeathed by the composer to the Bergen Public Library includes the following materials:

1 About 100 manuscripts, some of which have never been published. Grieg made it a condition of the bequest that these should remain unpublished and should not be circulated outside the Bergen Public Library;

2 About 5,000 letters to or from Edvard Grieg;

3 The composer's personal music library, consisting of about 2,700 volumes, some with his own annotations;

4 A large collection of first editions and pirated publications of Grieg's works.

Index

Abraham, Gerald, 70n, 152n, 164n
Abraham, Max, 53, 62, 63, 67, 86, 93, 234
Ældre og nyere Fjeldmelodier, 33, 135
Alfvén, 198
Alnæs, 100
Andersen, Hans Christian, 17, 21, 26, 33, 69, 165, 170, 172, 174, 234
Arnljot Gelline, 38, 39, 158
Artikler og Taler, vii, 36n, 40n, 100n, 194n, 201n

Bach, J. S., 25, 90, 92, 116, 148
Backer Gröndahl, Agathe, 29, 100, 197, 236
Backer-Grøndahl, Fridtjof, 116, 236
Bartók, 110, 125, 127,
Bax, 199
Beethoven, 5, 7, 9, 13, 26, 29, 60, 88, 92
Before a Southern Convent (Op. 20), 38, 103, 158
Bellaigue, Camille, 77, 77n, 202, 202n
Bellini, 24
Benzon, Otto, 95, 165, 192, 234
Berg, Theresa, 11
Bergen, 1, 2–3, 5, 6, 9n, 10, 11, 13–14, 13n, 15, 16, 17–18, 32, 45, 46, 62, 64–6, 73–4, 96, 98–102, 111, 117, 121, 150, 167n
Bergen Festival, 8, 99–100, 128
Bergen Public Library, 9, 137, 164, 191n, 245
Bergenposten, 48–50
Berggreen, A. P., 121
Bergliot (Op. 42), 38, 77, 92, 116, 154–5, 236
Bergslien, Nils, 67, 69
Bergtekne, Den (Op. 32), 56, 66–7, 158–61, 181
Berlin, 22, 23
Bernsdorf, 58–9, 69, 70n,
Beyer, Frants, 39n, 52, 64n, 65, 66, 67n, 68, 71, 73, 73n, 81, 82, 84, 90, 93, 93n, 95, 119, 123, 234
Bigeon, Maurice, 77, 105n
Birmingham Festival, 25, 74–5, 150
Bizet, 73, 77
Bjørnson, Bjørn, 45
Bjørnson, Bjørnsterne, 6, 14, 18, 16, 21, 22, 26, 28, 30, 30n, 36, 37–39, 41–2, 41n, 57n, 61, 75–6, 77, 79–80, 86, 102, 103, 111, 113, 115, 121, 140, 154, 156, 158, 165, 166, 175, 176, 177, 178, 234
Bloch, Andreas, 67
Bøgh, Gran, 196

Bøgh, Johan, 99
Bournonville, 15
Brahms, 50, 72, 72n, 87–8, 126, 131, 142, 169, 186, 187, 198
Brandes, Georg, 42
Brema, Maria, 116
Bridge, Frederick, 74n
Brodsky, Adolf, 69, 71–2, 72n, 88, 97–8, 101, 101n, 108, 118, 118n, 234
Brodsky, Anna, 158, 181n
Bull, Frances, 102n
Bull, Ole, 3, 5–7, 14, 17–18, 19, 20, 33, 34, 42, 46, 58, 60, 73, 75, 76, 121, 122, 139, 142, 176, 197, 235
Bull, Schak, 16n
Busoni, 88

Cappellen, 197
Carreño Tagliapietra, Teresita, 110–11
Casals, Pablo, 116
Chamisso, 17, 167, 172
Chopin, 5, 9, 132, 138, 146
Choral works:
  Album for Male Voices (Op. 30), 56, 118, 119, 120, 133, 134, 199
  Bear Hunt, The, 27
  Cantata for the unveiling of the Christie monument, 175n
  Cantata for the unveiling of the Kjerulf statue, 175n
  Four Psalms (Op. 74), 90, 115, 120, 133–5, 199, 201
  Hals Cantata, The, 30, 30n
  Land-sighting, 116
  Norse Seaman, The, 30
  Peace Oratorio, 80
  Serenade to Welhaven, 30
  See also *Before a Southern Convent*
Christiania, 13n, 15, 25, 27, 28, 29, 32, 39, 42–3, 45, 47, 53, 59, 61, 66, 83, 99, 102
Christiania Music Society, 21, 53, 99
Christiania Philharmonic Society, 26, 29, 40
Christiania School of Music, 26
Christiania Theatre and National Theatre, 26, 43, 43n, 102, 107, 111
Christie, W. F. K. 1, 30n
Clementi, 7
Colonne, Edouard, 63, 102, 103, 103n
Concertgebouw Orchestra, Amsterdam, 98, 99, 101, 115–16
Copenhagen, 14, 15, 18, 21n, 23, 25, 31, 44, 45, 59, 66, 67–8, 93, 128, 137, 169
'Cow-call' (string orchestra), 122
Cowen, Frederick, 73
Cuypers, Jules, 17n
Czerny, 7

Dahl, J. C., 3
Dale, Kathleen, 146n
Dale, Knut, 107, 108–9, 123, 124n
Dass, Petter, 1, 187
David, Ferdinand, 9
Debussy, 63, 78, 104–7, 104n, 127, 143, 144, 151, 155, 163–4, 201
Delibes, 147
Delius, 38, 72, 72n, 74, 81, 96, 96n, 104, 123, 151, 198, 199, 235
Denmark, 14, 16, 21–2, 27, 31, 33, 45, 64, 68, 137–8, 165
Desmond, Astra, 167n, 170, 180n

Donizetti, 24
Drachmann, Holger, 68–9, 69n, 79, 94, 165, 184–5, 186, 192, 235
Dreyfus case, 8, 86, 102–3, 104
Due, Fredrik, 235
Dvořák, 111, 129, 142, 161, 178

Edward VII, King of England, 112–13, 116
Eggen, Arne, 51n
Einstein, Alfred, 200, 200n
Elegiac Melodies (Op. 34), 58, 63, 73, 75, 103, 105–6, 182
Elling, 100
Euterpe, 20–1, 27

Fauré, 104
Feddersen, Benjamin, 21, 21n, 138
Figaro, Le, 104
Finck, Henry T., 5, 46n, 103n, 119, 120, 167n, 193, 201n
Flyveposten, 22
Franck, 142, 143
Frank, Alan, 143n, 164n
Frankfurter Zeitung, 103
Fritzsch of Leipzig (publisher), 31, 152, 152n
Funeral March in memory of Rikard Nordraak, 23, 24, 29, 117–18, 146–7, 200

Gade, Niels, 7, 9, 14–15, 21, 25, 27, 29, 67, 137, 138, 139, 140, 142, 148n, 149, 197, 235
Garborg, Arne, 94, 165, 166, 167, 189, 191, 191n, 235
Gaukstad, vii, 36n
Geibel, 169
Gil Blas, 104
Glinka, 129
Grainger, Percy, 81, 96, 98, 117, 123, 133, 134, 153n, 198, 235
Gray, Rev. W. A., 81, 81n
Greni, Liv, 18n, 19n, 24n
Grieg, Alexander (great-grandfather), 1–2
Grieg, Alexander (father), 2, 18
Grieg, Alexandra (daughter), 31
Grieg, Edvard:
harmonic style, 4–5, 9, 11, 20, 31, 57, 89–90, 91–2, 96, 121–2, 123, 125–7, 128–9, 131–2, 133, 134, 137, 138–9, 140, 144, 145, 146, 152, 153, 155, 159, 162, 169, 170, 172, 175, 177, 178, 179, 182, 184, 185, 187, 190, 199–200, 201
influence of folk-music, 5, 6–7, 20, 33–4, 55–6, 58, 60–1, 81, 82, 95, 104, 107–108, 115, Ch. 7, 140, 150–1, 186, 199, 201
nationalism, 6, 10, 18, 23–4, 25, 30, 31, 36, 38, 39, 42, 51–2, 56, 58–9, 69, 71, 76, 77, 81, 86, 88, 100, 106, 113–14, 119, 140, 141, 142, 152, 153, 176, 179, 181, 197, 199, 200–1
piano playing and concert giving, 4, 8, 9, 11, 12, 13, 17, 26, 53, 58, 61, 62, 63, 64, 66, 68, 71, 73–6, 79, 80, 84, 86, 97–8, 102, 103, 167n, 198
Grieg, Gesine (mother), 2, 4, 10, 33
Grieg, Harald, 1, 3, 3n
Grieg, John, 2
Grieg, John (brother), 5, 10, 17, 63, 66, 147n

Grieg, Nina (wife), 16–17, 26, 27, 29, 47–8, 61, 64, 68, 73, 83n, 84, 93, 98, 118, 138, 147n, 165, 167, 169, 181n, 192
Grieg, Nordahl, 1
Grimstad, Lauritz, 24
Grønvold, Aimar, 100–1
Grove, Sir George, 74–5
Gulbranson, Ellen, 103, 106, 168
Gundersen, Laura, 154, 236
Gurvin, Olav, 11n, 20, 137
Gyldendal, 1

Haakon VII, King of Norway, 113, 115
Haarklou, 197
Halvorsen, Johan, 18, 72, 108–10, 118, 119, 123, 124, 125, 236
Halvorsen-Grieg *Slåtter*, 18
Hansen (publisher), 129n
Hanslick, 46
hardanger-fiddle, 123–5
hardanger-fiddle tunes, etc., 18, 20, 25, 58, 81, 107–9, 119, 121, 123, 138, 140, 150
Hardanger visits, 53–5, 58, 69, 80–83, 90, 119
Harmonien (Bergen), 2, 6, 13, 14, 59–60, 63
Hartmann, Emil, 15
Hartmann, J. P. E., 15, 21, 38, 137, 139, 156, 197, 236
Haslund, Maren Regina, 2
Hauch, vi, 22n, 23n, 32n, 60n, 79n
Haugtussa cycle (Op. 67). *See under* Songs
Hauptmann, 7–8, 9, 12, 137
Heckmann, Robert, 56, 58, 162
Heine, 17, 167, 186
Heise, 166

Helsingfors conservatory (Sibelius Academy), 59
Hinrichsen, Max, 112, 115
Holberg, Ludvig, 3, 30n, 64–5, 102
Holberg Festival, 61, 65–6
Holberg suite, 62, 66, 74, 92, 147–8, 147n, 162
Holter, Iver, 59, 99, 100, 197
Hornbeck, Louis, 20, 23
Horneman, C. F. E., 10, 15, 20, 21, 67, 137, 197, 236
Hurum, H. J., 22n

Ibsen, Hendrik, 6, 14, 22, 24, 26, 30, 31, 36–7, 40, 41, 43–6, 47, 50–1, 57n, 61, 64, 67, 71, 72, 83, 86, 87, 99, 102, 153, 158, 165, 166, 175, 181, 236
In Autumn, 21, 24–5, 74, 103, 149, 150–1, 171
Incidental music: Frieriet paa Helgoland, 21. See also *Bergliot*, *Olav Trygvason*, *Peer Gynt*, *Sigurd Jorsalfar*
Indy, d', 202n
Ireland, John, 199

Janson, Kristoffer, 31
Joachim, 75
Johansen, Monrad, vi, 59n, 70n, 84, 150, 175
Josephson, Ludvig, 45, 236

Kajanus, Robert, 59
Karlshamn, 11
Keilhau, Wilhelm, 61–2, 61n, 187n
Kiel, Friedrich, 22
Kielland, Alexander, 76
Kinsarvik, Lars, 58,
Kjerulf, Halfdan, 26, 27, 28, 28n, 29, 30, 30n, 33, 34n, 38, 99,

100, 121–2, 133, 139, 166, 175, 176
Klengel, Julius, 63
Kortsen, Bjarne, 30n, 66n
Krag, Vilhelm, 61, 93–4, 165, 186, 236
Kretzschmar, Hermann, 97
Kuhlau, 7
Kullak, 19

Lalo, Édouard, 77, 77n
Lalo, Pierre, 104
Laloy, Louis, 105n, 202n
Lammers, Thorvald, 66, 67, 193, 237
Låndas, 5, 5n, 33, 39n, 64
Landkjenning. See *Land-sighting* under Choral
Landsmål, 31, 57, 57n, 94, 166, 181, 189
Landstad, M. B., 56, 158
Lange, D. de, 16–17
Langeleik, 33, 33n
Lange-Müller, Peter, 166
Langen, Albert, 103
Last Spring, The, 73, 118
Leeds Festival, 117
Leipzig, 23, 31, 58–9, 63, 69, 71–2, 87, 137, 169n, 198
Leipzig Conservatory, 5, 6, 7, 12, 13, 15, 26, 27, 61, 63, 72, 73, 88, 93, 110, 136, 149, 167
Leipzig Gewandhaus, 14, 58
Lenbach, Franz von, 69
Lie, Erika, 18, 19, 60, 66, 237
Lie, Jonas, 22, 76, 84, 105n, 176, 176n
Lindblad, 166
Lindeman, L. M., 14, 33–4, 34n, 56, 60, 96, 115, 119–20, 121, 122, 123, 127–8, 129, 131, 135, 237
Liszt, 6, 24, 32–3, 34–6, 38, 63, 131, 140, 152
Lumbye, H. C. L., 15
Lyric Suite, 95, 116, 145–6

Matin, Le, 70
Matthison-Hansen, Gottfried, 15, 20, 22, 25, 29, 32, 55, 60, 137, 197, 237
Mendelberg, 98, 99
Mendelssohn, 9, 10, 11, 14, 29, 60, 92, 131, 138
Messchaert, 93, 98
Meyer, Wilbecke, 13, 167n
Michelsen, 114
Moe, Jørgen, 17, 33, 165, 176
Moeran, 199
Morgenbladet, 26, 27
Mosafinn, Ola, 58
Moscheles, 7, 11, 13
Mountain-Thrall, The. See *Bergtekne Den*
Mozart, 5, 9, 17, 29, 53, 60, 90–2, 96, 190
Munch, Andreas, 24, 165, 174–5, 175n, 237
Munthe, Gerhard, 67
Mussorgsky, 19, 172

Nansen, 116
Neruda, Wilhelmina. *See* Norman-Neruda, Wilhelmina
Neupert, Edmund, 19, 31, 100, 237
Newspaper and periodical comment. See *Artikler og Taler; Bergenposten; Figaro, Le; Flyveposten; Frankfurter Zeitung; Gil Blas; Matin, Le; Morgenbladet; Revue musicale; Signale; Star, The; Temps, Le; Times, The*

Nielsen, 198
Nikisch, 91
Nissen, Erika Lie. *See* Lie, Erika
Nordraak, Rikard, 6, 10, 15, 18–20, 18n, 19n, 21, 22–3, 24n, 25, 26, 27, 28
Norges Melodier, 129
Norman-Neruda, Wilhelmina, 26, 74, 75, 237
Norse Theatre, 121
Norsk (Op. 53, No. 1), 184
Norsk Folkemusikk, 58n
Norsk Musikkgranskning Årbok, 11n, 21n, 43n, 76n, 107n, 137n
Norwegian National Theatre. *See* Christiania Theatre

Olav Trygvason, 15, 38, 39, 41, 45, 75–6, 85, 92, 100, 155–8
Olsen, Ole, 59, 100, 197
Oscar II, King, 40

Papperitz, 7
Paulsen, John, 24n, 48, 50–1, 51n, 55, 93, 180, 181, 186, 237
Peer Gynt (including orchestral suites), 28, 37, 41, 43–6, 43n, 50, 56, 62, 66, 67, 77, 78, 84, 85, 89, 103, 106, 112, 120–1, 128, 143, 153–4, 158, 179, 189, 199
Peters, Wilhelm, 54
Peters Edition, 31, 45, 53, 84, 152n, 162, 164, 180, 194
Philharmoniske Selskab, Det, 26
Piano Concerto in A minor, 25, 29, 31, 32, 33, 35, 46, 59, 60, 73, 75, 84, 88, 98, 100, 103, 104–5, 110, 116, 117, 132, 139, 140, 147n, 149, 152, 153n, 198
Piano Quintet, 142n
Piano works, in order of Opus Nos. (*See* Appendix B for individual titles):
Deux pièces symphoniques, 16, 149
Six Norwegian Mountain Melodies, 129
Smaastykker for Pianoforte, 11, 127, 136, 137
Three Piano Pieces, 11, 146
Four Piano Pieces (Op. 1), 9, 11, 13, 15, 136–7, 138
Poetic Tone-pictures (Op. 3), 119, 138
Humoresques (Op. 6), 20, 21, 26, 58, 119, 138, 139, 146, 164
Piano Sonata (Op. 7), 21, 23, 26, 112, 138, 139, 146, 168, 199
In Autumn, fantasia for four hands (Op. 11), 25, 27
Lyric Pieces (Op. 12), 29–30, 127
25 Norwegian Folksongs and Dances (Op. 17), 54, 119, 122–3
Scenes of Folk Life (Op. 19), 39, 39n, 58, 110, 128, 137, 138n
Ballade (Op. 24), 47, 88n, 92, 119, 131–2, 199
Album Leaves (Op. 28), 55, 58, 66
Improvisations on two Norwegian folksongs (Op. 29), 66, 119, 129
Norwegian Dances for piano duet (Op. 35), 60, 62, 66, 67, 77, 127–8
Valse-caprices (Op. 37), 145

From Holberg's Time (Suite, Op. 40), 65
Lyric Pieces (Op. 43), 68, 127, 144, 145
Old Norwegian Melody with Variations, for piano duet (Op. 51), 95, 120, 129–31
Lyric Pieces (Op. 54), 77–8, 95, 127, 144, 145
Lyric Pieces (Op. 57), 83, 127, 145
Symphonic Dances (Op. 64), 95, 122, 127, 128
Lyric Pieces (Op. 65), 84, 84n, 112, 127, 145
Nineteen Norwegian Folk-tunes (Op. 66), 82, 92, 95–96, 120, 122–3, 127, 133, 199, 201
Lyric Pieces (Op. 68), 145, 146
Lyric Pieces (Op. 71), 144, 145
Norwegian Peasant Dance-tunes (Op. 72), 18, 107, 108, 120, 123, 124–6, 146, 199, 210
'Moods' (Op. 73), 78, 96n, 107, 115, 146
Plaidy, 7
Pugno, Raoul, 103, 104

Rabe, Carl, 117
Rathen, Aberdeenshire, 1
Ravel, 145, 147, 153
Ravnkilde, Niels, 33, 238
Reinecke, Carl, 7, 9, 12, 238
Revue musicale, 202n
Richardt, Christian, 21, 150, 165, 171
Richter, E. F., 7, 9
Rolfsen, Nordahl, 94, 168, 187, 238
Röntgen, Julius, 55n, 63, 65, 81–3, 81n, 83n, 88, 88n, 93, 93n, 95–96, 96n, 99, 101n, 116, 116n, 117, 119, 123, 131n, 146, 147n, 164, 238
Ross, Kristian, 64
Rossini, 24, 90
Rubbra, Edmund, 134n
Rückblick (not extant), 13
Rungsted, 21, 22, 25, 169

Saint-Saëns, 95, 131, 131n
Schneider, Ludvig, 21n
Schiøtt, Ingolf, 84, 118
Schjelderup, Gerhard, 84n, 100, 238
Schjelderup-Ebbe, Dag, vii, 7n, 8, 8n, 20, 22n, 76n, 137, 139, 149, 151, 151n, 168n, 169n, 171, 172, 175, 200n
Schleinitz, H. C., 8, 8n, 9
Schröder-Devrient, 10, 93
Schubert, 40, 168, 170, 191
Schumann, 9, 10, 11, 13, 14, 29, 74n, 90, 92–3, 95, 131, 132, 136, 150, 152, 168, 171, 172, 180, 187
Schumann, Clara, 10, 93
Scriabin, 143, 145
Seidl, Anton, 95, 116, 145–6, 146n
Selmer, J. P., 100, 197, 238
Sgambati, G., 35, 238
Shaw, G. B., 85–6, 85n, 86n, 151
Sibelius, 151, 198
Signale, 58–9
Sigurd Jorsalfar, 27, 38–9, 56, 85, 102, 112, 115, 143, 154
Sinding, Christian, 59, 72, 81, 84, 100, 142n, 166, 187n, 197, 238
Sitt, Hans, 128, 128n
Sjögren, Emil, 166, 198

Slaalien, Gjendine, 82–3, 96, 123
Smetana, 35, 51
Söderman, August, 43n
Sommerfeldt, W. P., 47n
Sonatas. *See under* principal instrument
Songs, in order of Opus Nos. (*See* Appendix B for individual song titles):
  Four songs for Alto (Op. 2), 11, 13, 15, 167–8
  Six songs (Op. 4), 17, 167–8, 168n
  Melodies of the Heart (Op. 5), 17, 26, 169–70, 171
  Romances and Ballads (Op. 9), 24, 174–5
  Four Romances (Op. 10), 17, 169
  Romances (Op. 15), 31, 64, 169, 170
  Four Songs from *The Fisher Lass* (Op. 21), 38, 176, 177
  Six Songs (Op. 25), 47, 56, 64, 179–80, 198
  Five Songs (Op. 26), 48, 180–1
  Twelve Songs (poems by Vinje) (Op. 33), 57–8, 67, 69, 94, 161, 169, 177, 182–3 (4), 198
  Romances (Op. 39), 31, 37, 38, 168, 176–7, 178–9, 178n, 199
  Travel Memories from Mountain and Fjord (Op. 44), 69, 184–5
  Six Songs (Op. 48), 79, 168–9
  Six Songs (Op. 49), 79, 185
  Norway (Op. 58), 93, 181, 186
  Elegiac Poems (Op. 59), 93, 181, 186
  Songs (poems by Krag) (Op. 60), 93, 186–7, 188
  Children's Songs (Op. 61), 94, 187, 191
  Haugtussa Song Cycle (Op. 67), 61, 94–5, 184, 189–91, 191n, 198
  Five Poems (Op. 69), 95, 165, 191–2
  Five Poems (Op. 70), 95, 165, 191–3
Sontum, Bolette, 87, 87n
Spohr, 92
Stabbe-låten (string orchestra), 122
Star, The, 75
Strauss, Richard, 167
Strindberg, 41n, 42
String Quartet in F major (unfinished), 4, 56, 164
String Quartet in D minor (not extant), 9, 9n, 13
String Quartet in G minor, 34, 47, 55–6, 58, 72, 92, 162–4, 179, 201
Stub, Kjeld, 2
Stucken, Franz van der, 67
Sullivan, 74n
Svendsen, Johan Severin, 6, 27–8, 29, 31, 40, 60, 99, 100, 101, 142, 187, 197
Sweden, 11
'Swedish crisis', 8, 86, 113–15
Symphonic Dances. *See under* Piano works
Symphony in C minor, 15–16, 21, 26, 149

Tellefsen, Thomas, 76, 76n, 100, 238

Temps, Le, 104
Thoresen, Magdalene, 19n
Tidemand, 175
Times, The, 74
Tönsberg, 18, 18n
'Troldhaugen', 16, 66, 68, 69, 84, 87, 108, 109, 111, 117, 118, 148n, 153n, 176, 181n
Tchaikovsky, 72–3, 72n, 73n, 91, 129, 161, 198
Tua, Teresina, 69

Udbye, 51, 51n, 197
Uhland, 17, 167
Utne family, 54

Verdi, 88–90
Vikings of Helgeland, The, 51, 87
Vinje, Aasmund, 57–8, 67, 69, 74n, 94, 161, 165, 166, 167, 181–2, 184, 239
Violin Sonata in F major (Op. 8), 21, 23, 26, 33, 47, 59, 74, 75, 140–1, 164
Violin Sonata in G major (Op. 13), 27, 29, 34, 58, 75, 140, 141–2
Violin Sonata in C minor (Op. 45), 34, 69, 72, 75, 140, 142–3
Violoncello Sonata in A minor (Op. 36), 34, 62–3, 66, 116, 143, 147n, 154

Wagner, 10, 29, 41, 48–50, 51, 52, 54, 63, 77, 85, 90–1, 92, 103, 106, 156, 167
Warlock, 199
Weber, 5
Welhaven, J. S., 3, 14, 30, 51, 165, 239
Wenzel, E. F., 9, 93
Werenskiold, 81, 84
Wergeland, 121, 165, 239
Weyse, 166
William II, Kaiser, 111–12, 117
Winding, August, 15, 34, 68, 137, 197, 239
Winter-Hjelm, Otto, 26, 27, 100, 197, 239
Winther, Christian, 17, 165
Wolf, Hugo, 167
Wolff, Johannes, 75

Zschinsky-Troxler, v, vi, 53n, 62n, 67n, 86, 93n, 113n, 114n, 162n